NAVIGATION WORKBOOK
18465 Tr

Revised Edition

DAVID BURCH   LARRY BRANDT

STARPATH
starpathpublications.com

ISBN 978-0-914025-45-0

Published by

Starpath Publications

3050 NW 63rd Street, Seattle, WA 98107

Manufactured in the United States of America

www.starpathpublications.com

12   11   10   9   8

Table of Contents

Table of Contents Continued...

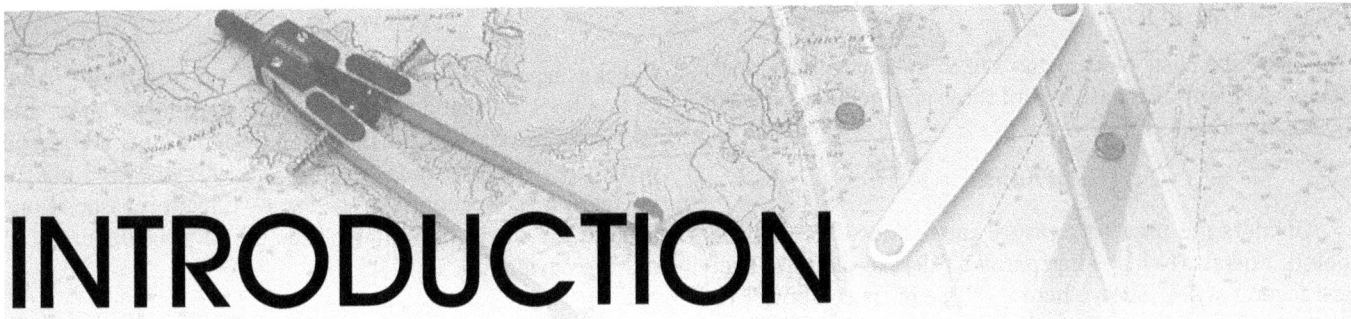

INTRODUCTION

Scope

These exercises are designed to help small-craft navigators hone their skills in both routine and special circumstances. They are practical exercises in chart reading and plotting, position fixing, dead reckoning, compass work, and the use of special resources such as online chart catalogs and tidal predictions, plus the traditional *Light Lists*, Local Notices to Mariners, *Chart No. 1*, *Navigation Rules*, and *U.S. Coast Pilots*. We show new procedures required now that NOAA has discontinued traditional paper charts as well as traditional tide and current tables.

These exercises can be incorporated into an ongoing navigation course or used by individuals on their own. This book along with a textbook of choice would then make up a self-study course. The chapters of this workbook correlate with those of the book *Inland and Coastal Navigation* by David Burch, but other books could also provide the necessary background.

The level of these exercises is about that required in the USCG Masters license exam for 100 GT, which in turn is about the same as that used in coastal navigation certification exams from the U.S. Sailing Association, American Sailing Association, Royal Yachting Association, and the Canadian Yachting Association.

Chart 18465 Tr

The exercises in this book that require a chart use NOAA training chart 18465 Tr, Strait of Juan de Fuca, Eastern Part. This is one of several historic NOAA training charts. This one is frozen in time to 1998, but is otherwise similar to what was, prior to 2024, the standard navigation chart of this region (No. 18465). Using a fixed training chart, the exercises do not become outdated with new chart versions.

The 18465 Tr is available at most of the historic print on demand chart dealers and from several online outlets (see Appendix A3.). This chart is used by many schools in the Pacific Northwest, but what is learned from this chart applies to all waterways around the country.

Except for this paper chart, which must be purchased separately, all other resource materials are provided in the Resources section, which includes excerpts for all publications needed.

You can also work the exercises with an electronic version of 18465 Tr, and for that solution we have an extended discussion in Appendix A1, which includes a source for the free echart. We encourage mariners to solve the charting exercises using both paper charts and electronic charts. Also provided are a few resources on the use of ECS (electronic charting system) for solving navigation problems.

Terminology

All references to miles are nautical miles. Sometimes this is stated as miles other places as nmi. One nautical mile is about 6,000 ft. (Exact is 1 nmi = 1852 m = (1852x100/2.54)/12 ft, which is about 6076.115 ft.)

General phrases like "north of" or "due east of," etc, always refer to true directions unless otherwise specified. Wind directions are labeled by the source of the wind, i.e., north wind flows from north to south, sea breeze blows from the sea toward the land. Wind waves and currents, on the other hand, are labeled with the true direction they flow toward. (Swells, as opposed to wind waves, are labeled by the direction they come from.)

Magnetic Variation

The magnetic variation on the 18465 Tr chart (frozen in 1998) covers magnetic variations that vary from 19.5° E to 19.75° E. To simplify the exercises, however, we use a fixed value of 20.0° E for all locations of the chart, and for all exercises.

Tides and Currents

In 2021, NOAA discontinued sanctioning third-party printing of tide and current tables, and in particular the list of corrections in the historical Tables 2, which are now all deprecated. Thus all exercises using those tables have been replaced in this edition, as further explained in Lesson 8.

Tools of the Trade

These are the basic plotting tools used in marine navigation. There are many alternatives, but these are the most common by far, worldwide, on all vessels.

Dividers

Dividers are used to measure the distance between two points, and also to help align parallel rulers or plotters. There are several styles. Shown here is a type of "speed bow." You can interchange one of the points with a pencil lead for drawing circles of position or other arcs.

A "bow" is a tool that will hold its point separation once set, and it is set by a rotating knob in the center of the tool—as opposed to conventional dividers which are just pulled open or squeezed closed. A "speed bow" is one that you can pull open or close by hand without having to use the center knob. In other words, you can override the fine control of the center knob by firmly pulling or pushing on the legs themselves.

This particular model has become the dividers of choice for the vast majority of professional navigators worldwide because of its ease of use and accuracy. This economic model is called (appropriately) "ultra light dividers."

Parallel Rulers

This is a tool that lets you draw one line parallel to another, some distance away from it. To use it, align one edge of the rulers with the base line, and then holding down that side of the tool, move the other side to the location of the new line. If the new location cannot be reached in one step, then you walk the rulers across the page to the destination.

It takes a bit of practice to manipulate these without slipping, but after some practice it is quite easy. There are numerous styles and sizes of these. A simple design, in clear plastic with small cork anti-slip pads, 15 inches long is a popular and functional option.

Weems Plotter

An alternative to parallel rulers is a rolling tool called a parallel plotter, or more specifically, the Weems parallel plotter, named after its inventor. These are designed to roll without sliding, which they generally do fairly well, with little practice. Unfortunately, rolling plotters do not work well near the edges of charts or over folds in the chart. A solution is always also carry parallel rulers underway and use the Weems plotter whenever possible, but immediately switch to parallel rulers if need be. On a large chart table (or kitchen table) many navigators find this tool faster and easier to use than parallel rulers.

Triangles

The most accurate chart plotting is often done with two matching navigation triangles. They take a bit more practice to master, but the larger protractor scale and more positive positioning does enhance the accuracy. They are popular with professional mariners.

For more Help

Check starpath.com/18465tr for news and resources related to this book as well as contact with the authors. Comments and suggestions will be much appreciated and addressed promptly. Training aids are available as well as links to navigation schools and navigation certification associations around the world that offer basic and advanced training in marine navigation.

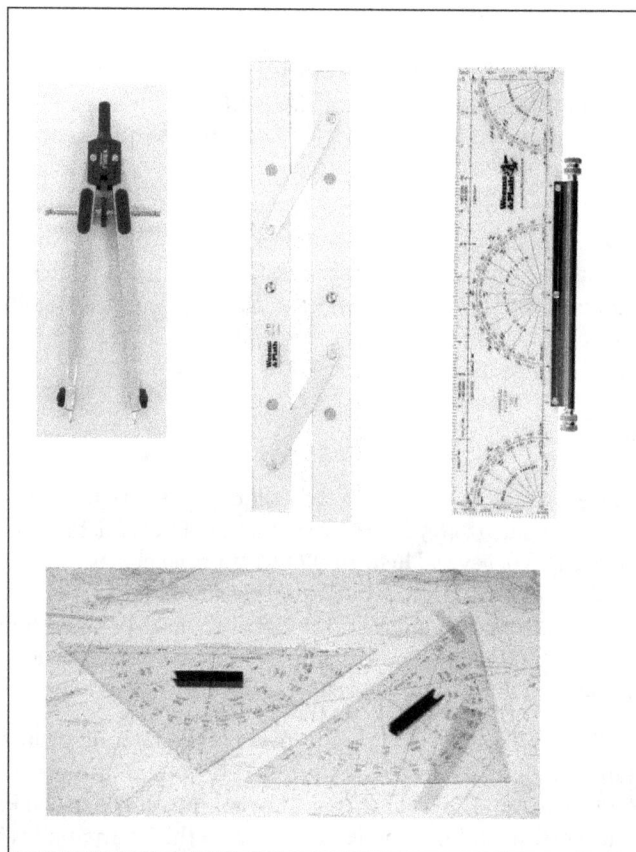

Plotting tools. *Dividers, parallel rulers, Weems Plotter, and triangles.*

EXERCISES

CHAPTER 1 – THE ROLE OF NAVIGATION

These questions are usually addressed in early chapters of a navigation text. Some are terminology, some philosophy.

1-1. The art of dead reckoning navigation lies in...

(A) Determining a best estimate for your position based on logbook records of course, distance and time.
(B) Determining your exact position based on course, distance and time.
(C) Estimating your position based on bearings to at least two known landmarks.
(D) Estimating your position based on identifying a buoy that you have just passed.

1-2. Piloting is the art of navigating a vessel...

(A) By reference to GPS courses and fixes.
(B) By reference to nearby landmarks and buoys.
(C) In heavy waves when the vessel may become airborne.
(D) By following other vessels of similar size and draft.

1-3. Choose from the following the one INCORRECT statement concerning The Navigation Rules:

(A) The Rules apply to stand-up-paddle boards.
(B) The Rules do not apply to kayaks, rowboats or jet skis.
(C) The Rules apply to submarines.
(D) The Rules apply to seaplanes when landing on the water or taking off from the water.

1-4. The numerical value of the direction to an object from your viewing location is called the...

(A) True bearing, if the value is read from the binnacle compass of your vessel.
(B) Relative bearing, if the value is referenced to Magnetic North.
(C) Magnetic bearing, if the value is referenced to the outer ring of an NCC chart's compass rose.
(D) Magnetic bearing, if the value is referenced to Magnetic North.

1-5. Arguably the most important book in navigation is...

(A) Bowditch's *New Practical American Navigator*.
(B) The *Navigation Rules*.
(C) *Chapman Piloting and Seamanship*.
(D) Latest editions of the *Tide Tables* and *Tidal Current Tables*.

1-6. When your vessel's accurate position at a particular time has been determined by some form of piloting or by electronic navigation using GPS or radar, and noted on a navigation chart, it is said to be...

(A) An estimated position (EP).
(B) An updated DR.
(C) A fix.
(D) A position forecast.

1-7. What is the approximate length of a nautical mile in feet that is very valuable for every navigator to know?

1-8. What is the most important reason for learning traditional navigation skills?

(A) Check the GPS.
(B) To use if the GPS receiver or display electronics fail.
(C) To use if the GPS signal is not available at our location.
(D) Good seamanship calls for us to be prepared to navigate in any condition.

1-9. A *small craft* is characterized by...

(A) Overall length under 65 ft.
(B) Maximum speed of 7 kts regardless of length.
(C) There is no single definition; it depends on the circumstances.
(D) Any shallow-draft vessel under 100 ft long.

2 Navigation Workbook 18465 Tr

1-10. Translate this into landsman language without using the word log: "We logged 20 miles according to the log, which I logged into the log."

1-11. Give at least one reason why the main challenge of modern navigation training is learning route planning and not position finding.

1-12. Which statement is true?

(A) For safe navigation I need the latest nautical charts.
(B) For safe navigation I need nautical charts and at least 3 books.
(C) A well designed electronic charting system can meet all of my needs for safe navigation.
(D) All statements are true.

1-13. Concerning the practical application of GPS compared to basic knowledge of piloting skills, give a few examples of where this thought might apply: "It is far more important to know for certain where you are not, than to know precisely where you are."

1-14. Looking ahead to some basics, looking at a chart or the special publication called Light List, (A) What is the color of even numbered buoys? (B) What is the color of odd numbered buoys?

1-15. Looking clear across the ocean, how do the British pronounce buoy?

CHAPTER 2 – NAUTICAL CHARTS AND CHART READING

These exercises require a copy of Chart No 1. *A full version in pdf format of this and other publications are online. Skim through the* Coast Pilot *excerpts in the Resources to become familiar with the chart. Use the* Light List *or* Coast Pilot *Indexes from the Resources to locate aids, marks or regions as needed—or use the super convenient ENC search function in qtVlm. Use magnetic variation 20.0° E for all locations on chart 18465 Tr. We include* Light List *excerpts needed for the exercises in the Resources, but it will be very instructive to download a full copy of the latest* Light List *and read the Introduction (about 20 pages). See www.starpath.com/navpubs. Note that NOAA Custom Paper Charts (NCC) are based on the ENC, but they use the traditional* Chart No.1 *paper chart symbols for all ATONs.*

2-1. One tenth of a nautical mile is how many (A) meters? (B) feet? (C) What is the unit called that is about 0.1 nautical miles? (D) What are the dimensions of training chart 18465 Tr in nmi?

2-2. What is the distance and magnetic bearing from Buoy R to Buoy RA marking the entrance into Rosario Strait shipping lanes?

2-3. What is the color of Buoy R?

2-4. What letters or numbers are printed on Buoy R?

2-5. What is the distance and true bearing from Buoy 2 at New Dungeness Spit to Buoy 4 just west of Port Angeles?

2-6. Buoy 4 just west of Port Angeles marks an underwater shelf. What is the charted depth of the water (A) 200 yards NE of the buoy and (B) 200 yards SW of the buoy?

2-7. What is the distance and magnetic bearing from Brotchie Ledge Light to Buoy V15, SE of Race Rocks?

2-8. Trace out this route and figure the total distance around it, leaving all marks to port: Start at Buoy S (north of Dungeness Spit), then travel to Buoy 1 at west end of Protection Island, then on around the south side to east end of Protection Island, then NE to Buoy SA, and from there to Minor Island Light, and then to Hein Bank Buoy DH, and on to Buoy R, and then back to Buoy S.

2-9. There is a buoy at Hein Bank labeled BR "DH". (A) What is the color of this buoy? (B) What is the purpose and instructions of the buoy? (C) Check out your answers in the Light List. Have we learned anything more there?

2-10. Looking at typical shipping lanes from Buoys S to SA, (A) what is the width of the inbound and outbound lanes? and (B) What is the width of the separation zone?

2-11. Looking at the shipping lanes north of Crescent Bay, (A) What is the width of the inbound lane? and (B) what is the width of the inshore zone at Crescent Bay?

2-12. What would our compass read if we were running westward along the inshore zone, parallel to the inbound shipping lane?

2-13. What is the width of the Strait from Tongue Pt. on the US side to Beechey Head on the Canadian side?

2-14. What is the compass bearing from the East end of Ediz Hook to the entrance to Victoria Harbor?

2-15. (A) What is the Lat, Lon of Buoy PA read from the chart? (B) What does the *Light List* give for its location?

2-16. (A) What is the distance and true bearing from 48° 08.42' N, 123° 15.65' W to 48° 12.42' N, 123° 15.21' W? (B) What is the nature of the bottom at the first point (southernmost)? (C) What is the bottom at the northern point? (D) What are "swirls"? (E) Roughly how much farther apart would these two points be if the lat of the north one was increased to 48° 12.43' N?

2-17. What is the Lat, Lon of the point 3.50 miles south of Buoy RA?

2-18. The Light List describes a light called "Discovery Island Light." Can this light be seen from Trial Island? Explain.

2-19. How many "miles per handspan" to a paper chart with scale (A) 1:20,000 and (B) 1:500,000?

2-20. Using starpath.com/getcharts (item 1.1), what is the (ENC) chart number for Neah Bay at the far western end of the Strait of Juan de Fuca (not shown on our paper training chart). The online interactive catalog has a useful search engine.

2-21. Using source of 2-20 above, what one chart (ENC) covers all of the Puget Sound? Hint: It spans Lat 47.0° to 48.3°, and Lon -123.4° to -122.1° (the viewer uses decimal degrees).

2-22. What does it mean when the seaward end of a jetty is shown dashed, like this = = = = = = ?

2-23. There are 4 shipwrecks between Dungeness Spit and Green Pt. Call them A to D, headed SW from easternmost one. Parts (A) to (D) are: what are the water depth and distance offshore of each one?

2-24. There are 6 rocks along the NW shore of Protection Island. Five are the same, one is different. (A) What is the difference between these two kinds of rocks? How high does the tide have to be to cover (B) all of them? (C) five of them?

2-25. (A) What is the elevation of Smith Island as read from chart 18465 Tr? (B) What is this elevation as discerned from the *Light List*? (C) What does the Coast Pilot tell us? See big hint in Figure 2-25. Note: this light has been moved, so we refer here to conditions at the time of our training chart, 18465 Tr (1998).

2-26. Read the notes on the chart (always a good idea) to answer these questions: (A) What does the green "NWR" mean on the NE shore of Protection Island? (B) What part of the chart 18465 Tr has the most accurate (latest) soundings measurements? (C) What is the copyright status of NOS nautical charts? (D) Running our dingy along shore about 5 miles due east of Smith Island (not shown on the chart) we see a series of red flags and lights. What do they mean?

2-27. (A) What is the true bearing from the Smith Island Light to the FL G 4s light at Davidson Rock? (B) What is the distance between the two?

2-28. There is a rock shown about one quarter of a mile west of Smith Island. (A) What is the depth at the site of that rock? (B) When the tide height is about 0 feet in that area, describe what the water will look like around that rock and between it and the island.

2-29. On Kulakala Pt (48° 06', 123° 04') there is something marked "E COR HO." What is that?

2-30. We call this the US Shore Route. It proceeds generally eastward from the Pacific Ocean toward Pt Wilson. We'll pick it up about Crescent Bay:

Waypoint	Location
1	0.25 miles N of Crescent Bay Buoy 2
2	Angeles Pt. Buoy 4
3	New Dungeness Buoy 2
4	Pt. Wilson Buoy 6

What is the compass course and distance of leg (A) 1 → 2, (B) 2 → 3, (C) 3 → 4?

2-31. What distinguishes BELL, GONG, WHISTLE, and HORN sounds?

2-32. Considering that a hand span is about 7 inches, and on a 1:10,000 scale paper chart that covers about 1 miles distance, what distance is covered by a hand span on a 1:40,000 scale chart?

2-33. One handspan on a 1:80,000 scale paper chart is about how many miles?

2-34. Is a 1:10,000 harbor chart a LARGER scale or a SMALLER scale chart than 1:1,000,000 oceanic chart?

2-35. For close inshore navigation, which chart scale, large or small, would better allow presentation of rocks, kelp beds, and other items of localized concern?

2-36. What is the link to where we create a backup paper chart called NOAA Custom Chart (NCC)?

2-37. Do the boundaries and scales of NCC have to match the discontinued traditional paper charts?

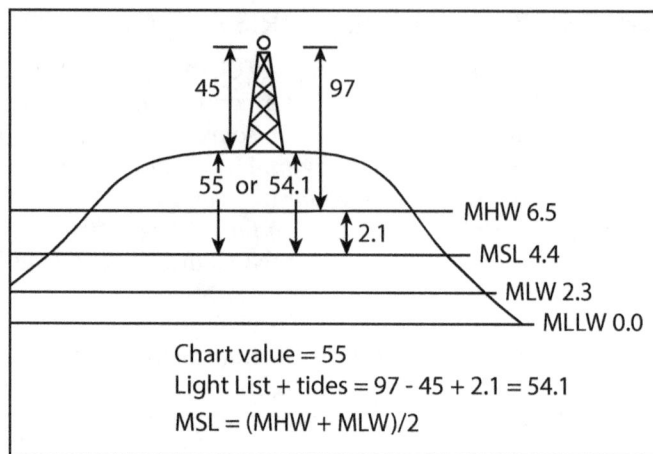

Figure 2-25. *Elevations vs heights. Light heights are relative to mean high water (MHW); land elevations are relative to mean sea level (MSL). The latter can be approximated as halfway between MHW and MLW. The water levels are on the chart. The Light List also includes structure heights above ground. See Answers for more details.*

2-38. How often are NOAA charts updated? These are the electronic navigational charts (ENC), as well as the data used to create the paper backup versions called NOAA Custom Charts (NCC).

(A) Daily.
(B) Weekly.
(C) Monthly.
(D) As needed.

2-39. Explain what the following light and buoy labels mean. (A) RW "NA" Mo (A) WHISTLE, (B) Fl G 4sec BELL, (C) G "31" FL G 4s GONG, (D) F R 25 ft "8", (E) FL 4sec 30ft 8M "2".

2-40. Which of the following statements concerning buoy location and number sequence is correct?

(A) Can be counted on as accurate and sequential, with no missing numbers.
(B) Is usually sequential, but may occasionally be missing numbers of the sequence.
(C) Can always be relied on for accurate location even though numbering may be off.
(D) Can always be relied on for sequential numbering even though position may be off.

2-41. When tracking a range indicated by painted boards and lights, which board and light set is the set closest to your vessel, the upper or the lower set?

2-42. Ranges can be very accurate aids to navigation but they are not always ahead of us where we need them. What must we do to follow a charted range if the range signals are astern of us?

2-43. Approaching the entrance to a harbor from offshore in restricted visibility you sight a buoy with vertical red and white colors, possibly with a white light atop. On which side must or may you leave this buoy as you pass it?

2-44. Regulatory markers are used for important communications, such as speed limits, no wake zones, etc. What does it indicate when you see a regulatory buoy with a crossed diamond on it?

2-45. What do the following navigation abbreviations mean? (A) C, (B) H, (C) R & B, (D) COG, (E) CMG, (F) Trk.

2-46. What are the definitions of the following terms: (A) Course, (B) Heading, (C) Bearing, (D) Course Over Ground, (E) Course Made Good, (F) Track.

2-47. A mark with two black spheres atop, typically black with red horizontal bands indicates what?

2-48. Cardinal marks* and buoys indicate which?

   (A) Navigable water to their named side.
   (B) Hazardous water to their named side.

We do not have cardinal marks on 18465 Tr, but they are common on international waters, including Canada. Use Chart No. 1 to answer these cardinal mark questions. The explanation of these marks shown in the latest edition of Chart No 1 refers to a "Point of Interest." If you change that to "The Danger Being Marked," it might help clarify the definitions.

2-49. A cardinal mark showing two triangles (cones) in a vertical line, point-to-point, indicates safe or hazardous water to which side?

   (A) Navigable water to the south.
   (B) Hazardous water to the west.
   (C) Navigable water to the west.
   (D) Navigable water to the east.

2-50. A cardinal mark at night showing a very quick sequence of 6 flashes on the top light and a quick series of flashes on the low light indicates what?

   (A) Navigable water to the south.
   (B) Navigable water to the west.
   (C) Navigable water to the north.
   (D) Hazardous water to the south.

2-51. What does "nominal range" mean when describing a light?

2-52. A hazard is marked on the approach into Sooke Inlet as a "deadhead". What does this term describe? What is the risk to a recreational vessel of, say, 12 meters LOA?

CHAPTER 3 – OTHER NAVIGATION AIDS

The following questions relate to the Coast Pilot, Light List, and LNM excerpts that appear in the Resources section. There is an Index at the end of the Coast Pilot selection to find locations or topics mentioned. In each case, you are using the Coast Pilot to identify or clarify some feature of the chart or to answer more general questions about the waters shown on the chart. These publications are available in full format online. See also the corresponding instructions to Chapter 2.

3-1. On 18465 Tr under the word "Smith" near Smith Island there is a "(55)" printed on the chart. What does that mean?

3-2. What river enters the Strait at Low Point?

3-3. There is a 480-ft tower on Angeles Pt. Are there any lights on that tower?

3-4. Just off of Observatory Point there is a "(20)" printed on the 18465 Tr. What does that mean?

3-5. With regard to Rules of the Road, do the Inland or International Navigation rules apply on the Strait of Juan de Fuca?

3-6. The Strait of Juan de Fuca is subject to a unique Pacific Northwest hazard called "deadheads." When are deadheads a particular hazard in this region?

3-7. What time of year is fog most likely at the western end of the Strait of Juan de Fuca?

3-8. How strong can the currents be in Race Passage? Hint: always check Coast Pilot as well as current tables when studying the currents of an area that is new to you.

3-9. What is the unique behavior of bell Buoy 2 off of New Dungeness Light?

3-10. Your height of eye above the water is 9 ft. The weather is clear and the seas calm. What is the maximum range you could see (A) Race Rocks Light and (B) New Dungeness Light? (C) Does the *Light List* and the 18465 Tr agree on the nominal ranges for these lights?

3-11. According to the Luminous Range Diagram, what is the Luminous Range of a 26-Mile light (Nominal Range = 26 mi.) when the prevailing atmospheric visibility is (A) 5.5 mi., (B) 1 mi., and (C) 500 yds.? Use the Luminous Range Diagram in the Light List Resources.

3-12. According to the Starpath approximate formula for Luminous Range given in the Resources, what are the answers to 3-11 (500 yds. = 0.25 mi.)?

3-13. From the top of a mast 49 ft above the water line, how far could you see the Race Rocks Light if the atmospheric visibility was 5.5 miles?

3-14. What do you do if you see a nav aid on the chart that is not in the Light List or vice versa?

3-15. Our chart 18465 Tr is not the best chart for entering Sequim Bay, but according to the Coast Pilot what depth can we count on for entering the channel with local knowledge?

3-16. You can see the Point Wilson Light while standing on the cabin top (height of eye about 15), but not from the cockpit (eye height about 8 feet). The water is calm, and it is a clear night. Roughly how far off the light are you?

3-17. From how far off could you see Protection Island (A) in clear weather? (B) In an atmospheric visibility of 4 miles? Use height of eye = 9 ft.

3-18. How far can you see a 5-mile light in 5 miles of visibility?

3-19. (A) If the nominal range of a buoy light is not given on the chart or *Light List*, what should you assume it is? and (B) more generally, how far off should you assume you can see a typical buoy light with no other information available?

3-20. A light is charted as Fl 4 sec, 27 ft, 19 M. I can see the light from the cabin top at an eye height of 12 ft, but not from the cockpit at an eye height of 7 ft. How far off the light am I?

3-21. In areas with a lot of fog, which electronic aid would likely be the most useful?

(A) AIS.
(B) Radar.
(C) Chartplotter.
(D) Depth sounder.

3-22. Besides the nautical charts, what are the five minimum publications or data sets we should have onboard for any extended voyage?

3-23 Referring to the Local Notices to Mariners (LNM) excerpt in the Resources section. Notice there is a sub section called Naval Activity. Then from the 11/5/25 LNM for District 13, Strait of Juan de Fuca section, (A) what lights identify the north and south boundaries of the Navy firing zone? Then identify this restricted area on the ENC and cursor pick it to learn: (B) How often does practice firing take place there?

3-24. In the same LNM used in 3-23, what is taking place in Haro Strait?

3-25. What percentage of the time is there fog (visibility < 2 nmi) off the coast of WA in August?

3-26. How strong can the current be at the south tip of Trial Islands?

CHAPTER 4 – COMPASS USE

Use variation of 20° E for all questions, unless otherwise stated. We just override the values listed on 18465 Tr, which vary by 0.5°. In modern times the variation has changed notably in this region. Give Lat, Lon answers to nearest tenth of a minute unless otherwise asked.

4-1. (A) According to 18465 Tr, what is the magnetic variation near Hein Bank in 1998? (B) Based on information on this chart, what will the variation be in the year 2015?

4-2. Assuming a local variation is 20° E. The true course to our destination is 330 T. What is the compass course assuming no deviation?

4-3. A typical compass rose on a chart has 3 circular scales around it. The outer is true in degrees, the middle is magnetic in degrees, what is the inner most scale represent?

4-4. Question on "boxing a compass." North is true course 000 or 360; East is 090. (A) What is SE (called southeast)? (B) What is W-SW (called west-southwest)? (C) What is NE x E (called northeast by east)?

4-5. Draw a course line from the R6 (Fl R 4s) just off Point Wilson to the R2 (Fl R 4s) off Dungeness Spit. (A) What is the magnetic course? (B) Assuming deviation to be 3° W, what is your True Course? (C) What is your Compass Course? (D) What is the distance of this leg?

4-6. Draw a course line from the R2 (Fl R 2.5s) off Ediz Hook to the VICTORIA HBR Light (Q R) in preparation for a crossing of the Strait of Juan de Fuca. Assume a deviation of 3° E on this heading. (A) What is the distance? (B) What is the Magnetic Course? (C) What is the True Course? (D) What is the Compass Course?

4-7. If you reason through these various problems on conversions you will have more practice than you will likely ever encounter again. Solve for the unknowns in each case. In part (A), for example, the true heading is known from the chart, and the compass is known from reading the compass, and the variation in the area is known from a chart. The problem, then, is to figure the proper magnetic heading and compass deviation. This type of problem can be solved using a TVMDC diagram and then filling in the blanks, or reason through each step using "Correcting, add East."

4-8. Hein Bank lighted Buoy DH bears 310M and Smith Island Light bears 047M. (A) Are you in the shipping lanes? (B) What is the charted depth at your location? (C) What is your Lat-Lon? (D) What is the course and distance from there to the east tip of Protection Island?

4-9. Sailing just east of Dallas Bank, McCurdy Pt. bears 098 M, Beckett Pt. bears 161 M, and Protection Island tank bears 206 M. (A) What is your Lat-Lon? (B) What is the distance to McCurdy Pt? (C) What is the charted depth? (D) from there, what is the range and bearing to Pt. Wilson Buoy 6?

4-10. You are headed straight toward Pt. Wilson Light on magnetic heading 100 M and McCurdy Pt. bears 150 M. What is your Lat, Lon?

4-11. On a rhumb line course from Pt. Wilson Buoy 6 to New Dungeness Buoy 2, what will be the magnetic bearing to the tank on Protection Island when you are half way there?

4-12. Following US Shore Route of problem 2-30 in reverse to the west (WP4 to WP1), select appropriate points (A, B, C) along each leg that would mark the approximate halfway point of the leg and identify a magnetic bearing at those points that would mark that location. Point A is between WP 4 and WP3, B is between WP3 and WP2, and C is between WP2 and WP1. Choose a landmark that is near the beam at each location. Give the name of the mark, the bearing to it, and briefly outline your reasoning for choosing it over others that might be possible. You can use the Coast Pilot to help with descriptions of the landmarks. You might also find it interesting to follow this route in Google Earth looking at the terrain. Also note, this exercise is tied to an earlier one so we kept the same waypoint numbers, but it is generally valuable to have your numbers increase along a route.

4-13. You are in Puget Sound where the magnetic variation is 21° E. Your compass course is 285, and it has no deviation on this heading. The sun is setting dead ahead. (A) What is

4-7 Conversion Exercise Table									
	A	B	C	D	E	F	G	H	I
True	280		007		114	138		049	
var	16 W	21 E		10 W		4 E	21 W		17 E
Magnetic		014		276	093		006		355
dev		5 E	8 W		5 W		0	0	
Compass	296		354	276		138		028	351

true bearing of the setting sun relative to due west? (B) Now a strange question: What time of year must this be?

4-14. Steering course 075 M from New Dungeness Spit Buoy 2, you measure a radar range of 4.5 miles at relative bearing 045R to the north tip of Protection Island. (A) What is your Lat-Lon? (B) Are you in the shipping lanes? (C) What is the charted depth? (D) What are the main contributions to the uncertainty in this position?

4-15. Sailing on course 070 M along the inshore zone, north of Crescent Bay, you make a radar observation of range and bearing to Observatory Pt., west end of Freshwater Bay. You get 3.40 miles at a relative bearing of 066 R. (A) What is your Lat-Lon? (B) How far outside of the shipping lanes are you? (C) What is the range and bearing to Tongue Pt. from your position (just aft of the beam)? (D) There is a purple wavy line in segments shown near your position. What does that signify?

4-16. Your course is 110 T, abeam Sooke Bay on the Canadian inshore zone. The radar range and bearing to Otter Point (on your port quarter) is 2.7 miles at 221 R. (A) What is your Lat-Lon? (B) What is the magnetic bearing to Sheringham Pt. Light from your position? (C) What is the magnetic bearing to Race Rocks Light (Fl 10s)?

4-17. (A) What does the rule "Correcting add east" mean? (B) Give at least two jingles that help us remember the meaning and order of compass corrections. (C) What is the correcting direction?

4-18. Assume you are in a place where the local variation is 15.0° W. The true course to our destination is 330 T. (A) What is the compass course assuming no deviation? (B) Same question with Dev = 4° E

4-19. *For extra practice, here are examples of the worst kind of compass correction problems you would ever run across on any vessel.* For these questions use Deviation Table 1. This one is from Bowditch, and shows rather large deviations, and almost certainly from a steel vessel. We have inserted extra spaces in the table to facilitate practice with interpolation.

In most vessels we cannot hope to steer a course to a tenth of a degree. In practice, we are good to *average* within 2° of our goal, but professional compass adjusters will measure and report the deviations precise to the tenth of a degree and some advanced navigation tests will require plotting to at least ±0.25°, and will often give compass questions to this precision. Thus it benefits us to have some practice at interpolation, as it comes up often in navigation whenever tables of any kind are used.

Also, real deviation curves are not always linear over the semi-quadrants shown here, so we are making an approximation with a simple linear interpolation, but this detail is not crucial for the purpose of this exercise. Underway, you may indeed only get two measurements over the region of interest

Deviation Table 1		
Compass	Deviation	Magnetic
000°	10.5° E	
015°		
030°		
045°	20.0° E	
060°		
075°		
090°	11.5° E	
105°		
120°		
135°	1.2° W	
150°		
165°		
180°	5.5° W	
195°		
210°		
225°	8.0° W	
240°		
255°		
270°	12.5° W	
285°		
300°		
315°	6.8° W	
330°		
345°		

and interpolation will be needed. You need only interpolate the deviations; the magnetic headings follow from these.

(A) Interpolate this table for the deviation at 015C and 030C. You can then skip to Parts B and C to learn the specific ones that are needed.

Refer to Appendix A2 Interpolation, or use any method of choice, to answer these questions. The questions assume a local variation of 15.0° W.

(B) What compass course would you steer to make a true course of (a) 340 T, (b) 032 T, (c) 152 T?

(C) What is the true course you are steering if the compass reads (d) 335 C, (e) 032 C, (f) 317 C, and (g) 285 C?

(D) Why can we reasonably guess that this table is from a steel vessel?

CHAPTER 5 – DEAD RECKONING

Recall our conventions that times are all 24-hour, i.e., 1402 means 2:02 PM; time intervals use h for hours, m for minutes, and s for seconds, as 1h 32m 32s. All miles are nautical miles. It does not matter how we solve the speed-time-distance problems, but we all need some consistent quick way so we are never reluctant to figure it out. Also included are some related issues in chart navigation.

5-1. Convert the following to decimal hours (i.e. 1h 30m = 1.50h): (A)3h 20m, (B)12h 54m, (C)2h 18m, (D)0h 38m, and (E)1h 5m. Convert the following to hours, minutes, and seconds (i.e. 1.57h = 1h+0.57*60m , etc.): (F)2.45h, (G)12.79h, (H)2.09h, (I)0.38h, and (J)1.73h.

Figure these time differences and sums. Use "today", "tomorrow," or "yesterday" as needed to describe the final time you get. Notation is 1205 = 12:05 = 12h 05m.

(K) 1934 - 0722, (L) 2312 - 0432, (M) 2312 + 0355, (N) 1425 - 0043, (O)1232 - 2139, (P) 2209 + 0658

5-2. (A) To average 200 miles per day what must your average speed be? (B) If your speed is 5 kts, how far do you travel in one day (24 hours)?

5-3. A Pilot Chart says the current drift is 15 miles per day. What is its speed in knots?

5-4. If Port Townsend is 37 miles away, how long will it take to get there at 4 kts?

5-5. (A) If Neah Bay is 110 miles away how long will it take to get there at 5 kts? (B) How long will it take if the first 50 miles is at 7 kts, you stop for 2 hr and the last leg is at 4 kts?

5-6. You have traveled 55 miles in 9 hr, what was your average speed?

5-7. You travel 12 miles in 3 hr 40 min, what was your average speed?

5-8. On a measured mile course you time the run from beginning to end, it takes 14 min 30 sec for the mile, what was your average speed?

5-9. You hold a steady 7 kts according to your knotmeter for a measured mile. (A) How long should it take to travel the course? (B) If the actual time was 2 minutes longer, how many knots or fraction of a knot was your knotmeter off? (C) What was its per cent error? (D) If this knotmeter reads 4 knots, what is your actual speed?

5-10. You want to check your speed. In calm water you approach a floating object and start a stop watch when it passes the bow and stop it when it passes the stern. The time was 4 sec. Your boat is 35 ft. long. Hint: use the rule that boat speed in knots equals boat speed in feet per second times 0.6. (A) What was your speed? (B) If your time was in error by 1 sec, how much in error would your speed be?

5-11. If you must sail a rhumb line distance of 18 miles to weather by tacking back and forth across the rhumb line, how long will take at 6.0 knots?

5-12. You must tack to weather for a distance of 4 miles at 5 knots, then reach on course for another distance of 8 miles at 6 knots. How long will it take to get there?

5-13. Consider this route: Leave Sequim Bay Entrance at 11:44 AM, sail east at 6.5 kts SOG to round Violet Pt. of Protection Island, then turn north to Minor Island with an SOG of 5.0 kts for that leg, then west to Hein Bank Buoy DH with SOG of 7.2 kts and then back south to Sequim Bay at 4.8 kts for this last leg. Parts (A) to (D) What are the distances, true courses, and time run for each of these 4 legs (each part has 3 answers)? And (E), when do you get back.

5-14. You are at Buoy SA NW of Pt. Wilson and your destination is Brotchie Ledge Light across the Strait to the NW at Victoria Harbor. Assume the current is slack for the entire route (which is, in fact, never the case for this passage) — later we re-do this with current corrections. (A) What is the rhumbline course and distance? (B) At 7 kts under power on the rhumbline route, how long will this passage take?

The following are a few sailor's questions. Think on these, and if you do not know how to work them, then just read through the answers and plot out the results to learn how to do these. These are fundamental matters for setting optimum sailing courses to weather.

(C) Sailor's question: assume the wind is steady from the northwest throughout the waterway for the time underway, and choose and plot a tacking route that will get you there. Assume you are tacking through 90°, which is equivalent to assuming you are sailing a true wind angle of 45°. After plotting the proposed route, figure the distance along it and the time it will take at a steady 7 kts.

(D) Plot the course with the minimum number of tacks and compare the time to sail it with a route that does not get more than about 5 miles off the rhumb line.

5-15. Leave Salmon Bank Buoy 3 close abeam and steer a steady course of 242 True from there across the Strait. Neglect current and leeway for this plotting exercise. (A) Where do you come ashore on the American side (Lat-Lon and landmark)? (B) What is the distance covered? (C) If you plot this route with a heading error of 1°, how far off will your answer be? (D) At an average speed of 3.2 kts for the first third of the trip, and 6.7 kts for the middle third, and 8.1 kts for the last third, how long will it take (hr and min)?

5-16. Your digital compass manual states that to calibrate your compass you must swing ship through 360°, uniformly (at constant speed) travel in a circle, taking at least 10 minutes to complete the circuit. Describe a way to do this by listing vessel speed, turning rate or step size, and then compute or plot the diameter of the entire path that you would be following according to your plan... or give any other method you can think of that will accomplish this and tell how to execute it.

5-17. I am traveling at 6.3 kts and I have 22.9 miles to go. How long will this take me?

5-18. It is nighttime and you are headed for Victoria Harbor. You are somewhere on the line created by the range of lights from Brotchie Ledge Light to the isophase 12-mile light near the Esquimalt Harbor entrance. You measure the bearing to the Trial Island Light (1.5 nmi off) to be 347 M. Use a variation of 20° E for this problem. (A) Locate your position along the range. What is your Lat-Lon? (B) Now assume the compass was in error by 3° and the correct bearing should have been 344 M. What is your Lat-Lon? (C) How much in error was this fix due to the compass error? (D) Compare this to 6-1 result. What is the message?

5-19. *This problem is a charting exercise. It is not necessarily a prudent navigational maneuver, as we shall see.* You are in Kanaka Bay on San Juan Island. It is thick fog in the middle of the night. You need to enter San Juan Channel on the other side of the peninsula. You choose to use your depth sounder to follow the steep drop off in depths, down and around the Salmon Bank Buoy 3.

(A) Verify that the 20 fathom contour will be a good guide to the region of the buoy.

(B) What will be your approximate magnetic course as you head toward Eagle Pt?

(C) If your log reads 707.0 as you leave Kanaka Bay, approximately what will it read as your depth contour course curves around to the south?

(D) As the contour begins to turn south, you confirm that your log reads close to what you expected (what does this signify?), so you decide to ease into the 10 fathom line. How close will this take you to gong Buoy 3?

(E) Will you be able to hear the gong as you pass? Explain.

(F) At the southern tip of the bank you turn north to follow the 10 fathom line up toward the channel, but as you proceed north, you very quickly notice that you cannot maintain 10 fathoms, and in a few minutes the depth is 60 fathoms? What is the likely explanation of this and what is the message?

(G) What would be your recourse in this circumstance, we still cannot see anything and the depth sounder is our only electronics.

5-20. Because you lost track of the 50 fathom line in the last situation, you decide to check your depth sounder. You are now somewhere just west of Buoy DH on Hein Bank. Discovery Island Lt bears 286 M. Your depth sounder shows 26 fathoms. Log = 07468.2, you head directly toward the light. When the depth sounder reads 30 fathoms a while later, the log reads 07472.8. Checking the chart, does it appear that the depth sounder is working properly? (Assume there is no tide)

5-21. Practice with DR and course plotting: You are 0.2 nmi south of G "V15" off Race Rocks and your log reads 5123.4. Lay out the course directly toward Racon Buoy VH south of Victoria Harbor. (A) What is the magnetic heading of this course? Now sail on this course for exactly 2.2 miles. (B) What will your log read now? (C) From this point what is the bearing to the light at Bn 2 F R in Pedder Bay? (D) What is the bearing to the Trial Island Lt? Now sail on toward the Racon Buoy until the Trial Island Lt bears 046 M. (E) What will the log read now? (F) How far are you from the Racon Buoy?

5-22. You plan to continue sailing, but starting from the same point where you left off in the last problem, you change course to 080 M, and sail on this new course until the log reads 5142.4. Now, take a bearing to Hein Bank Buoy DH. (A) What will this bearing be? Now change course to 226 M and sail for 5.5 miles, and then turn and head directly back for Racon Buoy VH. (B) What is your compass heading back on the last leg? (C) What is the distance back to Buoy VH from this last turn? (D) What will your log read when you arrive at a point a half mile before the buoy?

5-23. More DR plotting: Starting point is the Buoy 3 on Partridge Bank. Depart at 10:04 at 7 kts on course 004 M. At 10:30 change course to 249 M and reduce speed to 4 kts. At 11:15 change course again, returning to Buoy 3 directly at a speed of 10 kts. (A) What will be the bearing back to the buoy at 11:15? (B) What is the estimated time of arrival back at the buoy?

5-24. Plot the DR track on your chart that corresponds to the following section of the log book. Subtract successive log readings to find distance run on each leg; it is more accurate than speed x time.

Time	Log	Course	S-kts	Comments
12:00	51.0	182 M	6.0	Fix at 48° 28.6'N 122° 46.2' W
12:38	54.8	222 M	6.5	Turn to clear Dav Rk
13:12	58.5	274 M	7.0	Head towards Haro
14:30	67.6	205 M	7.0	Head into the Strait
15:30	74.6	205 M	7.0	Position Fix here

(A) What is the latitude and longitude of your DR position at log 74.6?

(B) You do a position fix at log 5674.6 and find that your true position at that time is (48° 20.2' N, 123° 10.8' W). What is the distance between your fix and your DR position at log 5674.6?

(C) What is the direction from the final DR position to the final fix position?

(D) Assume that your DR was wrong because you were in a current that set you off your DR track. Your first fix was at 12:00, the second at 15:30. What was the set (true direction) and drift (speed) of the current? The procedure is to assume that during the time you sailed your DR track, the water moved from your final DR position to your final fix position, thus accounting for the discrepancy.

(E) In practice, could you conclude from this work that the "current" you found this way was the true water current over the course you sailed? Explain.

CHAPTER 6 – PILOTING

These exercises can be worked in the traditional manner plotting on a paper chart, or they can be solved digitally using echart and electronic tools. Standard plotting tools are discussed in the Introduction. There is a review of echart solutions in Appendix A1. Recall we use var = 20° E for all locations. We do several piloting exercises using buoys, but we stress that this is primarily for convenient practice. Underway we should avoid using buoys whenever possible as their charted positions may not be correct.

6-1. As in 5-18, it is nighttime and you are headed for Victoria Harbor. You are somewhere on the line created by the range of lights from Brotchie Ledge Light to the isophase 12-mile light near the Esquimalt Harbor entrance. Use a variation of 20° E for this problem. With a hand-held compass you measure the bearing to the Discovery Island Light (4.2 nmi off) to be 028 M. Locate your position along this range. (A) What is your Lat-Lon? (B) Suppose now that this measurement was in error by 3° and the correct bearing should have been 025 M. Find your position from this bearing. What is your Lat-Lon? (C) How much was your first position fix in error? Compare to 5-18.

6-2. You are crossing Haro Strait from East to West and are approximately 1/2 mile south of Beaumont Shoal Buoy VD. Your intention is to approach through Baynes Channel and anchor in Cadboro Bay. You know from the Canadian local notice to mariners that the north lighted Buoy VK guarding Fulford Reef is "off station" and unavailable. To avoid the reef, you set up a danger bearing. Giving the deck watch a hand-bearing compass, you tell them that the QG Light on Cadboro Pt. Should bear : "No more than" or "No less than" this bearing _____. Choose the proper bearing restriction and give the bearing. (Assume you want to pass 0.2 nmi north of the proper location of Buoy VK.)

Note that problems 6-3 through 6-6 do not give an initial position, only an approximate location. To work these, estimate a position in the area based on what you know, lay off your course, and go on from there.

6-3. Running fix. You are sailing north from Rocky Point on the Miller Peninsula. Your heading is 332M. When your log reads 552.4, you take a bearing to bell Buoy 2 off Dungeness Spit, which is 297 M. You continue on course and later take a second bearing of the bell buoy which is then 262 M. The log now reads 556.4. Advance the first LOP to the second to find your position by running fix. (A) How far are you from the Buoy 2? (B) What is your distance off the northernmost point of the Dallas Bank 10 fathom depth contour? (C) What is the water depth where you are?

6-4. Bow angles. In problem 6-3 (A) What was the angle on the bow of the Buoy 2 at log = 552.4? (B) What was the angle on the bow at log 556.4? (C) What was the distance run between sights? (D) What does this tell you about your distance off the buoy at log 556.4? (E) Does this agree with 6-3?

6-5. Bow angles. You are sailing course 062 M off Victoria Harbor. You do not have a chart of the area (big mistake). The Victoria Harbor Light bears 020 M when the log reads 1672.5. (A) What is the angle on the bow of the light? (B) What will the bearing of the light be when you have doubled the angle on the bow staying on your original course? (C) Watching the light and your log, you note that the log reads 1674.2 when the light bears 338 M. What is your distance off the light?

6-6. Running fix. Referring to problem 6-5, now using the chart, verify your results by plotting and advancing the first LOP to form a running fix with the second.

6-7. Running fix, two targets. You are sailing course 050 M near Sheringham Pt. at speed 7 knots. It is foggy but calm. All you can see is Sheringham Pt. Light. You note that it is exactly on your beam at 18:55. (A) What must its magnetic bearing be at 18:55 if it's on your beam and you know your course heading? (B) You continue east on the same course at the same speed. The fog clears and you can just see the light at Race Rocks well off to starboard at 19:19, and it bears 080 M. How far have you traveled?

(C) Advance the first LOP to the second to find your position at 19:19 by running fix. What is your Latitude and Longitude? (D) What light should you be seeing dead ahead?

6-8. Practice with Small Angle Rule. If you steer the wrong course by 3° how far off your intended track will you be after sailing 20 miles?

6-9. If your compass had an error of 12° that you did not know about, how far off course would you be after traveling 45 miles? Use 6° rule, or plot it out to scale.

6-10. Vertical angle. You are approaching Race Rocks Lt. With a sextant you measure its height above the water (Hs) to be 1° 15'. How far off the light are you?

6-11. Vertical angle. You are north of the tower at Angeles Pt. Again, you use your sextant and measure its height above the water to be 2° 45'. What is your distance from the tower?

6-12. Bow angles. You are approaching the 120-foot-high Donaldson Island near Sooke Inlet. Your course is 272 M, the island bears 312 M when the log reads 6366.5. (A) What bearing to the island should you look for in order to double this angle on the bow? Continuing on a steady course, the log reads 6368.2 when the bow angle to the island has been doubled. (B) How far off the island are you now? (C) How close will you pass Otter Point if you hold a steady course?

6-13. Running fix. Your estimated position is 2 miles southeast of Beaumont Shoal Buoy VD, and your course is 000 M. The buoy bears 280 M when your log reads 6672.3, and after sailing for 1.5 miles on course 000 M, the Beaumont buoy bears 226 M. What is your latitude and longitude at the time of the second bearing?

6-14. Running fix. You are sailing on course 042 M at speed 6.0 kts. At 18:40, the Smith Island Lt bears 104 M. At 19:10, the Smith Island Lt bears 132 M. What is your latitude and longitude at 19:10?

6-15. As you sail west out of the Strait of Juan de Fuca, in the inshore zone on the south side, you can clearly see the highest point west of Murdock Creek, bearing 218 M. You measure it's height with your sextant and get 2° 20'. What is your latitude and longitude?

6-16. Running fix. You are SW of Buoy R sailing course 085 T at 6.0 kts. The buoy bears 043 T at 1235, and then 341 T at 1255. (A) How far off the buoy are you at 1255 assuming no current? (B) Same question assuming the current is 2.0 kts toward 295T and (C) same question with current = 1.0 kts due south?

6-17. Same question as 6-16, all three parts, but now assume there is in addition a fresh wind from 040T, which gives you a leeway of some 7°. A, B, and C, give the distances off the buoy.

6-18. Running fix. You are due north of the Ediz Hook Lt [Fl G (2) W 10s] which bearing 160M and you estimate your distance off the light as 2.5 miles. You then sail eastward at 048 M for 3 miles, then change course to 088 M and sail for 4.5 miles. Change again to course 022 M and sail for another 3.2 miles. Now you see the New Dungeness Lt which bears 084 M. (A) Advance your first LOP to the second one to find your running fix. (Latitude and Longitude) (B) From this position work backwards to find out what your actual distance off the light was when you estimated it to be 2.5 miles.

6-19. It is pea soup fog, but from a brief break in visibility you spot the white light on the Hein Bank Buoy north of you, at an estimated distance off of 1 to 3 nmi. Then it socks in again. Your speed is 6 kts and your course is 110 T. Shortly after that you noticed that your depth sounder dropped from something like 20 fathoms to 70 within a few minutes. This gives you the idea to look at the contours on the chart to see if you can figure out where you are from a line of soundings measurement as you cross the Eastern Bank, which you believe is somewhere ahead of you. Looking at the chart, you decide to concentrate on 20-fm and 50-fm contours

You confirm there is no forecasted currents expected at this time. The tide height and the sounder draft have been accounted for, so the recorded depths in the table below are the expected charted depths. (This measurement is best done with log readings rather than just times, because it will expedite the analysis. If you are running in a DR mode, assuming GPS has failed, then you can also drop a DR mark at each sounding record that will further simplify the analysis.)

Time	Log (nmi)	depth (fm)
13:15:00	0	93
13:25:16	1.03	50
13:27:15	1.23	20
13:37:04	2.21	11
13:43:43	2.87	11
13:46:24	3.14	20
13:54:41	3.97	50
14:06:18	5.13	50
14:09:44	5.48	20

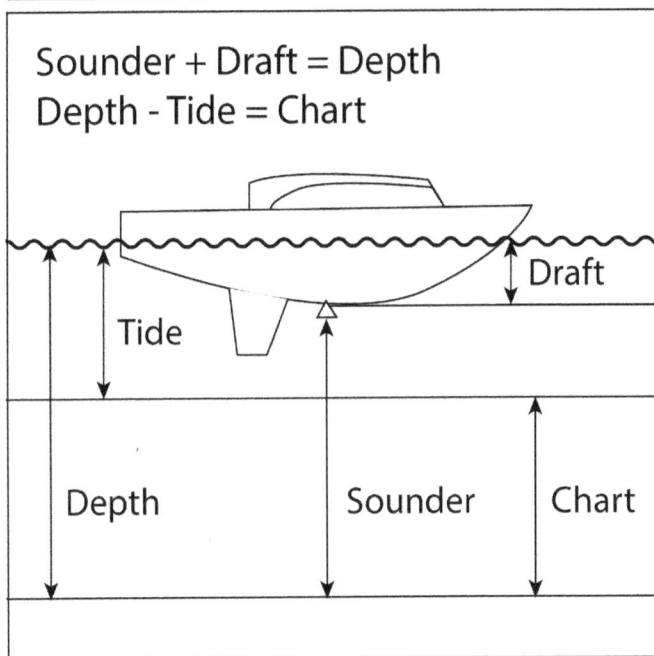

Sounder + Draft = Depth
Depth - Tide = Chart

(A) What is your estimated Lat-Lon at 14:09:44? (B) If you continue on this course, what will be the minimum depth ahead of you? (C) When will you reach that depth? (D) How accurate is this fix and how can we prove it?

6-20. If the tide predictions tell us that low water is 2.0 ft, and the charted depth is 2 fathoms, what is the depth of water in feet at low water?

6-21. If your compass had an error of 12° that you did not know about, how far off course would you be after traveling 45 miles? Use 6° rule, or plot it out to scale.

CHAPTER 7 – ELECTRONIC NAVIGATION

The basic electronic instruments we use for navigation are radar, GPS, and depth sounder, along with our knot-meter and log and wind instruments—which are just as valuable for power boats as they are for sail boats. Instrument manuals are often the main reference; they are usually online these days. It often helps to read manuals from other instrument makers, not just those of the brands you use. AIS receivers are also an important modern aid to navigation

7-1. Suppose you are following the US Shore Route of problem 2-30 reversed (4 to 3, 3 to 2, and 2 to 1) to the west starting at WP4 (Pt Wilson Buoy 6) with your GPS set to automatically switch to the next waypoint when you get within 0.25 miles of the target. Also suppose, as you depart WP4 intending for WP3, for some reason the chart plotter skipped WP3 and set WP2 as the next mark of the course. It is midnight and your speed is 8 knots. (A) What are some consequences of such a goof-up and (B) Name two ways that this type of thing could be avoided. [This is, by the way, a true story].

7-2. Sailing from McCurdy Pt region, NW across the Strait into Haro Strait you must cross two sets of lanes. (A) Set up a fake route that will guide you across these lanes. List the two waypoints for each route, and the XTEs that will mark the boundaries. (B) Can you think of a way that would simplify this process if you did a lot of navigation in this region? See a related reference article listed at starpath.com/18465tr.

7-3. What can be said about the relationship between vertical accuracy and horizontal accuracy of a GPS position? A. They are about the same, B. Vertical accuracy is only about half as good as horizontal accuracy, C. Vertical accuracy is about two times better than horizontal accuracy, D. There is no valuable way to make this comparison.

7-4. You are sailing east (090T) south of Donaldson Islet (48.35N, 123.71W) at a speed of 5.7 kts. From the radar you take a range and bearing to the islet at 1300 and get 3.50 nmi at 321R (relative). (A) What is your lat and lon? (B) at 1400 you do it again and get 2.67 nmi at 235R. What is your new lat and lon? and (C) What was the current you were sailing in?

7-5. Sailing due west (270 T) at 12 kts, south of Donaldson Islet, you measure radar range to Donaldson Islet to be 3.20 nmi and at the same time *(within a few seconds)* the range to Monument Point on Beechey Head is 2.40 nmi. What is your lat and lon?

7-6. You are sailing on course 300 T, south of Donaldson Is, at a speed of 12 kts. At 1410 you measure the range to Otter Point near dead ahead and get 4.80 nmi. At 1413 you measure the range to Donaldson Is near the beam and get 1.10 nmi. (A) what is your Lat and Lon at 1413 if you *do not* take into account the times of the measurements? (B) What is your Lat and Lon if you plot this correctly as a running fix? (C) How much error was in method A?

7-7. What is the typical accuracy we might expect from a GPS fix without any differential enhancement?

(A) ± 2 ft
(B) ± 20 ft
(C) ± 40 ft
(D) ± 80 ft

7-8. A currently operational differential GPS system that considerably improves resultant fix accuracy is called...

(A) GLONASS
(B) Enhanced LORAN
(C) Wide Area Augmentation System
(D) Radio Direction Beacon

7-9. What is the most likely reason that a fix from a handheld GPS unit is not as good as it was just some time in the recent past?

(A) Batteries are low.
(B) A satellite is temporarily not transmitting.
(C) The relative bearings of the satellites you have been using are no longer as favorable as before.
(D) You have sailed into a region or moved the instrument in such a way that part of the sky is now blocked from view of its antenna.

7-10. Your vessel has a small portable chartplotter and GPS navigation system that is quite accurate when used. However, like most electronics, it has some weaknesses. What is the most likely weakest link in your navigation system?

(A) The cigarette lighter socket and wiring.
(B) The navigation chart memory chip.
(C) The VHF microphone exposed to sea water.
(D) The GPS satellite constellation.

7-11. Your very well-equipped vessel has a chartplotter with a WAAS-enabled GPS input; however the chartplotter gets its directional references from the GPS, not from a flux-gate compass. Your accurately swung helm compass often indicates a significantly different direction from the vessel icon on the chartplotter. Why?

7-12. Which type of radar fix is the fastest to achieve for comparison with the GPS?

(A) Two bearings
(B) One range and one bearing
(C) Two ranges
(D) All are the same.

7-13. Which type of radar fix is the most accurate for comparison with the GPS?

    (A) Two bearings
    (B) One range and one bearing
    (C) Two ranges
    (D) All are the same.

7-14. Explain how an electronic charting system (ECS) can be extremely valuable to you even if you do not plan to use any underway, or in fact do not even have any on the boat?

7-15. When sailing with both radar and ECS, what is the fastest way to identify your approximate location (situation awareness)?

7-16. What information do we learn from a basic AIS receiver about vessel targets in the region?

7-17. Which statement concerning Automatic Identification System is NOT true?

(A) Fast AIS Class B vessels can outrun their AIS position broadcasts, much to the annoyance of other mariners, particularly pilots of large ships.

(B) AIS data accessed over the Internet via smart phone or tablet computer is at risk of latent delay and sudden outage.

(C) AIS Class B relies of transmission of vessel position and heading every 5 seconds.

(D) AIS is not to be considered a replacement for the capabilities of traditional marine radar.

7-18. What is the typical range from which we can receive AIS signals from a typical AIS receiver on a recreational vessel?

7-19. List at least three important differences between Raster Navigation Charts (RNC) and Electronic Navigation Charts (ENC). *Both are available from the link you can find at www.starpath.com/getcharts.*

CHAPTER 8 – TIDES AND CURRENTS

In 2020, NOAA discontinued sanctioning third party printing of annual tide and current predictions, and also discontinued predictions for waters outside of the US. Any such books seen in print now should be used with caution. In particular, what was called "Table 2, Tide and Current Differences" is no longer valid after 2020. The intended procedure is now to get the primary data from the NOAA site tidesandcurrents.noaa.gov for each station you care about. There is also the option to print your own Annual Table for that station for use away from the internet. We use samples of that type of printout for these exercises. See Resources Section for helpful tips. Tides and currents can also be found conveniently from within most electronic charting systems, ECS, (see Appendix), but we should always check those sources at least once with the official NOAA data. Instructions for the use of the NOAA online data are at starpath.com/18465tr.

8-1. If the tide predictions tell us that low water is 2.0 ft, and the charted depth is 2 fathoms, what is the depth of water in feet at low water?

8-2. What are the local times and heights in feet for high and low waters at Port Townsend on (A) April 17, 2022 and (B) June 17th, 2022?

8-3. The ocean is calm and no bad weather is forecast. You want to go dinghy exploring in the rocks in and around Aleck Bay on Lopez Island. You want plenty of water for exploring the entire vicinity. (A) What are the precise local times and heights of the evening high water at Aleck Bay on April 2, 2022? (B) According to chart 18465 Tr, what will be the water depth at the rocks in the back bay area at that time?

8-4. There is a prominent house about 2 miles SW of Dungeness Spit visible from the water. The bearing to this house is 110M. Your depth sounder reads 90 feet. (A) Assume this is the charted depth at your location and figure how far off shore you are (off the coast line, not off the house). (B) Now assume the depth sounder is 1 foot below the water and the tide height is 13 feet at the moment. Now how far offshore are you?

8-5. Make an approximate tide height table for every hour or so from about noon till about 8 pm at Port Townsend on May 18, 2022.

8-6. The tidal data box on the chart refers to a place called Gardiner, Discovery Bay. What is the charted depth at the exact Lat-Lon given?

8-7. Find heights in feet and local times of lower low water (LL) and higher high water (HH) at (A) Port Townsend and (B) Aleck Bay for April 17, 2022.

8-8. (A) Our training chart (18465 Tr) is not adequate to enter Sequim Bay. What chart does it tell us to use? (B) What does the Coast Pilot tell us is the minimum charted depth along the marked channel into the Bay? (C) If we draw 6 ft and want an under keel clearance of at least 6 ft, what time window do we have for entering the Bay on Oct 1, 2022? (D) What is unusual about the tides on this day and others in this Bay?

8-9. There is a bridge in Port Townsend, just out of sight of this chart, which is labeled to have a vertical clearance of 58 feet. The high tide at the bridge is currently 10 feet. What is the actual clearance under this bridge at this time?

8-10. If your sailboat has a mast height of 62 ft, what would be your time window to pass under the bridge in 8-9 with a safety margin of 1 foot on June 2, 2022?

8-11. (A) What is the difference between Mean Lower Low Water (used as the sounding reference for US waters) and Lowest Normal Tides used in Canadian Waters?

8-12. (A) Mark the location of all tide and current stations on your chart within 5 miles of Iceberg Point. (B) What is the nearest tide station to Iceberg Point? HINT: The tidal currents app in any ECS should plot these out for you, else we need to get the data from the NOAA web page.

8-13. (A) What is the nearest current station to 48° 20' N, 123° 2' W? (B) What would be the best current station to use for waters south of Protection Island? HINT: need to check NOAA site, or use currents app in an ECS.

8-14. (A) What are the local times of the slacks before and after the mid-day ebb at Station PUG1635 (2.8 mi NNW of New Dungeness Light) on Sept 1, 2022? (B) What is the time and speed of the peak midday ebb? (C) Are these local times PDT or PST? (D) In the official definition of the station location, are the miles referred to statute miles or nautical miles?

8-15. What are times (PDT) and speeds of peak currents and slack water times at Lopez Pass (PUG1730) on July 2, 2022? (B) What are the mean flood and ebb directions at this station?

8-16. We want to go under power starting from halfway between Decatur Island and Belle Rock (top right of chart 18465 Tr), down around the south end of Lopez Island and up through the San Juan Channel to a destination just west of Rock Point. Assume the current forecast at Rosario Strait (PUG1702) describes the general flow along the east side of the islands, and that the forecast at San Juan Channel, south entrance (PUG1703) describes the current flow along the west side. (A) Not counting for current, roughly how long would this trip take at 5 kts? (B) With those broad assumptions about the current, what would be the best time of day on May 1, 2022 to make the trip and get the best benefit of the current flow? Explain your logic. (C) Accounting for the current with an engine speed of 5 kts what would be an estimate of the current-corrected transit time?

8-17. Use an echart program with a tidal currents app or go online to tidesandcurrents.noaa.gov to answer the question: What is unique about the currents at current station PUG1634, Smith Island, 3.4 mi ENE of (depth 20 ft)?

8-18. Use an echart program with a tidal currents app or go online to tidesandcurrents.noaa.gov to answer the question: (A) What is name and number of the station in Cape Cod, MA that forecasts the currents at the east end of the Cape Cod Canal? (B) Is the current pattern at that station diurnal, semidiurnal, or mixed semidiurnal? (C) Comparing flood and ebb strengths throughout the year, are the floods much stronger, much weaker, or about the same strength as the ebbs at this location?

8-19. Use an echart program with a tidal currents app or go online to tidesandcurrents.noaa.gov to answer the question: (A) What is name and number of the station in Alabama at the entrance to the Mobile River that forecasts the currents? (B) Is the current pattern at that station diurnal, semidiurnal, or mixed semidiurnal? (C) Comparing flood and ebb strengths throughout the year, are the floods much stronger, much weaker, or about the same strength as the ebbs at this location?

8-20. Is the tide station at Sequim Bay (No. 944555) inside or outside of Travis Spit that extends off of Kiapot Pt. defining the top border of Sequim Bay?

8-21. Tides at Sequim Bay are essentially the same as at Discovery Bay, about 5 nmi to the east. Thus we can assume these represent the tide height at the location of the Kanem Pt current station (PUG1630), about halfway between them. Review the textbook sections on progressive wave vs. standing wave tides, and then compare times of tides at Sequim with times of currents at Kanem Pt on Nov 3, 2022 to determine if the tides in this area are standing wave type or progressive wave type? We need to know this if we are to correlate current times with tide times.

8-22. The currents at the San Francisco Bay entrance are rotary; they are given in the Resources. (A) What would you expect the rotary tidal current component to be on average (set and drift) when the tide height at the Golden Gate was at the lower low? (B) Same question when the tide as at higher high?

8-23. (A) At what stage of the San Francisco tide would you expect the rotary tidal current component at the entrance to be the strongest? (B) What is the approximate set and drift during that period?

8-24. (A) On what day of March, 2011 would you expect the rotary tidal current contribution at San Fransisco Bay entrance to be up to 40% stronger than average? (B) On which day in June, 2011 would you expect these currents to be up to 40% less than average?

8-25. What is the predicted set and drift of the rotary tidal current at the entrance to San Francisco Bay at about 0815 on May 16, 2011? May, 2011 tide data are included in the discussion of rotary currents in Resources.

8-26. Coastal currents, especially near an entrance, are a complex combination of rotating tidal current, wind-driven current, and unseasonal river runoff. Though each of these are relatively small, what is the maximum reported current at the entrance to San Francisco Bay in the vicinity of the entrance buoy SF (former location of the lightship and now the rotary current reference station?

8-27. Practice with the 50-90 Rule explained in the Current Resources. It is the counterpart for currents of the Rule of Twelfths for tides. Consider a hypothetical place where we have the following current data:

0443	Slack
0817	2.3F
1131	Slack
1412	1.7E

(A) Find the current speed at 0543, 0630, and 0717. These times are an hour from the turning points as well as the midpoint. Use Table 3 of the Current Tables (Table A) and compare the results you get with the Starpath 50-90 Rule for making these estimates. (B) Then do the same in the next cycle which goes back to slack at 1131 (i.e. 0917, 0954, and 1031). (C) And for more practice, repeat for the next cycle which peaks at 1.7 ebb at 1412. (i.e. 1231, 1251, and 1312).

8-28. Based on our sample currents data for selected days in 2022 for the San Juan Channel, which of the days listed have a full moon?

8-29. We see two half moons on Sept 3 and 17 in the currents data. They have different sides lit up. Which one is waning (growing less full) and which is waxing (growing fuller)?

CHAPTER 9 – NAVIGATION IN CURRENTS

Current sailings are usually vector problems that can be solved by basic plotting or by dedicated calculators programmed for the job. Alternatively, they can be quickly solved with ECS displays as outlined in Appendix A1. There are also approximations listed in the Resources for quick estimates adequate for most practical work, keeping in mind we do not often know the currents very precisely. Chapters 5 and 6 have related exercises.

9-1. At 0915, you depart the New Dungeness Sand Spit lighted bell Buoy 2 (48° 11.5' N, 123° 05.7' W) on a course of 090° M toward Dallas Bank & McCurdy Pt. You are sailing on a broad reach in calm seas making 6.0 knots through the water. At 1045, you find yourself close aboard the McCurdy Point Buoy 4 (48° 08.7' N, 122° 50.7' W). What has been the set and drift of the current during the trip?

9-2. You are located 3.0 nmi due north of the Dungeness Spit Light. Your goal is to figure the initial magnetic course to steer (CTS) to take you to Buoy 1 at the SW tip of Protection Island, taking into account the tidal currents. You will be motoring at a knotmeter speed of 5.5 kts. It is 10:15 local time on July 1, 2022. Variation is 20 E. (A) What is the length of this route in nmi, and what is the magnetic bearing from start to finish? (B) How long would this leg take with no current at a speed of 5.5 kts? (C) What is the nearest current station to the starting point, and will the current be helping us (ie faster than without current) or slowing us down? Current data in the Resources section. (D) Use the 50-90 rule to make an estimate of the current speed during the first hour of this trip. (E) Now use some method to find the CTS in a current of 1.5 kts toward 273T when your speed through the water is 5.5 kts and you make good the course of 121M. Try both plotting and some numerical solution. (F) If the current remains the same all the way to Buoy 1, what time will you get there? (G) Look for the closest current station to the destination at Buoy 1, to see if it was reasonable to treat the current as constant over this leg. In other words, what was the current at 1219 on July 1, 2022 near the Buoy 1, SW tip of Protection Island?

9-3. Using a net tidal current vector (which means you assume the current is the same over the full run of all entries), plot your estimated 1552 position from the following Deck Log entries, assuming the current is 1.1 kt @ 270° T.

Time	Log	Course	Wind	Remarks
1330	10.5	050°M	270° T @ 15 kts	Close aboard Y "VF" 48° 14.1' N, 123° 31.9' W
1430	16.0	110°M	270° T @ 15 kts	Jibed to Starboard Tack
1518	20.4	050°M	270° T @ 15 kts	Jibed to Port Tack
1552	23.5	050°M	270° T @ 15 kts	Since 1330 current has been constant: 1.1 kt @ 270° T

(A) From the 1552 EP, what is the range and true bearing to New Dungeness Light if there were no current present?

(B) What is this same range and bearing after you correct the DR for the set and drift?

9-4. Current is on your port beam at about 2 kts. Your compass reads 200 and your knotmeter reads 6.0 knots. (A) What is a quick estimate of your CMG? (B) Will your SMG be larger or smaller than your knotmeter speed? (C) What is your exact CMG and SMG from plotting?

9-5. Current is on your starboard quarter at about 2 kts. Your compass reads 200 and your knotmeter reads 6.0 knots. What is your approximate CMG?

9-6. Your knotmeter speed is 5.0 knots. You want to cross a current that you estimate is about 1.5 knots on your beam. How many degrees should you point into the current to track straight across the current?

9-7. Sailor's question: You are beating to weather in strong southerly winds on a port tack. You estimate that your leeway is 10°. There is a current flowing to the north at about 2.0 knots. Your compass reads 205 and your knotmeter reads 6.0 knots. (A) What is your CMG? (B) If you know you tack through 90° in such conditions, what should the compass bearing to a windward buoy be if you intend to pass to weather of it when you tack?

9-8. On a mountain hike you wish to cross a large open meadow to a tree in the far corner. Explain how you might navigate this walk across the field in the least number of steps without being distracted by the beautiful hills and mountains on the other side.

9-9. You want to go across a large open area to your destination, which you can see on the horizon. You know there are currents present but have no idea what they are. You pass by a lighthouse just as you start your crossing. That is, just as you enter the currents the lighthouse is dead astern. Your destination is dead ahead and your compass reads 340. The back bearing to the lighthouse is 160°. After traveling some time you notice that the lighthouse is no longer dead astern, though your destination still lies dead ahead because it is so far away, and your compass course hasn't changed. Using a hand-held bearing compass you find the bearing to the lighthouse is now 135°. What compass course should you steer to get back on track toward your destination? (A long problem with a quick and easy solution.)

9-10. During a passage in tidal waters you notice a prominent tide rip some distance ahead. What can you expect the current to do upon crossing that rip line?

9-11. The following are standard current sailing problems. H= boat heading, S=knotmeter speed. All directions true.

(A) Fill in the missing data. For example in #1 you are steering 200 T at a knotmeter speed of 6.0 and the tables tell you to expect a current of 2.0 kts in direction 150. What do you anticipate will be your CMG and SMG in these conditions. In #4, you want to cross a current of 2.0 kts in direction 150 making good a course of 200, running at a knotmeter speed of 6.0. What course should you steer and what will be your SMG on this course? In #7, you are steering a steady course of 180 with a steady knotmeter speed of 7.4, but your trail of past positions shows you are making good a steady 205 and your SOG on the GPS shows that you have had a steady SOG of 6.8. If this difference is due to current alone, what would be the set and drift of this current?

#	S	H	Set	Drift	CMG	SMG
1	6.0	200	150	2.0		
2	5.0	100	315	1.5		
3	7.5	350	260	1.8		
4	6.0		150	2.0	200	
5	5.0		315	1.5	100	
6	7.5		260	1.8	350	
7	7.4	180			205	6.8
8	6.2	130			110	5.6
9	6.2	130			110	7.0

(B) Compare the headings you get from 4, 5, and 6 with those of 1, 2, and 3 to evaluate how accurate it is to just assume the correction to make good a course is just the opposite of what happens if you do not correct the course. That is, if I am being set 15° to the right, I can correct by steering 15° to the left. (C) Compare the answers you get to 1 through 7 with the simple Starpath 40-60 Rule for current sailing.

9-12. You are sailing in a region with only one current station covering the full area you will be transiting. The current report for this reversing current pattern is as follows:

2103	slack
0035	1.7 F
0326	slack
0613	1.4 E

Practice using the 50-90 Rule given in the Resources to answer these questions: (A) If you were sailing in this current from slack to slack (about 2100 to 0330) what would be an equivalent average current that could be used for figuring an average SMG during this period? (B) Same question, but now entering the current at 0130 (about an hour after the peak) and leaving it at 0330 (about slack)?, and (C) Entering at 0230 (about an hour before slack) and leaving at 0530 about an hour before next peak

9-13. This is an important exercise, because sometimes we need to transit a pass that has strong currents so we must be there at specific times, which are in fact easy to look up. But if the Pass is some distance off and there are weaker but significant currents along the way, the harder part of the navigation is planning though these changing currents on the way to the Pass so we get there on time. Thus we have here an exercise in the process of figuring effects of currents by deciding what time of day is best for a trip and how will the currents along the way affect our ETA. The chartlet we need is shown in Figure 9-13, which includes enough information to work the exercise, but a printable version is noted in the caption.

We consider the trip from Mats Mats to Pt Hudson, located in the Admiralty Inlet to Puget Sound, WA. The date is Oct 16, 2021. The current data needed are in the Figure. The active stations are small squares, linked to the station numbers, with the true directions of the flood and ebb beside them. Speeds are in kts; times in PDT. NOAA always lists ebb currents as negative, but this is not related to practical applications. Effect on our routes could be plus or minus.

Without current, this 11+ nmi route takes about 2 hr at 6 kts with no current. But current is significant in this area, so the question arises about what time of day would be most efficient at 6 kts under power.

We have the choice of a morning trip starting about 5 am PDT or midday starting about 11 am PDT. Divide the route up with waypoints as shown in Figure 9-13, so the route legs can be associated with a specific current forecast.

(A) Make a Route Plan for the route of Figure 9-13.

(B) What currents do you expect along each leg of the route starting at 11 am? Check the answers to get hints on how to organize this exercise. We used the actual plot from NOAA to do this, but you can also use the 50-90 rule (plenty good enough for this) or any current app that lets you look at past current patterns.

(C) Estimate these same currents along the route starting at 5 am.

(D) Using these currents, figure the speed made good (SMG) at a knotmeter speed of 6.0 along each leg for both 5 am run and 11 am run.

(E) Using length of each leg and SMG on each leg figure time on each leg, and then sum them up for a total ETA corrected for current for 5am and 11 am departures.

(F) Which departure time has the fastest total time and how much do you save choosing one over the other?

Notes on this exercise and how to improve it.

1. Often you do not need much math to decide if current is helping or hurting at specific times, but there are often times

DEPTHS IN FEET   **Mats-Mats to Pt Hudson**   WGS 84

PCT511	F100, E 275	
00:44	slack	-
04:05	ebb	-1.23
06:14	slack	-
10:21	flood	1.67
14:26	slack	-
17:35	ebb	-1.24
19:44	slack	-
22:57	flood	0.88

PUG1619	F129, E 349	
01:00	slack	-
05:30	ebb	-3.25
08:36	slack	-
12:00	flood	4.41
15:36	slack	-
18:24	ebb	-3.16
21:30	slack	-

PUG1615	F162, E 357	
00:48	slack	-
04:54	ebb	-2.87
08:24	slack	-
11:12	flood	2.46
13:30	slack	-
17:30	ebb	-1.87
22:30	slack	-

PUG1611	F149, E 342	
00:06	flood	0.57
02:24	slack	-
05:54	ebb	-1.07
08:42	slack	-
11:48	flood	1.08
14:36	slack	-
17:48	ebb	-1.12
22:06	slack	-

1.0 nmi

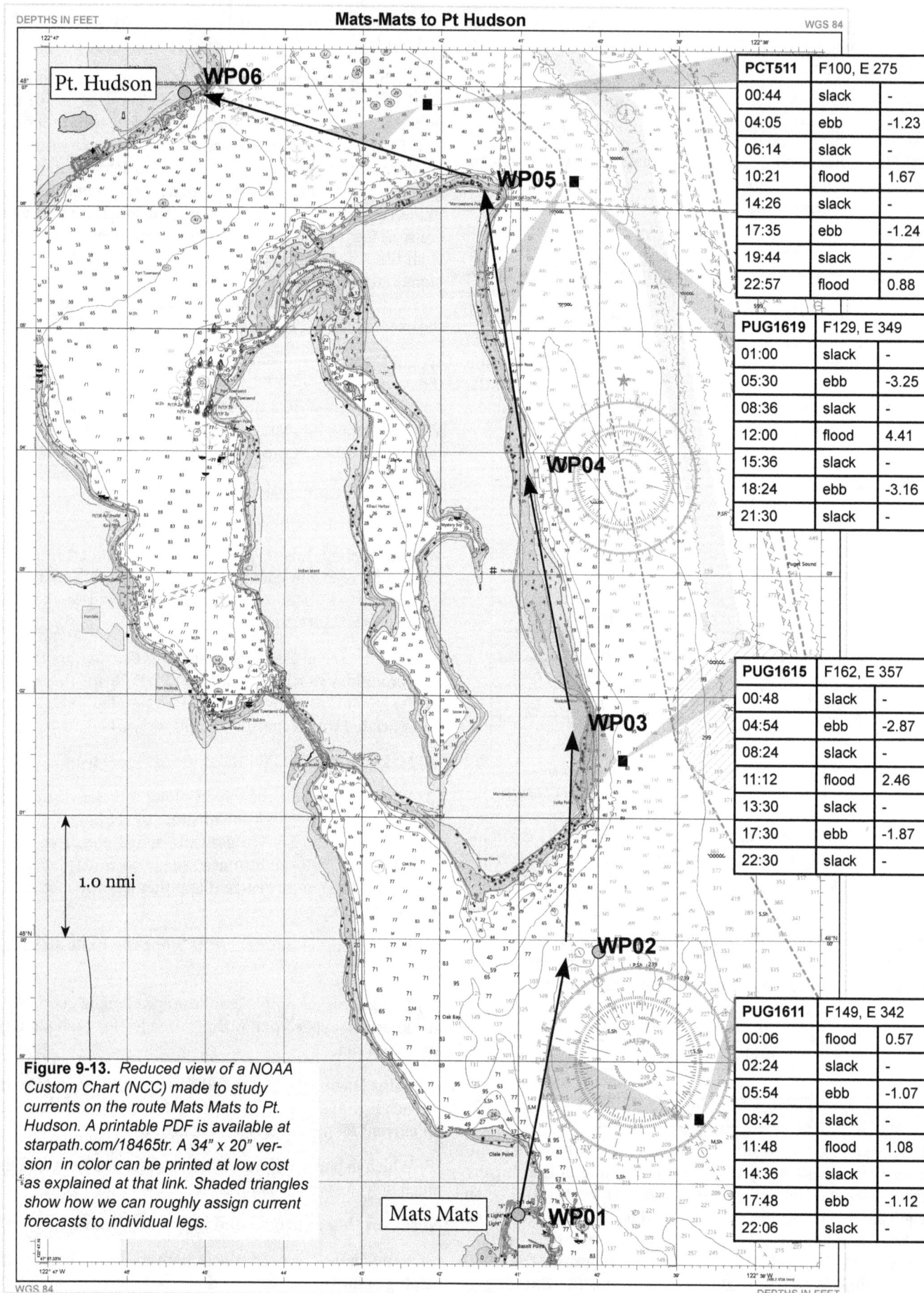

Figure 9-13. *Reduced view of a NOAA Custom Chart (NCC) made to study currents on the route Mats Mats to Pt. Hudson. A printable PDF is available at starpath.com/18465tr. A 34" x 20" version in color can be printed at low cost as explained at that link. Shaded triangles show how we can roughly assign current forecasts to individual legs.*

WGS 84   DEPTHS IN FEET

when it is valuable to know how much the difference is so some form of this analysis is valuable.

2. The 50-90 Rule is generally all you need to estimate currents at specific times.

3. For this short run, we assumed an average current for each leg, and did not change the current times based on when we got there. For longer runs, this is best done in steps. Start at the beginning, figure a SMG, then use that to get to the next current station and then look up the currents for that time.

4. Any program that shows currents can get us the data much faster than the NOAA tables, but we must at some point, double check that the software is correct—and the implication is valid, namely some popular apps do not have accurate tide and current data.

9-14. A running fix with course changes and in a current. Here is the logbook. We are navigating by log and compass, so there is no speed recorded here, but generally that would be included in the logbook.

Time	Log	Course	Notes
1220	52.0	207M	Race Rks Light bears 264M
1237	53.9	290M	Tack to port
1257	56.1	215M	Tack to starboard
1303	56.8	215M	Race Rocks Light bears 053M

Part A. Find your position at log 56.8 assuming no current.

Part B. Find position at log 56.8 assuming a current over the full run of 1.7 kts in direction 098T. (Remember courses are M and current is T.)

CHAPTER 10 – NAVIGATION RULES

Refer to the Navigation Rules to answer these questions. An electronic copy (any format) would be convenient for finding answers. These questions are selected from the USCG database of license exam questions. Each question applies to both the International Rules and to the US Inland Rules, thus if the Rules differ you must choose the answer with the common rules. The Answers list the specific Rules that apply.

Nav Rules Parts A and B.
Definitions and Right of Way

10-1. If you are the stand-on vessel in a crossing situation, you may take action to avoid collision by your maneuver alone. When may this action be taken?

(A) At any time you feel it is appropriate.
(B) Only when you have reached *extremis*.
(C) When you determine that your present course will cross ahead of the other vessel.
(D) When it becomes apparent to you that the give-way vessel is not taking appropriate action.

10-2. Which statement is true concerning a vessel equipped with operational radar?

(A) She must use this equipment to obtain early warning of risk of collision.
(B) The radar equipment is only required to be used in restricted visibility.
(C) The use of a radar excuses a vessel from the need of a lookout.
(D) The safe speed of such a vessel will likely be greater than that of vessels without radar.

10-3. A vessel must proceed at a safe speed...

(A) in restricted visibility.   (B) in congested waters.
(C) during darkness.   (D) at all times.

10-4. A sailing vessel is overtaking a tug and tow as shown in DIAGRAM 43. Which statement is correct?

(A) The sailing vessel is the stand-on vessel because it is overtaking.
(B) The sailing vessel is the stand-on vessel because it is under sail.
(C) The tug is the stand-on vessel because it is being overtaken.
(D) The tug is the stand-on vessel because it is towing.

10-5. The word "vessel", in the Rules, includes...

(A) sailing ships.   (B) nondisplacement craft.
(C) seaplanes.   (D) All of the above.

10-6. If two sailing vessels are running free with the wind on the same side, which one must keep clear of the other?

(A) The one with the wind closest abeam.
(B) The one with the wind closest astern.
(C) The one to leeward.
(D) The one to windward.

10-7. The *NAVIGATION RULES* define a "vessel not under command" as a vessel which...

(A) from the nature of her work is unable to keep out of the way of another vessel.
(B) through some exceptional circumstance is unable to maneuver as required by the rules.
(C) by taking action contrary to the rules has created a special circumstance situation.
(D) is moored, aground or anchored in a fairway.

10-8. A vessel "restricted in her ability to maneuver" is one which...

(A) from the nature of her work is unable to maneuver as required by the rules.
(B) through some exceptional circumstance is unable to maneuver as required by the rules.
(C) due to adverse weather conditions is unable to maneuver as required by the rules.
(D) has lost steering and is unable to maneuver.

10-9. You are seeing another vessel and its compass bearing does not significantly change. This would indicate that...

(A) you are the stand-on vessel.
(B) risk of collision exists.
(C) a special circumstances situation exists.
(D) the other vessel is dead in the water.

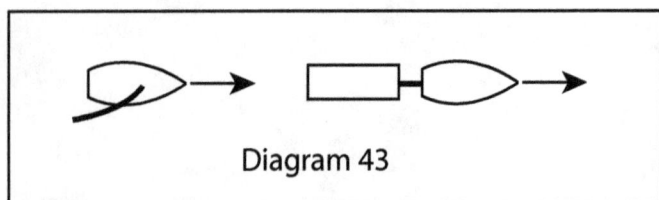

Diagram 43

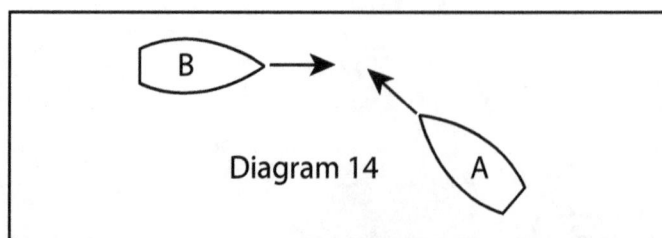

Diagram 14

10-10. You are the watch officer on a power-driven vessel and notice a large sail vessel approaching from astern. You should...

(A) slow down.
(B) sound one short blast and change course to starboard.
(C) sound two short blasts and change course to port.
(D) hold course and speed.

10-11. You are underway on vessel "A" and sight vessel "B" which is a vessel underway and fishing. Which statement is true? (see DIAGRAM 14)

(A) Vessel "A" must keep out of the way of vessel "B" because "B" is to port.
(B) Vessel "A" must keep out of the way of vessel "B" because " B" is fishing.
(C) Vessel "B" must keep out of the way of vessel "A" because "A" is to starboard.
(D) In this case, both vessels are required by the Rules to keep clear of each other.

10-12. If it becomes necessary for a stand-on vessel to take action to avoid collision, she shall, if possible...

(A) not decrease speed.
(B) not increase speed.
(C) not turn to port for a vessel on her own port side.
(D) not turn to starboard for a vessel on her own port side.

10-13. Your vessel is NOT making way, but is not in any way disabled, another vessel is approaching you on your starboard beam. Which statement is true?

(A) The other vessel must give way since your vessel is stopped.
(B) Your vessel is the give-way vessel in a crossing situation.
C . You should be showing the lights or shapes for a vessel not under command.
(D) You should be showing the lights or shapes for a vessel restricted in her ability to maneuver.

10-14. Two vessels meeting in a "head on" situation are directed by the Rules to...

(A) alter course to starboard and pass port to port.
(B) alter course to port and pass starboard to starboard.
(C) decide on which side the passage will occur by matching whistle signals.
(D) slow to bare steerageway.

10-15. A vessel is "engaged in fishing" when...

(A) her gear extends more than 100-meters from the vessel.
(B) she is using any type of gear, other than lines.
(C) she is using fishing apparatus which restricts her maneuverability.
(D) she has any fishing gear on board.

10-16. When shall the stand-on vessel change course and speed?

(A) The stand-on vessel may change course and speed at any time as it has the right-of-way.
(B) After the give-way vessel sounds one blast in a crossing situation.
(C) When action by the give-way vessel alone cannot prevent collision.
(D) When the two vessels become less than one-half mile apart.

10-17. Which factor is listed in the Rules as one which must be taken into account when determining safe speed?

(A) The construction of the vessel.
(B) The maneuverability of the vessel.
(C) The experience of vessel personnel.
(D) All of the above.

10-18. Which statement is true concerning seaplanes on the water?

(A) A seaplane must show appropriate lights but need not exhibit shapes.
(B) A seaplane should exhibit the lights for a vessel constrained by her draft.
(C) In situations where a risk of collision exists, a seaplane should always give way.
(D) A seaplane on the water shall, in general, keep well clear of all vessels.

10-19. A vessel approaching your vessel from 235 degrees relative is in what type of situation?

(A) Meeting.   (B) Overtaking.
(C) Crossing.   (D) Passing.

10-20. Vessels "A" and "B" are crossing as shown in DIAGRAM 26. Which statement is true?

(A) The vessels should pass starboard to starboard.
(B) Vessel "B" should pass under the stern of vessel "A".
(C) Vessel "B" should alter course to the right.
(D) Vessel "A" must keep clear of vessel "B".

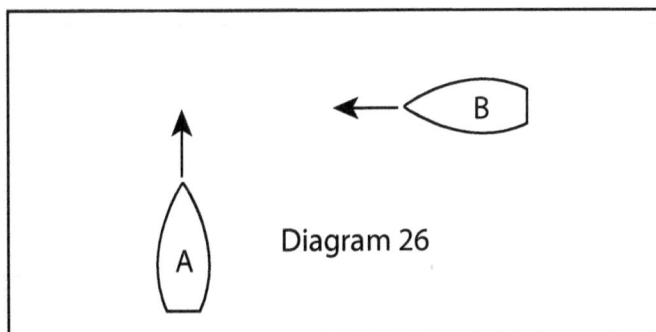

Diagram 26

10-21. In the situation illustrated in DIAGRAM 2, Vessel I is a power-driven vessel. Vessel II is a sail vessel with the wind dead aft. Which of the following statements about this situation is correct?

(A) Vessel I should keep out of the way of Vessel II.
(B) Vessel II should keep out of the way of Vessel I.
(C) Vessel II would normally be the stand-on vessel, but should stay out of the way in this particular situation.
(D) The Rules of Special Circumstances applies, and neither vessel is the stand-on vessel.

10-22. You are aboard vessel "A" on open waters and vessel "B", a sailing vessel, is sighted off your port bow as shown in DIAGRAM 27. Which vessel is the stand on vessel?

(A) Vessel "A" because it is towing.
(B) Vessel "A" because it is to starboard of vessel "B".
(C) Vessel "B" because it is sailing.
(D) Vessel "B" because it is to port of vessel "A".

10-23. You are on vessel "A" and approaching vessel "B" as shown in DIAGRAM 15. You are not sure whether your vessel is crossing or overtaking vessel "B". You should...

(A) change course to make the situation definitely either crossing or overtaking.
(B) consider it to be a crossing situation.
(C) consider it to be an overtaking situation.
(D) consider it a crossing situation if you can cross ahead safely.

10-24. The term "restricted visibility" as used in the Rules refers...

(A) only to fog.
(B) only to visibility of less than one-half of a mile.
(C) to visibility where you cannot see shore.
(D) to any condition where visibility is restricted.

10-25. Which statement(s) is (are) true concerning the Rules of the Road?

(A) Distress signals are in the Annexes of the Rules.
(B) Spacing and positioning requirements for lights are in the Annexes to the Rules.
(C) Radar information is in the main body of the Rules.
(D) All of the above.

10-26. According to the Navigation Rules, you may depart from the Rules when...

(A) no vessels are in sight visually.
(B) no vessels are visible on radar.
(C) you are in immediate danger.
(D) out of sight of land.

10-27. Which statement is true concerning two sailing vessels?

(A) A sailing vessel with the wind forward of the beam on her port side shall keep out of the way of a sailing vessel with the wind forward of the beam on the starboard side.
(B) When both vessels have the wind on the same side, the vessel to leeward shall keep out of the way.
(C) A sail vessel with the wind aft of the beam must keep out of the way of a vessel sailing into the wind.
(D) None of the above.

10-28. You are aboard vessel "A" which is towing on open waters when vessel "B", a sailing vessel, is sighted off your port bow, as shown in DIAGRAM 20. Which vessel has the right of way?

(A) Vessel "A" is the stand-on vessel because it is towing.
(B) Vessel "A" is the stand-on vessel because it is to starboard of vessel "B".
(C) Vessel "B" is the stand-on vessel because it is sailing.
(D) Vessel "B" is the stand-on vessel because it is to port of vessel "A".

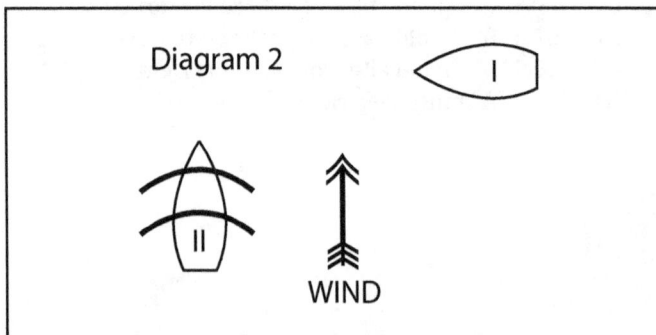

Diagram 2

WIND

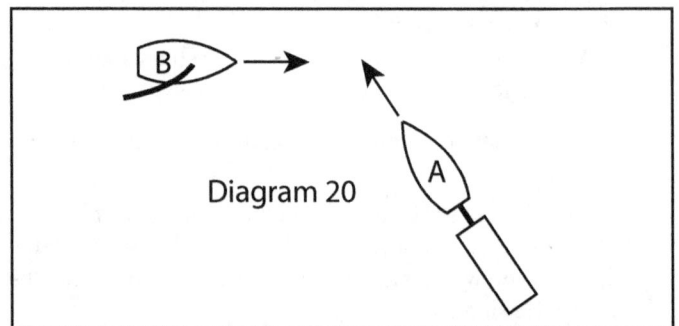

Diagram 20

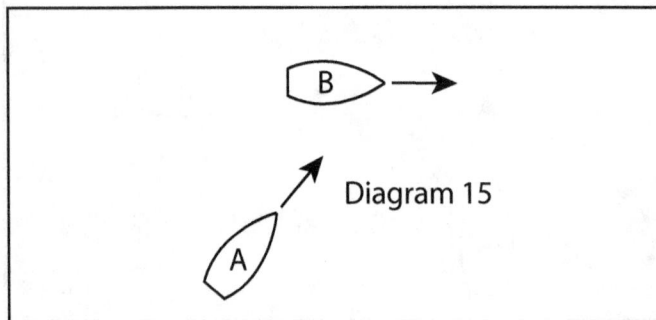

Diagram 15

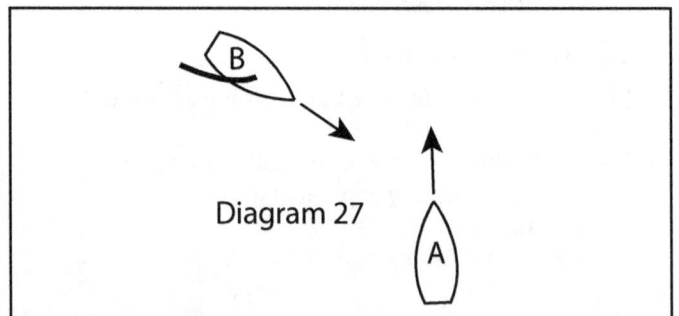

Diagram 27

10-29. When underway in a channel, you should keep....

(A) in the middle of the channel.
(B) to the starboard side of the channel.
(C) to the port side of the channel.
(D) to the side of the channel that has the widest turns.

10-30. When navigating in restricted visibility, a power-driven vessel shall...

(A) if risk of collision does not exist, still stop her engines when hearing a fog signal forward of her beam.
(B) have her engines ready for immediate maneuver.
(C) when making way, sound one prolonged blast at intervals of not more than one minute.
(D) operate at a speed to be able to stop in the distance of her visibility.

10-31. A vessel is "in sight" of another vessel when...

(A) she can be observed visually or by radar.
(B) she can be observed visually from the other vessel.
(C) she can be seen well enough to determine her heading.
(D) her fog signal can be heard.

10-32. Which statement is true concerning two sailing vessels approaching each other?

(A) A sailing vessel overtaking another is the give-way vessel.
(B) When each is on a different tack, the vessel on the starboard tack shall keep out of the way.
(C) A sailing vessel seeing another to leeward on an undetermined tack shall hold her course.
(D) All of the above.

10-33. A power-driven vessel has on her port side a sailing vessel which is on a collision course. The power-driven vessel is to...

(A) maintain course and speed.
(B) keep clear.
(C) sound one blast and turn to starboard.
(D) stop her engines.

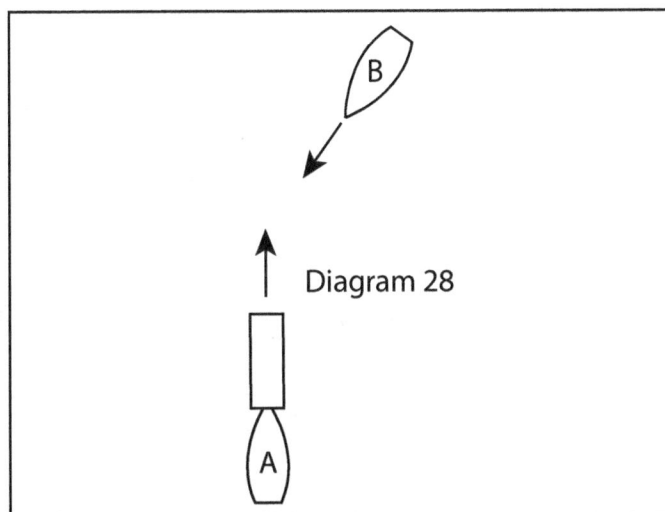

10-34. A sailing vessel is NOT required to keep out of the way of a...

(A) power-driven vessel.
(B) vessel not under command.
(C) vessel restricted in her ability to maneuver.
(D) vessel engaged in fishing.

10-35. In DIAGRAM 28, vessel "A" is underway and towing, when vessel "B" is sighted off the starboard bow. Which vessel is the stand-on vessel?

(A) Vessel "A" is the stand-on vessel because it is to port.
(B) Vessel "A" is the stand-on vessel because it is towing.
(C) Vessel "B" is the stand-on vessel because it is to starboard of vessel "A".
(D) Neither vessel is the stand-on vessel.

10-36. A sailing vessel is meeting a vessel engaged in fishing in a narrow channel. Which statement is true?

(A) The fishing vessel shall not hinder the passage of the sail vessel.
(B) The fishing vessel has the right of way.
(C) Each vessel should move to the edge of the channel on her port side.
(D) Each vessel should be displaying signals for a vessel constrained by her draft.

10-37. Vessel "A" is overtaking vessel "B" as shown in DIAGRAM 9. Which vessel is the stand-on vessel?

(A) Vessel "A".
(B) Vessel "B".
(C) Neither vessel.
(D) Both vessels must keep clear of the other.

10-38. A vessel is being propelled both by sail and by engines. Under the Rules, the vessel is...

(A) considered a "special circumstance" vessel.
(B) not covered under any category.
(C) considered a sail vessel.
(D) considered a power-driven vessel.

10-39. The rule regarding lookouts applies...

(A) in restricted visibility.
(B) between dusk and dawn.
(C) in heavy traffic.
(D) All of the above.

10-40. When taking action to avoid collision, you should...

(A) make sure the action is taken in enough time.
(B) not make any large course changes.
(C) not make any large speed changes.
(D) All of the above.

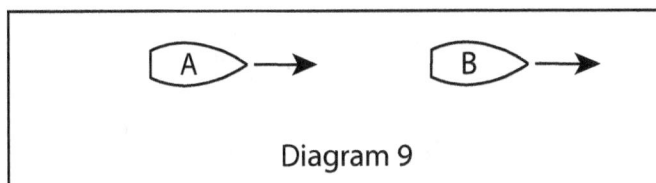

Diagram 28

Diagram 9

10-41. A vessel transferring cargo while underway is classified by the Rules as a vessel...

(A) not under command.
(B) in special circumstances.
(C) restricted in her ability to maneuver.
(D) constrained by her draft.

10-42. Which vessel is "underway" under the Rules of the Road?

(A) A vessel at anchor with the engine running.
(B) A vessel with a line led to a tree onshore.
(C) vessel drifting with the engine off.
(D) A vessel aground.

10-43. You are on watch in the fog. The vessel is proceeding at a safe speed when you hear a fog signal ahead of you. The Rules require you to navigate with caution until the danger of collision is over and to...

(A) slow to less than 2 knots.
(B) reduce to bare steerageway.
(C) stop your engines.
(D) begin a radar plot.

10-44. In order for a stand-on vessel to take action in a situation, she must determine that the other vessel...

(A) is restricted in her ability to maneuver.
(B) has sounded the danger signal.
(C) is not taking appropriate action.
(D) has not changed course since risk of collision was determined.

Nav Rules Part C. Lights and Dayshapes

10-45. At night, a barge being towed astern must display...

(A) red and green sidelights only.
(B) a white sternlight only.
(C) sidelights and a sternlight.
(D) one all-round white light.

10-46. Which of the following may be used as a distress signal?

(A) Directing the beam of a searchlight at another vessel.
(B) A smoke signal giving off orange colored smoke.
(C) A whistle signal of one prolonged and three short blasts.
(D) International Code Signal PAN.

10-47. A pilot vessel on pilotage duty at night will show sidelights and a sternlight...

(A) when at anchor.
(B) only when making way.
(C) at any time when underway.
(D) only when the identifying lights are not being shown.

10-48. A vessel which displays the day signal as shown in DIAGRAM 6 is engaged in...

(A) submarine cable laying.   (B) pilotage duty.
(C) fishing.   (D) mine sweeping.

10-49. A vessel displaying the dayshapes illustrated in DIAGRAM 11, is...

(A) towing.   (B) conducting underwater operations.
(C) drifting.   (D) aground.

10-50. Which vessel must show forward and after masthead lights when making way?

(A) A 75-meter vessel restricted in her ability to maneuver.
(B) A 100-meter sailing vessel.
(C) A 150-meter vessel engaged in fishing.
(D) A 45-meter vessel engaged in towing.

10-51. A light signal of three flashes means...

(A) "I am in doubt as to your actions".
(B) "My engines are full speed astern".
(C) "I desire to overtake you".
(D) "I am operating astern propulsion".

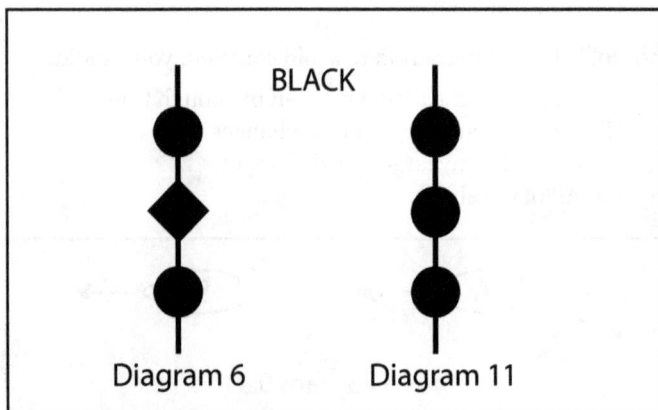

Diagram 6   Diagram 11

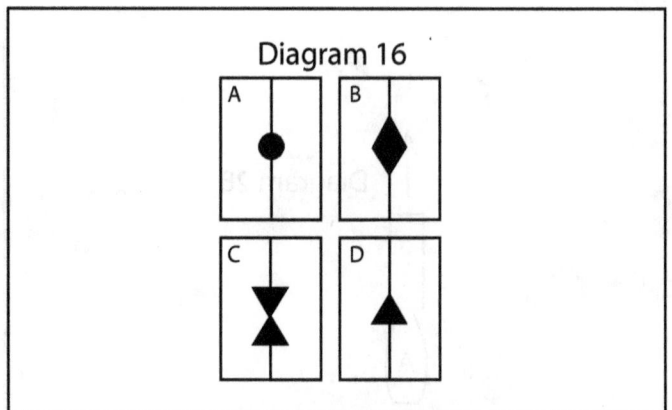

Diagram 16

10-52. If a towing vessel and her tow are severely restricted in their ability to change course, they may show lights in addition to their towing identification light. These additional lights may be shown if the tow is...

(A) pushed ahead.
(B) towed alongside.
(C) towed astern.
(D) Any of the above.

10-53. Additional light signals are provided in the Annexes to the Rules for vessels...

(A) engaged in fishing.
(B) not under command.
(C) engaged in towing.
(D) under sail.

10-54. Which vessel may combine her sidelights in one lantern on the fore and aft centerline of the vessel?

(A) A 16-meter sail vessel.
(B) A 25-meter power-driven vessel.
(C) A 28-meter sail vessel.
(D) Any non-self propelled vessel.

10-55. Which of the following dayshapes, in DIAGRAM 16, indicates a vessel with a tow exceeding 200-meters in length?

(A) A.   (B) B.   (C) C.   (D) D.

10-56. What lights are required for a barge being towed alongside?

(A) Sidelights and a stern light.
(B) Sidelights, a special flashing light, and a sternlight.
(C) Sidelights and a special flashing light.
(D) Sidelights, a towing light, and a sternlight.

10-57. A towing vessel pushing a barge ahead which is rigidly connected in composite unit shall show the lights of...

(A) a vessel towing by pushing ahead.
(B) a power-driven vessel, not towing.
(C) a barge being pushed ahead.
(D) either answer A or answer B.

10-58. You see a vessel's green sidelight bearing due east from you. The vessel might be heading...

(A) east.
(B) northeast.
(C) northwest.
(D) southwest.

10-59. A vessel shall be deemed to be overtaking when she is in such a position with reference to the vessel she is approaching that she can see, at night...

(A) only the sternlight of the vessel.
(B) the sternlight and one sidelight of the vessel.
(C) only a sidelight of the vessel.
(D) any lights except the masthead lights of the vessel.

10-60. A vessel trawling will display a...

(A) red light over a white light.
(B) green light over a white light.
(C) white light over a red light.
(D) white light over a green light.

10-61. The rules concerning lights shall be complied with in all weathers from sunset to sunrise. The lights...

(A) shall be displayed in restricted visibility during daylight hours.
(B) need not be displayed when no other vessels are in the area.
(C) shall be set at low power when used during daylight hours.
(D) need not be displayed by unmanned vessels.

10-62. You are in charge of a power-driven vessel navigating at night. You sight the red sidelight of another vessel on your port bow. Its after masthead light is to the right of the forward masthead light. You should...

(A) hold course and speed.
(B) alter course to port.
(C) stop engines.
(D) sound the danger signal.

10-63. A 30-meter tug is underway and not towing. At night, this vessel must show sidelights and...

(A) one masthead light and a sternlight.
(B) two masthead lights and a sternlight.
(C) three masthead lights and a sternlight.
(D) a sternlight.

10-64. A vessel at anchor shall display between sunrise and sunset on the forward part of the vessel where it can best be seen...

(A) one black ball.
(B) two black balls.
(C) one red ball.
(D) two orange and white balls.

10-65. Which vessel must exhibit three white masthead lights in a vertical line?

(A) Any vessel towing astern.
(B) A vessel whose tow exceeds 200-meters astern.
(C) A vessel not under command, at anchor.
(D) A vessel being towed.

10-66. Which vessel must show an after masthead light, if over 50-meters in length?

(A) A vessel engaged in fishing.
(B) A vessel at anchor.
(C) A vessel not under command.
(D) A vessel trawling.

10-67. A "flashing light" is a light that...

(A) is red in color.
(B) is visible over an arc of the horizon of 360 degrees.
(C) flashes at regular intervals at a frequency of 120.
flashes or more per minute.
(D) All of the above.

10-68. An authorized light to assist in the identification of submarines operating on the surface is a/an...

(A) blue rotating light.
(B) intermittent flashing amber/yellow light.
(C) flashing white light.
(D) flashing sidelight.

10-69. During the day, a dredge will indicate the side on which it is safe to pass by displaying...

(A) two balls in a vertical line.
(B) two diamonds in a vertical line.
(C) a single black ball.
(D) no shape is shown during the day.

10-70. What type of vessel or operation is indicated by a vessel showing two cones with the apexes together?

(A) Sailing vessel.
(B) Vessel trawling.
(C) Mineclearing.
(D) Dredge.

10-71. A vessel, which is unable to maneuver due to some exceptional circumstance, shall exhibit...

(A) during the day, three balls in a vertical line.
(B) during the day, three shapes, the highest and lowest being balls and the middle being a diamond.
(C) when making way at night, two all-round red lights, sidelights, and a sternlight.
(D) when making way at night, masthead lights, sidelights, and a sternlight.

10-72. One of the signals, other than a distress signal, that can be used by a vessel to attract attention is a/an...

(A) searchlight.
(B) continuous sounding of a fog-signal apparatus.
(C) burning barrel.
(D) orange smoke signal.

10-73. A lantern combining the two sidelights of a vessel's running lights may be shown on a...

(A) 15-meter sailing vessel.
(B) 20-meter vessel engaged in fishing and making way.
(C) 25-meter power-driven vessel trolling.
(D) 25-meter pilot vessel.

10-74. A vessel engaged in fishing during the day would show...

(A) one black ball.
(B) two cones with bases together.
(C) a cone, point downward.
(D) two cones, points together.

10-75. By day, when it is impracticable for a small vessel engaged in diving operations to display the shapes for a vessel engaged in underwater operations, it shall display...

(A) three black balls in a vertical line.
(B) two red balls in a vertical line.
(C) a black cylinder.
(D) a rigid replica of the International Code flag "A".

10-76. A vessel will NOT show sidelights when...

(A) underway but not making way.
(B) making way, not under command.
(C) not under command, not making way.
(D) trolling underway.

10-77. Which vessel may show two masthead lights in a vertical line?

(A) A vessel less than 50-meters in length with a 20-meter tow.
(B) A sail vessel towing a small vessel astern.
(C) A vessel restricted in her ability to maneuver.
(D) A vessel engaged in dredging.

10-78. What dayshape should a vessel being towed exhibit if the tow EXCEEDS 200-meters?

(A) Two balls.
(B) Two diamonds.
(C) One ball.
(D) One diamond.

10-79. Which statement is true when you are towing more than one barge astern at night?

(A) Only the last barge in the tow must be lighted.
(B) Only the first and last barges in the tow must be lighted.
(C) Each barge in the tow must be lighted.
(D) Only manned barges must be lighted.

10-80. The white masthead light required for a power-driven vessel under the Rules is visible over how many degrees of the horizon?

(A) 22.5 degrees.
(B) 112.5 degrees.
(C) 225.0 degrees.
(D) 360.0 degrees.

10-81. Which statement is true concerning lights and shapes for towing vessels?

(A) If a tow exceeds 200-meters in length, the towing vessel will display a black ball during daylight.
(B) When towing astern, a vessel will carry her identification lights at the masthead in addition to her regular masthead light.
(C) When towing astern, the towing vessel may show either a sternlight or a towing light, but not both.
(D) If the towing vessel is over 50-meters in length, she must carry forward and after masthead lights.

10-82. A vessel may use any sound or light signals to attract the attention of another vessel as long as...

(A) white lights are not used.
(B) red and green lights are not used.
(C) the vessel signals such intentions over the radiotelephone.
(D) the signal cannot be mistaken for a signal authorized by the Rules.

10-83. Which vessel may exhibit identifying lights when not actually engaged in her occupation?

(A) a trawler.　　(B) a fishing vessel.
(C) a tug.　　(D) none of the above.

10-84. What lights, if any, would you exhibit at night if your vessel was broken down and being towed by another vessel?

(A) none.
(B) same lights as for a power driven vessel underway.
(C) a white light forward and a white light aft.
(D) side lights and a stern light.

Nav Rules Part D. Sound Signals

10-85. While underway in fog, you hear a prolonged blast from another vessel. This signal indicates a...

(A) sailboat underway.
(B) vessel underway, towing.
(C) vessel underway, making way.
(D) vessel being towed.

10-86. Reserved.

10-87. If your vessel is approaching a bend and you hear a prolonged blast from around the bend, you should...

(A) back your engines.
(B) stop your engines and drift.
(C) answer with one prolonged blast.
(D) sound the danger signal.

10-88. Failure to understand the course or intention of an approaching vessel should be indicated by...

(A) one short blast.
(B) one prolonged blast.
(C) no less that five short blasts.
(D) not less that five prolonged blasts.

10-89. If your vessel is underway in fog and you hear one prolonged and three short blasts, this is a...

(A) vessel not under command.
(B) sailing vessel.
(C) vessel in distress.
(D) vessel being towed.

10-90. A power-driven vessel underway in fog making NO way must sound what blast(s) on the whistle ?

(A) One long.
(B) Two prolonged.
(C) One prolonged.
(D) One prolonged and two short.

10-91. Which of the following is a distress signal?

(A) A triangular flag above or below a ball.
(B) The International Code Signal of distress indicated by JV.
(C) A green smoke signal.
(D) Flames on the vessel as from a burning tar barrel.

10-92. A sailing vessel with the wind abaft the beam is navigating in fog. She should sound...

(A) three short blasts.
(B) one prolonged blast.
(C) one prolonged and two short blasts.
(D) two prolonged blasts.

10-93. Which of the following actions would indicate a distress signal?

(A) Firing of green star shells.
(B) Deploying dye marker in the water.
(C) Answering a one blast signal with two blasts.
(D) Sounding 5 short blasts on the whistle.

10-94. The duration of a prolonged blast of the whistle is...

(A) 2 to 4 seconds.　　(B) 4 to 6 seconds.
(C) 6 to 8 seconds.　　(D) 8 to 10 seconds.

10-95. When underway in restricted visibility, you might hear, at intervals of two minutes, any of the following fog signals EXCEPT...

(A) one prolonged blast.
(B) two prolonged blasts.
(C) one prolonged and two short blasts.
(D) ringing of a bell for five seconds.

10-96. What is the identity fog signal which may be sounded by a vessel engaged on pilotage duty?

(A) 2 short blasts.　　(B) 3 short blasts.
(C) 4 short blasts.　　(D) 5 short blasts.

10-97. A bell is used to sound a fog signal for a...

(A) power-driven vessel underway.
(B) sailing vessel at anchor.
(C) vessel engaged in fishing.
(D) vessel not under command.

10-98. You are on lookout watch, when you sight a vessel displaying the code flag "LIMA" below which is a red ball, this indicates...

(A) a vessel with trolling lines out.
(B) a vessel getting ready to receive aircraft.
(C) a vessel aground.
(D) a vessel in distress.

10-99. You are underway in fog when you hear the rapid ringing of a bell for five seconds followed by the sounding of a gong for five seconds. This signal indicates a vessel...

(A) aground.
(B) more than 100-meters in length, at anchor.
(C) fishing while making no way through the water.
(D) fishing in company with another vessel.

10-100. The wind is ESE, and a sailing vessel is steering NW. What tack is she on, and what fog signal should she sound?

(A) Port tack - one blast at one-minute intervals.
(B) Starboard tack - one blast at one-minute intervals.
(C) Starboard tack - two blasts at one-minute intervals.
(D) Starboard tack - one prolonged and two short blasts at two-minute intervals.

10-101. You are underway and sight a vessel which is continuously sounding its fog whistle. This indicates...

(A) the other vessel desires to communicate by radio.
(B) the other vessel desires a pilot.
(C) a distress signal.
(D) the vessel is aground.

10-102. A tug is towing three barges in line in restricted visibility. The second vessel of the tow should sound...

(A) one prolonged and two short blasts.
(B) one prolonged and three short blasts.
(C) one short blast.
(D) no fog signal.

10-103. You are approaching another vessel on crossing courses. She is about one mile distant and is on your starboard bow. You believe she will cross ahead of you. She then sounds a whistle signal of five short blasts. You should...

(A) answer the signal and hold course and speed.
(B) reduce speed slightly to make sure she will have room to pass.
(C) make a large course change, and slow down if necessary.
(D) wait for another whistle signal from the other vessel.

10-104. You are underway in fog and hear a fog signal of two prolonged blasts on your starboard quarter. You should...

(A) stop your vessel.
(B) change your course to the left.
(C) change course to the right.
(D) hold your course and speed.

10-105. You are underway, in fog, when you hear a whistle signal of one prolonged blast followed by two short blasts. This signal could indicate a vessel...

(A) not under command.   (B) being towed.
(C) aground.   (D) All of the above.

10-106. A 35-ft power-driven vessel must carry for sound signaling...

(A) Whistle.
(B) Bell.
(C) Bell and Whistle.
(D) Any device that makes an efficient sound.

10-107. A 35-ft sailing vessel must carry for sound signaling...

(A) Whistle.
(B) Bell.
(C) Bell and Whistle.
(D) Any device that makes an efficient sound.

10-108. Which of the following statements is true concerning the danger signal?

(A) Vessels must be in sight of each other in order to use the danger signal.
(B) Only the stand-on vessel can sound the danger signal.
(C) Distress signals may be used in place of the danger signal.
(D) The danger signal consists of 4 or more short blasts of the whistle.

10-109. A distress signal...

(A) consists of 5 or more short blasts of the fog signal apparatus.
(B) may be used separately or with other distress signals.
(C) consists of the raising and lowering of a large white flag.
(D) is used to indicate doubt about another vessel's intentions.

10-110. What is the danger signal?

(A) A continuous sounding of the fog signal.
(B) Firing a gun every minute.
(C) Five or more short rapid blasts on the whistle.
(D) One long blast on the whistle.

10-111. At specified intervals, a 40-ft vessel anchored in fog shall sound...

(A) no sound signal needed.   (B) bell.
(C) any efficient sound.   (D) bell and gong.

10-112. Continuous sounding of a fog whistle by a vessel is a signal...

(A) that the vessel is anchored.
(B) for a request that the draw span of a bridge be opened.
(C) of distress.
(D) that the vessel is broken down and drifting.

10-113. Which statement is true concerning the light used with whistle signals?

(A) Use of such a light is required.
(B) The light shall have the same characteristics as a masthead light.
(C) It is only used to supplement short blasts of the whistle.
(D) All of the above.

10-114. What is the minimum sound signaling equipment required aboard a vessel 14-meters in length? [*ed. note: sailing both Inland and International waters*]

(A) A bell only.
(B) A whistle only.
(C) A bell and a whistle.
(D) Any means of making an efficient sound signal.

10-115. When should the fog signal of a vessel being towed be sounded?

(A) After the towing vessel's fog signal.
(B) Before the towing vessel's fog signal.
(C) Approximately one minute after the towing vessel's fog signal.
(D) If the towing vessel is sounding a fog signal, the vessel towed is not required to sound any fog signal.

10-116. Which vessel may sound the danger signal?

(A) The stand-on vessel in a crossing situation.
(B) The give-way vessel in a crossing situation.
(C) A vessel at anchor.
(D) All of the above

10-117. The duration of each blast of whistle signals used in meeting, and crossing, situations is...

(A) about 1 second.   (B) 2 or 4 seconds.
(C) 4 to 6 seconds.   (D) 8 to 10 seconds.

10-118. A fog signal of one short, one prolonged, and one short blast can be sounded by...

(A) a vessel at anchor.   (B) a vessel aground.
(C) a trawler shooting its nets. (D) All of the above.

10-119. While underway in fog you hear a whistle signal consisting of one prolonged blast followed immediately by two short blasts. Such a signal is sounded in fog by...

(A) vessels at anchor, not engaged in fishing.
(B) vessels underway and towing.
(C) vessels in danger.
(D) pilot vessels.

10-120. When a vessel signals her distress by means of a gun or other explosive signal, the firing should be at intervals of approximately...

(A) 10 minutes.   (B) 1 minute.
(C) 1 hour.   (D) 3 minutes.

10-121. Your vessel is underway in reduced visibility. You hear, about 30 degrees on the starboard bow, a fog signal of another vessel. Which of the following actions should you take?

(A) Alter course to starboard to pass around the other vessel's stern.
(B) Slow your engines and let him pass ahead of you.
(C) Reduce your speed to bare steerageway.
(D) Alter course to port and pass him on his port side.

10-122. A power-driven vessel making way through the water sounds a fog signal of ...

(A) one prolonged blast at intervals of not more than two minutes.
(B) two prolonged blasts at intervals of not more than two minutes.
(C) one prolonged blast at intervals of not more than one minute.
(D) two prolonged blasts at intervals of not more than one minute.

10-123. In restricted visibility, a vessel fishing with nets shall sound at intervals of two minutes...

(A) one prolonged blast.
(B) one prolonged followed by two short blasts.
(C) one prolonged followed by three short blasts.
(D) two prolonged blasts in succession.

10-124. You are underway and approaching a bend in the channel where vessels approaching from the opposite direction cannot be seen. You should sound...

(A) one blast, 4 to 6 seconds in duration.
(B) three blasts, 4 to 6 seconds in duration.
(C) one continuous blast until you are able to see around the bend.
(D) one blast, 8 to 10 seconds in duration.

10-125. Fog signals, required under the Rules for vessels underway, shall be sounded...

(A) only on the approach of another vessel.
(B) only when vessels are in sight of each other.
(C) at intervals of not more than one minute.
(D) at intervals of not more than two minutes.

10-126. Five or more short blasts on a vessel's whistle indicates that she is...

(A) in doubt that another vessel is taking sufficient action to avoid a collision.
(B) altering course to starboard.
(C) altering course to port.
(D) the stand-on vessel and will maintain course and speed.

10-127. A person aboard a vessel, signaling by raising and lowering his outstretched arms to each side, is indicating...

(A) danger, stay away.
(B) all is clear, it is safe to pass.
(C) the vessel is anchored.
(D) a distress signal.

CHAPTER 11 – NAVIGATION PLANNING AND PRACTICE

This chapter includes exercises that review topics covered in earlier chapters, presented sequentially along a hypothetical boat trip. Use information from the Resources section of this workbook as needed. With sequential problems that rely to some extent on previous answers, it might be best to check the solutions as you proceed, rather than working through all of them before looking at the solutions.

Trip 1.

The following are examples of questions asked on USCG deck license exams. There is no order to the presentation. Use magnetic variation 20.0 E unless otherwise stated.

11-1. Your eye height is 25 feet (7.6 meters). The visibility is 5.5 nmi. (A) What is the luminous range of Trial Island Light? (B) For outside study you may check the latest Light List for the present range of this light. What is the current range of this light, and the new luminous range in this same visibility?

11-2. (A) What chart gives the most detail for Port Angeles harbor? (B) What is its scale? (C) Is this considered a LARGE scale or a SMALL scale chart?

11-3. Near Telegraph Cove, northeast of the city of Victoria, BC, are two dashed lines leading off the chart approximately NE. What do these lines indicate, and what is their significance?

11-4. You are on course 356 M. Your speed is 7.0 kts. You passed 0.4 nmi abeam the Y "SA" Fl Y 4sec RACON (- -) buoy (48° 11.5' N, 122° 49.8' W) at 2010, headed up the traffic lane towards Rosario Strait. It is now 2114. You see a prominent flashing white light on your port beam. (A) What is the name of this light? (b) Approximately how far off is it?

11-5. What is the nature of the seabed in the center of Discovery Bay?

11-6. You are on course 160 M in Haro Strait. You establish a fix from a 214 hand bearing compass check to the Q G 21ft 5M Ra Ref at Cadboro Point, and another bearing 124° to the buoy at Beaumont Shoal (assumed to be properly on station). (A) What is your Lat Lon? Proceeding on course sometime later you notice that the Cadboro Bay flashing green disappears. (B) What is your approximate Lat when that happens? (C) What is the bearing and distance to Discovery Island Light when that happens?

11-7. At 0725 your position is 48° 12.5' N, 123° 35.3' W. What is the range and true bearing to Race Rocks light?

11-8. At 1425 you are heading 054 T and Trial Island light is abeam to port at 3.1 nmi. The current is 135 T at 1.8 kts. (A) At a knotmeter speed of 8.0 which true course must you steer to make good 048 T? (B) What is the corresponding compass course? Use deviation table on the right.

11-9. At 1130 you are located near Partridge Bank on course 195 T. You take a bearing to Point Partridge light of 127 T. What is the relative bearing to that point? (A) 292 R, (B) 142 R, (C) 068 R, (D) 277 R

11-10. At 0825 your position is 48° 20.7' N, 123° 05.7' W and your heading is 080 T. You see a buoy at a relative bearing of 340 R. What does this buoy mark?

11-11. You continue on the course established in the previous problem. Your depth sounder draft is 2 ft and the tide is 4.0 ft. What is the minimum depth you expect to see on your depth sounder?

11-12. Departing Port Angeles harbor and then turning west down the Strait of Juan de Fuca toward open sea, at what point are you in waters governed by the International Rules?

11-13. At 0845 you are passing about 1 nmi south of the G "V15" Q G buoy near Race Rocks. You plan to rendezvous with a boat at 1200 at a meeting point 1 nmi SE of Sheringham Point Light. (A) What is your present Lat Lon? (B) What is the Lat Lon of the meeting point? (C) What is the true course to the meeting point? (D) What is the distance to the meeting point? (E) Assuming still water, what knotmeter speed should you hold to arrive at the meeting point at 1200?

11-14. You want to make good a course of 172 T. An east wind is causing 3° of leeway and the current is 1.2 kt setting toward 320 T. What true course should you steer to make good 172 at a knotmeter speed of 9.0 kts?

Deviation Table	
Heading Mag	Deviation
000°	2.0°E
030°	3.0°E
060°	4.0°E
090°	2.0°E
120°	1.0°E
150°	1.0°W
180°	2.0°W
210°	3.5°W
240°	3.0°W
270°	1.5°W
300°	0.0°
330°	1.5°E

11-15. Referring to Figure 11-15, your sailboat is exiting Discovery Bay on course 360T bound for Victoria on the other side of the Strait, under sail at a speed of 5 kts, and is presently passing 0.6 nmi east of Violet Point, Protection Island at 1015 local time. From your AIS, you spot a freighter to the west at Lat 48° 10.9' N, Lon 123° 13.4' W, inbound under pilot at 18 kts on course 077T, presumably intending to merge with the traffic lane at Buoy S and then follow the lane to the east toward Admiralty Inlet. Figure what time you expect to cross and from that answer this: Which of the following statements is true if both vessels maintain speed?

(A) No close quarters situation will develop.
(B) You are the stand-on vessel because sail has right of way over power
(C) You are the stand-on vessel because you are coming from the right.
(D) You are the give-way vessel.

11-16. Now assume that in the situation presented by the previous problem both vessels are operating in restricted visibility and each is tracking the other vessel by radar alone. Which of the following statements is true?

(A) No close quarters situation will develop.
(B) Sail is the stand-on vessel even in restricted visibility.
(C) The freighter is the stand-on vessel.
(D) There is no "right of way" nor stand on vessel in the fog. Both vessels must adhere to Rule 19d and maneuver accordingly.

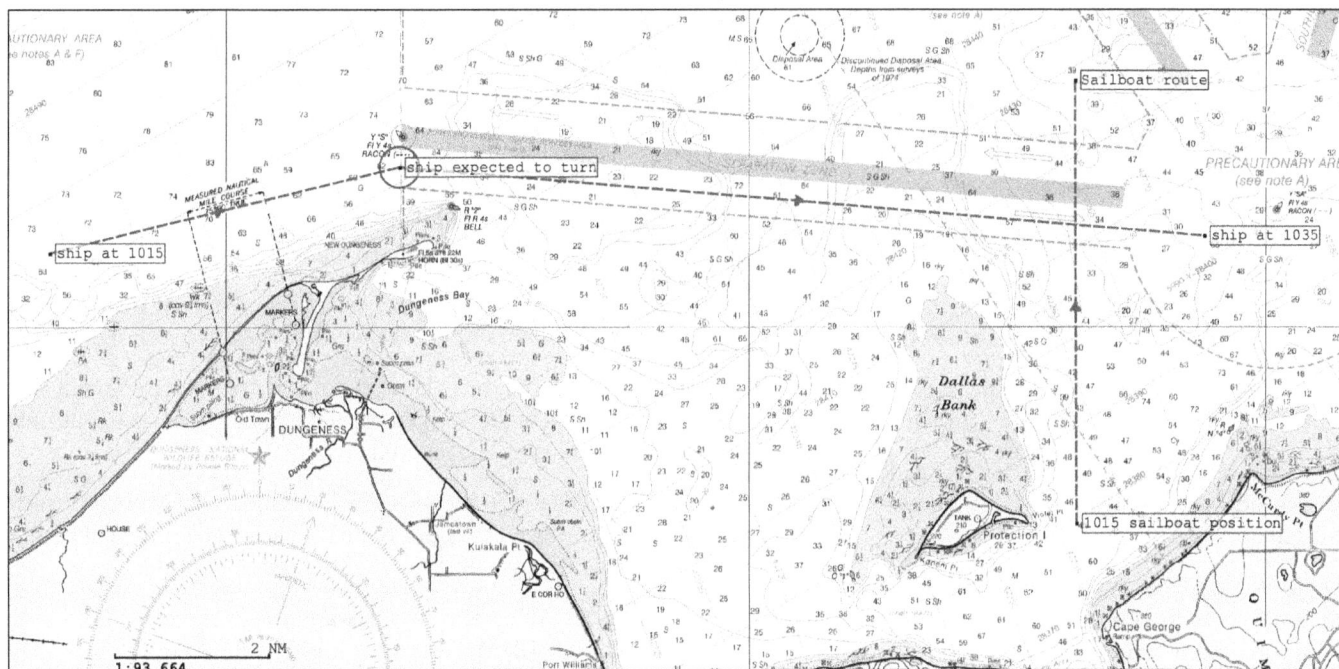

Figure 11-15. *Perspective of questions 11-15 and 16.*

CHAPTER 12 – IN DEPTH...

This section is a review of basics and some new material on special topics.

12-1. What is the most important book in navigation?

12-2. (A) What are the three primary electronic navigation instruments?

12-3. (A) Which of the following is the most accurate LOP?

(a) compass bearing to a lighthouse,
(b) natural range between an exposed rock and the lighthouse,
(c) depth contour at known tide height,
(d) radar bearing to an islet.

(B) Which is the least accurate?

12-4 (A) What would be a fair estimate of your DR uncertainty when traveling at 5 kts for 24h in coastal waters? (B) Same question when traveling at 12 kts for 24 hr?

12-5. Of all the many options for plotting tools, which would most navigators consider the two basic tools?

12-6. What is the navigator's trick play for notes and labels?

12-7. (A) What is the sailor's formula for a quick estimate of an ETA to weather when tacking, for example? (B) The buoy upwind of you that you must go around is 2 miles away; your speed is 6 kts; how long will it take to get to the buoy?

12-8. What is the approximate speed of a wind-created current after it has blown in the same direction for about a day?

12-9. Your compass deviation is 5° E headed south. Without further information, what would you guess your deviation is headed north?

12-10. What is the name of the free software program from National Geodetic Center that calculates accurate magnetic variation for any time and place?

12-11. You just motored along a measured mile in still water and calm wind at a constant rpm with your knotmeter reading 6.0 ± 0.05 kts. This took you 9m and 23 sec. (A) is your knotmeter correct, high, or low? (B) If incorrect, what is the percentage correction you must apply?

12-12. (A) At 6 kts, what is your speed in miles in minutes per mile? (B) At 10 kts, what is your speed in minutes per mile? (C) At 1 kt, what is your speed in feet per min?

12-13. What is the difference between ECDIS and ECS?

12-14. Which statements are True and which are False? (Hint: Read all carefully before answering any.)

(A) Current affects both our CMG and our SMG.
(B) Leeway affects both our CMG and our SMG.
(C) To find our distance made good during a given time accounting for current, we must correct our compass course steered and the logged distance run.
(D) To find our distance made good during a given time accounting for leeway, we must correct our compass course steered and the logged distance run.
(E) To find our best estimated position, the correction for current depends on our heading.
(F) To find our best estimated position, the correction for leeway depends on our heading.
(G) Sailing to weather with a 6° leeway, a 6° current set into the wind direction cancels out the leeway leaving our DR accurate.
(H) I can change my heading to minimize the effect of current.
(I) I can change my heading to minimize the effect of leeway.
(J) I can measure a usable value of the current underway using the GPS.
(K) I can measure a usable value of the leeway underway using GPS.
(L) Leeway is only important in strong winds.
(M) A specific current correction on inland waters is rarely the same for more than an hour or so.

12-15. VMG is commonly used in two different ways in modern instruments. What is the distinction between them.

12-16. Assuming all else is equal and assumed to remain constant, what is the derived parameter that we want to optimize when choosing the favored tack?

12-17. What are the two VHF channels that you can use to communicate with both recreational and commercial vessels after contact is made on Channel 16?

12-18. (A) What are three advantages of the new POD nautical charts? (B) What are two disadvantages of the new POD nautical charts?

12-19. (A) A NOAA current prediction at a specific midchannel station reports a max ebb of 2.7 kts at 1220 EST. What is the range of variance from this prediction in speed and time that we can fairly expect right at the location of the current station? (B) What are the same variances in max speed and time (and direction) we might expect along the shoreline nearest to this station, which is about 1 mile away?

12-20. List at least three advantages AIS offers to supplement a radar.

12-21. It is generally a good approximation to assume the correction for a set detected on the GPS will be the same as the set itself. That is, you are under power steering 045 T at knotmeter speed 6.0, but your COG is 055 T and your SOG is 6.5. You are getting set 10°, so a first guess would be to turn 10°

into the current (steer 035) and you will hope to then track at the desired course of 045. (A) Solve for the current (set and drift) and (B) then with that information figure what your heading should be to make good 045 at knotmeter speed 6.0. (C) Then compare the proper correction with the approximation to see how close it was.

12-22. You are in pea soup fog navigating only by radar. (A) You see a target approaching from 045R. Who has the right of way. (B) Once you see that risk of collision might develop with this target, what should you do? (C) Later you see a similar target approaching from 315R on the radar. What should you do? (D) Later another target approaches from 200R, clearly overtaking you, what should you do, and (E) Later a target is seen you approaching from 165 R, overtaking you on a parallel course, estimated to pass within just under half a mile on your starboard side. What should you do?

12-23. As a stand on vessel in a close encounter, you have a right to maneuver to avoid collision when...

(A) you decide the other vessel is not going to obey the Rules.
(B) you decide that the only way to avoid a collision is your own maneuver.
(C) the vessel has approached into what you have defined as your "close quarters" range for this encounter.
(D) Any of the above reasons can be used to justify your maneuver.

12-24. Which of the following are true about the 5-short blast danger signal.

(A) It can be used by both sail and power vessels.
(B) It can be used in both fog and clear weather.
(C) A long steady blast is more effective in most situations.
(D) We should be stopping by the time we sound it a second time.

12-25. What is the advantage of showing both a tricolor sidelights at the masthead and deck sidelights when sailing?

(A) Better visibility.
(B) Indicates you are under sail.
(C) Confuses your racing competitors.
(D) None. It is illegal and you will be fined.

12-26. What is the closest distance off you can pass a cruise ship in a harbor, even traveling dead slow?

12-27. What can be said about folding charts?

(A) There is a specific optimum way to fold them.
(B) We should not fold charts, only roll them.
(C) Usually we must fold them, but it really doesn't matter how.
(D) We should fold them so the large chart name and number printed on the chart shows in the corner.

12-28. It is now 1525, sunset is 1907, your steady speed is 7.4 kts, how far can you travel before sunset?

12-29. Use your best estimate of a range of values for each. (A) What is typical best accuracy of a GPS fix in feet? (B) What is a typical poor accuracy of a GPS fix in feet?

12-30. Give two conditions necessary for your GPS to use the WAAS system for enhanced accuracy?

12-31. What are various factors that might account for your VMG into the wind to be different on one tack compared to the other?

Notes:

RESOURCES

The following are excerpts from standard resources used in navigation. The Light List *and* Coast Pilot *also have custom made indices that just cover the sections excerpted.*

Times and Distances in NOAA Tide and Current Tables

LST_LDT denotes "local time," which means standard time in the winter and daylight time in the summer. In the Pacific region of our chart, it is PST (UTC-8h) and PDT (UTC-7h). The US rule for all time zones is we switch systems at 2 am on the second Sunday of March and on the first Sunday of November. Almost every year the Congress discusses (without action) changing this or eliminating the two systems completely! See time.gov for an official depiction of the time zone boundaries in the US. The *Nautical Almanac* (not part of this course) is where we learn time keeping policies in other nations.

Distances given in station names, such as "Cattle Point, 1.2 nm SE of" or "Cattle Point, 2.8 mi SSW of," are sometimes in statute miles and other times in nautical miles!

Tide and Current Apps in Electronic Charting Systems

NOAA data at tidesandcurrents.noaa.gov remains the primary source, but many navigation programs (called electronic charting systems, ECS) include apps or plugins that compute tides and currents for any time and place in US waters based on harmonic constants. Two examples of free programs that work on both Mac and PC are OpenCPN and qtVlm. These are very convenient solutions showing the stations at the correct places on the charts, providing digital values for any time. It is crucial, however, that before relying on any such program, the data should be checked with official NOAA data for several stations at several dates. A check that takes just minutes to complete.

Current Sailing Resources

These resources originate from *Inland and Coastal Navigation* (Starpath Publications).

The 50-90 Rule for Current Speeds

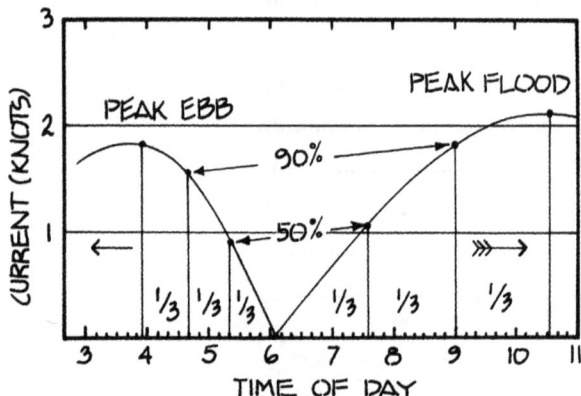

Divide the time between slack water and peak flow into three steps. In many cases, each step will be approximately one hour long. During the first step the current increases to 50 percent of its maximum value, and during the next step it increases to 90 percent of its maximum value. The same procedure will reproduce the fall in current speed after maximum flow.

The 40-60 Rule for Estimating Current Set

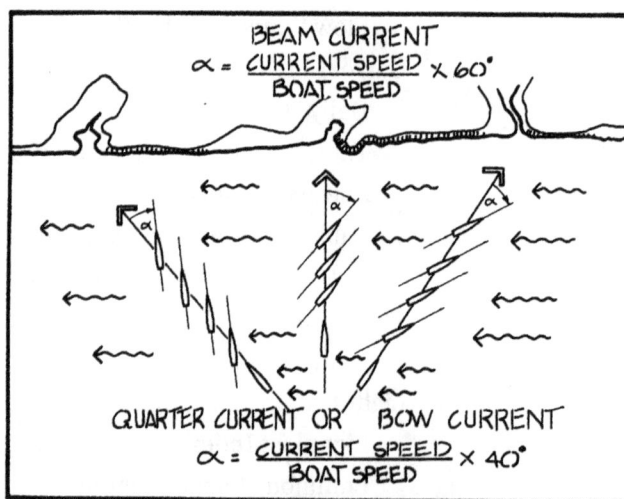

To solve current sailing problems by approximation, we define the following relative bearings of the current with your boat headed toward your destination: current "on the beam" means current points toward your beam, about 90° off the bow. Current "on the bow" means the current points to about 45° off the bow (stem) of the boat, current "on the quarter" means current points to about 45° off the stern.

The rule works adequately well for set angles up to 42° or so, which is equivalent to limiting its use to currents that are less than some three quarters of your boat speed. In most cases, knowledge of current speed and direction is not accurate enough to justify precise vector solutions. This formula is useful and easy to remember. Bow and quarter currents take less of a correction, but they are the same in each case. The only difference is the resulting SMG. Bow currents slow you down, quarter currents speed you up. Bow, beam, and quarter current directions are defined for this application with the boat pointed toward the destination, as in the starting position shown on each route.

Effect of a Changing Current on Net Progress

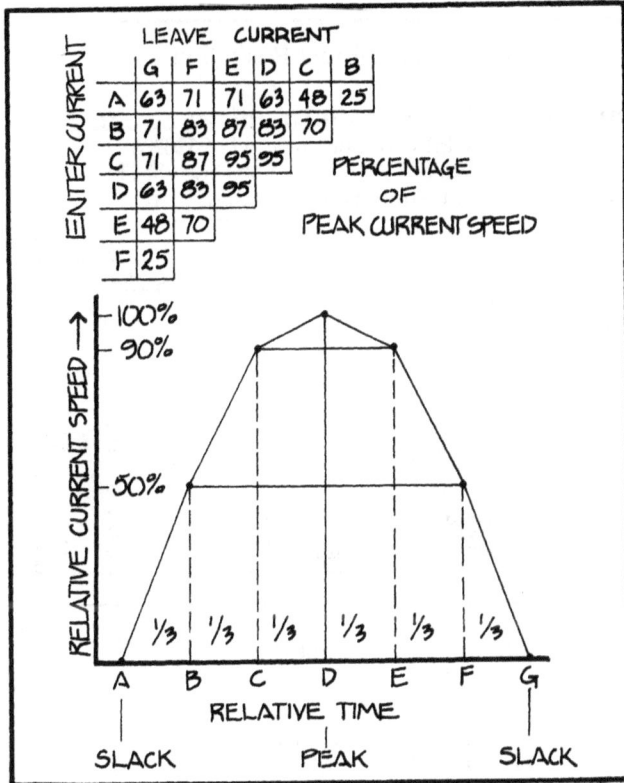

Here we use the 50-90 Rule to estimated the total effect of progress crossing a changing current. Divide the duration of the cycle into six parts, then use data from the inset to find the constant current speed that is equivalent to the changing current of the cycle. Sailing in a current with a peak speed of 3 knots from relative point B to point E, the current would be increasing from 1.5 knots to 3 knots and then decreasing to 2.7 knots during this time. From the inset, you can assume that this will move the boat as if in a constant current of 0.87 times 3, or 2.6 knots.

Note that staying in a current from slack to peak (A to D) or slack to slack (A to G) is equivalent to sailing in a constant current of 0.63 times the peak current speed.

Slow Water Rule for Estimating Duration of Slack

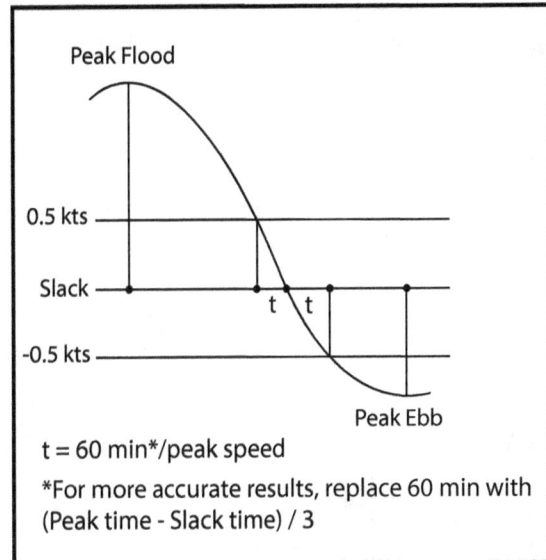

t = 60 min*/peak speed

*For more accurate results, replace 60 min with (Peak time - Slack time) / 3

The Slow Water Rule states that the current stays less than 0.5 kts on either side of slack for a time (in minutes) equal to 60 minutes divided by the peak current speed in knots. This period is usually different on each side of the slack for mixed semidiurnal tides. That very simple form assumes the period from peak to slack is equal to the global semidiurnal average of 3 hr, but there are many cases where this varies from just 2 hr to over 5 hr. Thus to make the Rule more accurate, replace the 60 min with one third of the actual time interval between peak and slack—this Rule is derived from the 50-90 Rule, which accounts for that adjustment.

A cycle that is roughly 3 hr peak to slack, with a peak current of 2 kts, will stay less than 0.5 kts on that side of slack for 60/2 = 30 min. If the cycle was 4 hr, then the slow water time would be 80/2 = 40 min, where 4/3 = 1.33 hr = 80 min.

Current Predictions

NOAA Tidal Current Predictions

Station ID: PUG1703 Depth: 75 feet
Source: NOAA/NOS/CO-OPS
Station Type: Harmonic
Time Zone: LST/LDT

San Juan Channel, south entrance, 2022
Latitude: 48.4610° N Longitude: 122.9520° W
Mean Flood Dir. 347° (T) Mean Ebb Dir. 168° (T)
Times and speeds of maximum and minimum current, in knots

April

Day	Slack (h m)	Maximum (h m)	knots
1 F ●	00:24	03:06	3.4F
	05:48	09:18	-3.6E
	12:54	15:42	3.5F
	18:30	22:00	-4.0E
2 Sa	01:18	03:48	2.8F
	06:18	09:48	-3.4E
	13:30	16:30	3.7F
	19:24	22:54	-3.8E
3 Su	02:18	04:30	2.2F
	06:48	10:12	-3.2E
	14:06	17:18	3.6F
	20:18	23:42	-3.6E
16 Sa ○		02:24	2.8F
	04:48	07:48	-3.9E
	11:54	15:06	3.5F
	17:54	21:06	-3.4E
17 Su	00:42	03:06	2.5F
	05:18	08:30	-4.2E
	12:30	15:48	3.9F
	18:48	21:54	-3.4E
18 M	01:30	03:48	2.3F
	05:54	09:12	-4.4E
	13:12	16:36	4.2F
	19:42	22:48	-3.2E

May

Day	Slack (h m)	Maximum (h m)	knots
1 Su	01:18	03:18	1.8F
	05:24	08:54	-3.5E
	12:48	16:06	4.3F
	19:18	22:36	-3.6E
2 M	02:12	04:00	1.4F
	05:48	09:18	-3.4E
	13:24	16:48	4.2F
	20:06	23:24	-3.4E
3 Tu	03:00	04:30	0.9F
	06:06	09:48	-3.4E
	14:00	17:30	4.1F
	20:54		
16 M ○	00:30	02:42	1.9F
	04:30	08:00	-4.8E
	12:06	15:36	4.8F
	18:48	21:54	-3.1E
17 Tu	01:24	03:24	1.7F
	05:06	08:42	-5.0E
	12:48	16:18	5.1F
	19:42	22:48	-3.1E
18 W	02:18	04:12	1.4F
	05:48	09:30	-5.1E
	13:36	17:06	5.3F
	20:42	23:48	-3.0E

June

Day	Slack (h m)	Maximum (h m)	knots
1 W	02:54	03:54	0.4F
	05:00	09:06	-3.8E
	13:18	16:54	4.7F
	20:30	23:42	-3.1E
2 Th	04:00	04:30	0.1F
		09:42	-3.7E
	13:42	17:30	4.6F
	21:06		
3 F		00:30	-3.1E
		05:06	-0.2E
		10:18	-3.5E
	14:18	18:06	4.5F
	21:42		
16 Th	02:24	03:54	0.9F
	05:12	09:06	-5.3E
	13:12	16:48	6.0F
	20:24	23:42	-3.3E
17 F	03:30	04:48	0.7F
	06:00	10:00	-4.9E
	14:00	17:36	5.8F
	21:12		
18 Sa		00:36	-3.5E
	04:36	05:48	0.5F
		11:00	-4.2E
	14:48	18:24	5.3F
	21:54		

NOAA Tidal Current Predictions

Station ID: PUG1730 Depth: 15 feet
Source: NOAA/NOS/CO-OPS
Station Type: Harmonic
Time Zone: LST/LDT

Lopez Pass, 2022
Latitude: 48.4797° N Longitude: 122.8189° W
Mean Flood Dir. 286° (T) Mean Ebb Dir. 90° (T)
Times and speeds of maximum and minimum current, in knots

July

Day	Slack (h m)	Maximum (h m)	knots
1 F	02:24	03:42	0.5F
	05:36	09:48	-3.2E
	13:30	16:24	2.5F
	20:30	23:42	-1.7E
2 Sa	03:06	04:30	0.5F
	06:24	10:24	-3.2E
	14:06	16:54	2.5F
	21:06		
3 Su		00:18	-1.7E
	03:54	05:18	0.5F
	07:06	11:06	-3.1E
	14:42	17:30	2.5F
	21:36		
16 Sa	02:06	03:54	1.2F
	06:12	10:06	-3.8E
	13:42	16:42	3.1F
	20:42		
17 Su		00:00	-2.6E
	03:06	04:54	1.2F
	07:12	10:54	-3.4E
	14:24	17:24	2.9F
	21:18		
18 M		00:42	-2.8E
	04:06	06:00	1.1F
	08:24	11:42	-2.9E
	15:12	18:06	2.7F
	21:54		

August

Day	Slack (h m)	Maximum (h m)	knots
1 M	03:06	04:54	0.9F
	07:12	10:42	-3.1E
	14:00	16:54	2.8F
	20:36	23:48	-2.5E
2 Tu	03:54	05:42	1.0F
	08:12	11:24	-2.7E
	14:36	17:30	2.6F
	21:00		
3 W		00:18	-2.8E
	04:36	06:36	1.1F
	09:18	12:12	-2.2E
	15:12	18:06	2.4F
	21:18		
16 Tu		00:00	-3.3E
	03:30	05:48	1.6F
	08:30	11:24	-2.4E
	14:42	17:24	2.4F
	20:54		
17 W		00:36	-3.3E
	04:24	06:54	1.7F
	09:36	12:18	-1.8E
	15:30	18:06	1.8F
	21:18		
18 Th		01:12	-3.1E
	05:12	08:00	1.7F
	10:48	13:24	-1.3E
	16:42	18:54	1.2F
	21:48		

September

Day	Slack (h m)	Maximum (h m)	knots
1 Th	03:30	06:00	1.9F
	09:18	11:54	-2.0E
	14:54	17:36	1.9F
	20:12		
2 F		00:00	-3.5E
	04:06	06:48	2.0F
	10:24	12:48	-1.6E
	16:00	18:24	1.4F
	20:36		
3 Sa ◐		00:42	-3.3E
	04:54	07:48	2.1F
	11:36	14:00	-1.3E
	17:24	19:24	0.9F
	21:18		
16 F		00:06	-2.9E
	04:12	07:12	2.0F
	10:30	13:24	-1.4E
	17:00	18:30	0.5F
	20:36		
17 Sa ◑		00:36	-2.5E
	05:00	08:12	1.9F
	11:36	15:24	-1.3E
	18:54	19:42	0.1F
	20:48		
18 Su		01:24	-2.1E
	05:54	09:24	1.7F
	12:48	17:00	-1.4E
	21:00		

NOAA Tidal Current Predictions

Station ID: PUG1635 Depth: 52 feet
Source: NOAA/NOS/CO-OPS
Station Type: Harmonic
Time Zone: LST/LDT

New Dungeness Light, 2.8 mi. NNW of, 2022
Latitude: 48.2335° N Longitude: 123.1334° W
Mean Flood Dir. 66° (T) Mean Ebb Dir. 273° (T)
Times and speeds of maximum and minimum current, in knots

July

Day	Slack (h m)	Maximum (h m)	knots
1 F		03:06	-0.3E
		09:48	-1.6E
	14:54	18:06	1.4F
	21:18		
2 Sa		00:30	-0.9E
		04:00	-0.3E
		10:48	-1.5E
	15:18	18:36	1.3F
	21:30		
3 Su		00:54	-1.0E
		05:36	-0.3E
		11:24	-1.4E
	15:54	19:00	1.2F
	21:48		
16 Sa	04:48	10:36	-2.1E
	14:48	18:06	1.8F
	21:00		
17 Su	06:00	00:12	-1.1E
		11:36	-1.9E
	15:30	18:42	1.6F
	21:30		
18 M	06:18	00:42	-1.3E
	07:36	12:30	-1.6E
	16:18	19:18	1.3F
	22:00		

August

Day	Slack (h m)	Maximum (h m)	knots
1 M	05:18	00:00	-1.3E
	06:24	11:36	-1.3E
	15:18	18:12	1.1F
	20:42		
2 Tu	05:06	00:12	-1.4E
	07:42	06:24	-1.9E
		12:12	-1.2E
	16:00	18:36	0.9F
	21:00		
3 W	05:24	00:18	-1.4E
		06:54	0.2F
		12:42	-1.1E
	16:48	18:54	0.7F
	21:24		
16 Tu	04:36	06:48	0.5F
	08:30	12:30	-1.5E
	16:06	18:42	0.9F
	20:48		
17 W	05:18	00:18	-1.4E
	09:36	07:42	0.5F
		13:18	-1.2E
	17:00	19:06	0.5F
	21:06		
18 Th	06:06	00:36	-1.3E
	10:48	08:54	0.5F
		14:30	-1.0E
	18:06	19:18	0.1F
	20:48		

September

Day	Slack (h m)	Maximum (h m)	knots
1 Th	04:06	06:42	0.6F
	09:06	12:30	-1.1E
	16:30	18:18	0.5F
	20:12		
2 F	04:54	07:24	0.6F
	10:06	13:06	-0.9E
	17:12	18:48	0.3F
	20:30		
3 Sa ◐	05:54	00:30	-1.7E
		09:06	0.5F
	14:18	14:18	-0.6E
	18:00	19:18	0.2F
	20:42		
16 F	05:12	06:24	0.7F
	10:54	14:12	-0.8E
		18:18	-0.1E
17 Sa ◐	06:24	00:06	-1.3E
		09:42	0.6F
	12:12	15:42	-0.6E
		18:36	-0.2E
18 Su	08:00	00:36	-1.3E
		10:48	0.7F
	14:00	16:36	-0.5E
			-0.3E

Station ID: PUG1702 Depth: 47 feet
Source: NOAA/NOS/CO-OPS
Station Type: Harmonic
Time Zone: LST/LDT

NOAA Tidal Current Predictions

Rosario Strait, 2022
Latitude: 48.4581° N Longitude: 122.7501° W
Mean Flood Dir. 357° (T) Mean Ebb Dir. 190° (T)
Times and speeds of maximum and minimum current, in knots

April

Day	Slack h m	Max h m	knots	Day	Slack h m	Max h m	knots
1 F ●	01:42	04:18	2.2F	16 Sa ○	01:00	03:42	1.8F
	07:06	10:42	-2.8E		06:18	10:00	-3.1E
	14:18	16:36	1.8F		13:54	16:24	2.0F
	19:18	22:54	-2.5E		19:12	22:12	-2.0E
2 Sa	02:30	04:54	1.9F	17 Su	01:42	04:18	1.6F
	07:30	11:12	-3.0E		06:30	10:30	-3.5E
	14:48	17:18	2.0F		14:24	17:06	2.5F
	20:18	23:48	-2.1E		20:12	23:06	-1.7E
3 Su	03:12	05:24	1.5F	18 M	02:30	04:48	1.2F
	07:42	11:42	-3.2E		06:48	11:06	-3.9E
	15:24	18:00	2.2F		14:54	17:48	2.9F
	21:18				21:18		

May

Day	Slack h m	Max h m	knots	Day	Slack h m	Max h m	knots
1 Su	02:24	04:12	1.0F	16 M ○	01:24	03:30	0.9F
	06:06	10:18	-3.7E		05:12	09:48	-4.5E
	14:12	17:00	2.7F		13:48	16:48	3.4F
	20:48	23:54	-1.4E		20:42	23:12	-1.2E
2 M	03:12	04:42	0.6F	17 Tu	02:24	04:12	0.6F
	06:12	10:48	-3.8E		05:30	10:24	-4.6E
	14:42	17:36	2.8F		14:24	17:30	3.7F
	21:42				21:36		
3 Tu		00:42	-1.1E	18 W		00:12	-1.1E
	04:12	05:12	0.3F		03:42	04:48	0.3F
	06:12	11:18	-3.8E		05:48	11:06	-4.5E
	15:18	18:12	2.8F		15:06	18:12	3.8F
	22:30				22:30		

June

Day	Slack h m	Max h m	knots	Day	Slack h m	Max h m	knots
1 W		00:48	-0.7E	16 Th	04:00	00:06	-1.0E
		04:36	-0.1E		14:42	10:42	-4.5E
	14:48	10:36	-4.0E		22:18	17:54	3.9F
	22:30	17:48	3.0F				
2 Th		01:30	-0.6E	17 F		01:06	-1.2E
		05:06	-0.3E			05:24	-0.1E
	15:18	11:12	-3.8E		15:30	11:30	-4.1E
	23:06	18:24	2.8F		23:06	18:42	3.6F
3 F		02:12	-0.6E	18 Sa		02:06	-1.4E
		05:36	-0.4E			06:24	-0.3E
	16:00	11:48	-3.5E		16:24	12:24	-3.5E
	23:42	19:06	2.6F		23:48	19:36	3.3F

Station ID: PUG1630 Depth: 22 feet
Source: NOAA/NOS/CO-OPS
Station Type: Harmonic
Time Zone: LST/LDT

NOAA Tidal Current Predictions

Kanem Point, 1.5 mi. SW of Protection Island, 2022
Latitude: 48.1077° N Longitude: 122.9736° W
Mean Flood Dir. 117° (T) Mean Ebb Dir. 279° (T)
Times and speeds of maximum and minimum current, in knots

October

Day	Slack h m	Max h m	knots	Day	Slack h m	Max h m	knots
1 Sa	03:00	00:00	-1.6E	16 Su	03:18	00:12	-1.3E
	10:00	05:42	1.1F		11:30	05:54	0.7F
	19:06	13:30	-1.0E		20:12	15:18	-1.0E
2 Su	03:36	00:36	-1.6E	17 M ◐	04:00	00:48	-1.1E
	10:54	06:24	1.2F		12:18	06:30	0.6F
	20:00	14:30	-1.0E		21:00	16:24	-1.0E
		20:00	-0.2E				
3 M ◐	04:18	01:18	-1.4E	18 Tu	05:00	01:36	-1.0E
	11:54	07:24	1.3F		13:24	07:54	0.5F
	20:48	15:48	-1.0E		21:36	17:18	-0.9E
		20:48	-0.2E				

November

Day	Slack h m	Max h m	knots	Day	Slack h m	Max h m	knots
1 Tu ◐	03:54	00:54	-1.4E	16 W ○	03:42	00:12	-1.1E
	11:24	07:00	1.3F		11:36	07:18	0.4F
	20:12	14:54	-1.1E		19:36	15:12	-0.7E
2 W	05:12	01:54	-1.3E	17 Th	05:36	01:12	-1.0E
	12:18	08:24	1.1F		12:30	08:36	0.4F
	20:00	16:00	-1.0E		19:24	16:00	-0.7E
	22:18	21:06	0.1F		22:00	20:42	0.2F
3 Th	06:54	03:18	-1.2E	18 F	07:12	09:36	0.4F
	13:24	09:42	0.9F		13:18	16:36	-0.9E
	20:12	17:06	-1.1E		19:36	21:24	0.4F
		22:00	0.4F		23:30		

December

Day	Slack h m	Max h m	knots	Day	Slack h m	Max h m	knots
1 Th	04:24	00:54	-1.3E	16 F ○	05:30	00:54	-1.1E
	10:42	07:24	0.8F		11:12	08:18	0.4F
	17:42	14:06	-1.1E		18:24	14:36	-0.8E
	21:48	19:48	0.4F		21:54	20:12	0.3F
2 F	06:06	02:30	-1.2E	17 Sa	06:42	02:24	-0.9E
	11:30	08:36	0.7F		11:42	09:00	0.4F
	18:30	15:12	-1.2E		19:00	15:30	-1.1E
		20:48	0.6F		23:48	21:06	0.4F
3 Sa	00:00	04:18	-1.3E	18 Su	07:30	04:18	-0.9E
	07:30	09:36	0.6F		12:12	09:42	0.5F
	12:18	16:12	-1.5E		19:36	16:18	-1.4E
	19:18	21:48	0.8F			21:54	0.6F

Station ID: PUG1630 Depth: 22 feet
Source: NOAA/NOS/CO-OPS
Station Type: Harmonic
Time Zone: LST/LDT

NOAA Tidal Current Predictions

Kanem Point, 1.5 mi. SW of Protection Island, 2022
Latitude: 48.1077° N Longitude: 122.9736° W
Mean Flood Dir. 117° (T) Mean Ebb Dir. 279° (T)
Times and speeds of maximum and minimum current, in knots

July

Day	Slack h m	Max h m	knots	Day	Slack h m	Max h m	knots
1 F	04:18	09:30	-1.6E	16 Sa	01:54	03:30	0.2F
	12:30	15:00	0.8F		13:06	09:54	-1.8E
	20:42	23:30	-0.8E		20:12	16:18	1.2F
						23:06	-1.2E
2 Sa	04:48	10:18	-1.5E	17 Su	02:30	04:30	0.4F
	13:36	16:30	0.7F		06:30	11:00	-1.7E
	21:24				14:24	17:36	1.0F
					21:00	23:54	-1.2E
3 Su	04:18	00:06	-0.8E	18 M	03:12	05:36	0.5F
	06:24	11:12	-1.5E		08:00	12:06	-1.5E
	14:42	18:18	0.6F		15:42	18:42	0.8F
	22:00				21:36		

August

Day	Slack h m	Max h m	knots	Day	Slack h m	Max h m	knots
1 M	02:36	04:48	0.3F	16 Tu	02:36	05:24	0.7F
	06:42	11:00	-1.5E		08:36	12:12	-1.4E
	14:42	18:06	0.6F		15:54	18:30	0.7F
	21:12				20:54		
2 Tu	03:24	00:00	-1.0E	17 W	03:42	00:12	-1.5E
	07:48	05:36	0.3F		10:00	06:30	0.7F
	15:36	11:54	-1.3E		17:00	13:30	-1.1E
	21:36	18:54	0.6F		21:36	19:24	0.6F
3 W	04:18	00:48	-1.2E	18 Th	04:42	01:00	-1.6E
	08:54	06:36	0.4F		11:30	07:42	0.6F
	16:24	12:48	-1.0E		18:12	14:42	-1.0E
	22:00	19:42	0.5F		22:12	20:12	0.5F

September

Day	Slack h m	Max h m	knots	Day	Slack h m	Max h m	knots
1 Th	03:24	00:06	-1.5E	16 F	03:54	00:18	-1.6E
	09:06	05:54	0.6F		11:18	07:00	0.6F
	16:06	12:36	-0.9E		18:12	14:36	-1.0E
	21:00	19:00	0.4F		21:24	19:48	0.3F
2 F	04:06	00:48	-1.6E	17 Sa ◐	04:30	01:00	-1.4E
	10:12	06:30	0.7F		12:18	07:48	0.6F
	17:30	13:36	-0.8E		19:36	15:06	-1.0E
	21:18	19:42	0.3F		21:48	20:42	0.2F
3 Sa ◐	04:36	01:24	-1.6E	18 Su	05:06	01:36	-1.2E
	11:18	07:24	0.8F		13:18	08:24	0.5F
	19:36	14:54	-0.8E		20:54	17:06	-1.0E
	21:24				22:06		

TABLE 3.—SPEED OF CURRENT AT ANY TIME

TABLE A

Interval between slack and maximum current

Interval between slack and desired time (h. m.)	1 20	1 40	2 00	2 20	2 40	3 00	3 20	3 40	4 00	4 20	4 40	5 00	5 20	5 40
	knots	knots	knots	knots	knots	knots	knots	knots	knots	knots	knots	knots	knots	knots
0 20	0.4	0.3	0.3	0.2	0.2	0.2	0.2	0.1	0.1	0.1	0.1	0.1	0.1	0.1
0 40	0.7	0.6	0.5	0.4	0.4	0.3	0.3	0.3	0.3	0.2	0.2	0.2	0.2	0.2
1 00	0.9	0.8	0.7	0.6	0.6	0.5	0.5	0.4	0.4	0.4	0.3	0.3	0.3	0.3
1 20	1.0	1.0	0.9	0.8	0.7	0.6	0.6	0.5	0.5	0.5	0.4	0.4	0.4	0.4
1 40	----	1.0	1.0	0.9	0.8	0.8	0.7	0.7	0.6	0.6	0.5	0.5	0.5	0.4
2 00	----	----	1.0	1.0	0.9	0.9	0.8	0.8	0.7	0.7	0.6	0.6	0.6	0.5
2 20	----	----	----	1.0	1.0	0.9	0.9	0.8	0.8	0.7	0.7	0.7	0.6	0.6
2 40	----	----	----	----	1.0	1.0	1.0	0.9	0.9	0.8	0.8	0.7	0.7	0.7
3 00	----	----	----	----	----	1.0	1.0	1.0	0.9	0.9	0.8	0.8	0.8	0.7
3 20	----	----	----	----	----	----	1.0	1.0	1.0	0.9	0.9	0.9	0.8	0.8
3 40	----	----	----	----	----	----	----	1.0	1.0	1.0	0.9	0.9	0.9	0.9
4 00	----	----	----	----	----	----	----	----	1.0	1.0	1.0	1.0	0.9	0.9
4 20	----	----	----	----	----	----	----	----	----	1.0	1.0	1.0	1.0	0.9
4 40	----	----	----	----	----	----	----	----	----	----	1.0	1.0	1.0	1.0
5 00	----	----	----	----	----	----	----	----	----	----	----	1.0	1.0	1.0
5 20	----	----	----	----	----	----	----	----	----	----	----	----	1.0	1.0
5 40	----	----	----	----	----	----	----	----	----	----	----	----	----	1.0

TABLE B

Interval between slack and maximum current

Interval between slack and desired time (h. m.)	1 20	1 40	2 00	2 20	2 40	3 00	3 20	3 40	4 00	4 20	4 40	5 00	5 20	5 40
	knots	knots	knots	knots	knots	knots	knots	knots	knots	knots	knots	knots	knots	knots
0 20	0.5	0.4	0.4	0.5	0.3	0.3	0.3	0.3	0.2	0.2	0.2	0.2	0.2	0.2
0 40	0.8	0.7	0.6	0.5	0.5	0.5	0.4	0.4	0.4	0.4	0.3	0.3	0.3	0.3
1 00	0.9	0.8	0.8	0.7	0.7	0.6	0.6	0.5	0.5	0.5	0.4	0.4	0.4	0.4
1 20	1.0	1.0	0.9	0.8	0.8	0.7	0.7	0.6	0.6	0.6	0.5	0.5	0.5	0.5
1 40	----	1.0	1.0	0.9	0.9	0.8	0.8	0.7	0.7	0.7	0.6	0.6	0.6	0.6
2 00	----	----	1.0	1.0	0.9	0.9	0.9	0.8	0.8	0.7	0.7	0.7	0.7	0.6
2 20	----	----	----	1.0	1.0	1.0	0.9	0.9	0.8	0.8	0.8	0.7	0.7	0.7
2 40	----	----	----	----	1.0	1.0	1.0	0.9	0.9	0.9	0.8	0.8	0.8	0.7
3 00	----	----	----	----	----	1.0	1.0	1.0	0.9	0.9	0.9	0.9	0.8	0.8
3 20	----	----	----	----	----	----	1.0	1.0	1.0	1.0	0.9	0.9	0.9	0.9
3 40	----	----	----	----	----	----	----	1.0	1.0	1.0	1.0	0.9	0.9	0.9
4 00	----	----	----	----	----	----	----	----	1.0	1.0	1.0	1.0	0.9	0.9
4 20	----	----	----	----	----	----	----	----	----	1.0	1.0	1.0	1.0	0.9
4 40	----	----	----	----	----	----	----	----	----	----	1.0	1.0	1.0	1.0
5 00	----	----	----	----	----	----	----	----	----	----	----	1.0	1.0	1.0
5 20	----	----	----	----	----	----	----	----	----	----	----	----	1.0	1.0
5 40	----	----	----	----	----	----	----	----	----	----	----	----	----	1.0

Use table A for all places except those listed below for table B.
Use table B for Deception Pass, Seymour Narrows, Sergius Narrows, Isanotski Strait. and all stations in table 2 which are referred to these points.

1. From predictions find the time of slack water and the time and velocity of maximum current (flood or ebb), one of which is immediately before and the other after the time for which the velocity is desired.
2. Find the interval of time between the above slack and maximum current, and enter the top of table A or B with the interval which most nearly agrees with this value.
3. Find the interval of time between the above slack and the time desired, and enter the side of table A or B with the interval which most nearly agrees with this value.
4. Find, in the table, the factor corresponding to the above two intervals, and multiply the maximum velocity by this factor. The result will be the approximate velocity at the time desired.

ASTRONOMICAL DATA, 2022

January

	d	h	m
P	1	23	..
S	2	14	..
●	2	18	33
E	8	23	..
◐	9	18	11
A	14	09	..
N	16	11	..
○	17	23	48
E	23	15	..
◑	25	13	41
S	30	00	..
P	30	07	..

February

	d	h	m
●	1	05	46
E	5	07	..
◐	8	13	50
A	11	03	..
N	12	17	..
○	16	16	56
E	19	20	..
◑	23	22	32
S	26	07	..
P	26	22	..

March

	d	h	m
●	2	17	35
E	4	17	..
◐	10	10	45
A	10	23	..
N	12	01	..
○	18	07	18
E	19	03	..
☉m	20	15	33
P	24	00	..
◑	25	05	37
S	25	12	..

April

	d	h	m
E	1	01	..
●	1	06	24
A	7	19	..
N	8	09	..
◐	9	06	48
E	15	12	..
○	16	18	55
P	19	15	..
S	21	18	..
◑	23	11	56
E	28	08	..
●	30	20	28

May

	d	h	m
A	5	13	..
N	5	16	..
◐	9	00	21
E	12	22	..
○	16	04	14
P	17	15	..
S	19	02	..
◑	22	18	43
E	25	14	..
●	30	11	30

June

	d	h	m
N	1	23	..
A	2	01	..
◐	7	14	48
E	9	07	..
○	14	11	52
P	14	23	..
S	15	11	..
◑	21	03	11
☉j	21	09	14
E	21	19	..
●	29	02	52
N	29	05	..
A	29	06	..

July

	d	h	m
E	6	14	..
◐	7	02	14
S	12	22	..
P	13	09	..
○	13	18	38
E	19	02	..
◑	20	14	19
N	26	10	..
A	26	10	..
●	28	17	55

August

	d	h	m
E	2	19	..
◐	5	11	07
S	9	07	..
P	10	17	..
○	12	01	36
E	15	10	..
◑	19	04	36
N	22	16	..
A	22	22	..
●	27	08	17
E	30	00	..

September

	d	h	m
◐	3	18	08
S	5	14	..
P	7	18	..
○	10	09	59
E	11	20	..
◑	17	21	52
N	18	23	..
A	19	15	..
☉s	23	01	04
●	25	21	55
E	26	06	..

October

	d	h	m
S	2	20	..
◐	3	00	14
P	4	17	..
E	9	05	..
○	9	20	55
N	16	07	..
A	17	10	..
◑	17	17	15
E	23	15	..
●	25	10	49
P	29	15	..
S	30	02	..

November

	d	h	m
◐	1	06	37
E	5	12	..
○	8	11	02
N	12	15	..
A	14	07	..
◑	16	13	27
E	20	01	..
●	23	22	57
P	26	02	..
S	26	09	..
◐	30	14	37

December

	d	h	m
E	2	18	..
○	8	04	08
N	9	22	..
A	12	00	..
◑	16	08	56
E	17	10	..
☉d	21	21	48
●	23	10	17
S	23	19	..
P	24	08	..
E	29	23	..
◐	30	01	21

LUNAR DATA

- ● -- new Moon
- ◐ -- first quarter
- ○ -- full Moon
- ◑ -- last quarter
- A -- Moon in apogee
- P -- Moon in perigee
- N -- Moon farthest north of Equator
- E -- Moon on Equator
- S -- Moon farthest south of Equator

SOLAR DATA

- ☉m -- March equinox
- ☉j -- June solstice
- ☉s -- September equinox
- ☉d -- December solstice

Greenwich mean time (GMT) or universal time (UT) is the mean solar time on the Greenwich meridian reckoned in days of 24 mean solar hours written as 00^h at midnight and 12^h at noon. To convert the above times to those of other standard time meridians, add 1 hour for each 15° of east longitude of the desired meridian and subtract 1 hour for each 15° of west longitude. This table was compiled from data supplied by the Nautical Almanac Office, United States Naval Observatory.

TABLE 5. ROTARY TIDAL CURRENTS EXPLANATION

Offshore and in some of the wider indentations of the coast, the tidal current is quite different from that found in the more protected bays and rivers. In these inside waters the tidal current is of the reversing type. The current sets in one direction for a period of 6 hours after which is ceases to flow momentarily and then sets in the opposite direction during the following 6 hours. The offshore tidal current, not being confined to a definite channel, changes its direction continually and never slows to a true slack water. Thus in a tidal cycle of 12.5 hours it will have set in all directions of the compass. This type of current is referred to as a rotary current.

A characteristic feature of the rotary current is the absence of slack water. Although the current generally varies from hour to hour, this variation from greatest current to least current and back again to greatest does not give rise to a period of slack water. When the speed of the rotary tidal current is least, it is known as the minimum current, and when it is greatest it is known as the maximum current. The minimum and maximum speeds of the rotary current are related to each other in the same way as slack and strength of current. A minimum speed of the current follows a maximum speed by an interval of approximately 3 hours and followed in turn by another maximum after a further interval of 3 hours.

The following table provides the direction and speed of the rotary current for each hour at a number of offshore stations. The times and speeds are referred to predictions for a reference station in Table 1. All times are in local standard time for the secondary station.

The speeds given in the table are the average speeds for the station. The Moon when new, full, or at perigee tends to increase the speeds 15 to 20 percent above average. When perigee occurs at or near the time of new or full Moon, the current speeds will be 30 to 40 percent above average. The Moon when at first and third quarter or at apogee tend to decrease the current speeds below average by 15 to 20 percent. When apogee occurs at or near the first or third quarter Moon, the currents will be 30 to 40 percent below average.

The speeds will be about average when apogee occurs at or near the time of the new or full Moon and also when perigee occurs at or near quadrature. (See table of astronomical data.) '

The direction of the current is given in degrees, true, reading clockwise from 00 at north, and is the direction toward which the water is flowing. The speeds and directions are for tidal current only and do not include the effect of the wind. When a wind is blowing, a wind-driven current will be set up as is superimposed on the normal tidal current. The actual current encountered will thus be a combination of the wind-driven current and the tidal current. See the chapters (in the NOAA Current Tables) on "Wind-Driven Currents" and "The Combination of Currents".

Below is a table created by the authors to help apply the astronomical data. On the next page is an example of figuring rotary current speed taking into account these factors.

Age[2]	Astronomical Adjustments to Rotary Currents[1]		HP[2]
28, 29, 00	◗ New Moon	x1.2 → x1.4 @ Perigee	>60.0'
06, 07, 08	◗ First Quarter	x0.8 → x0.6 @ Apogee	<55.0'
13, 14, 15	○ Full Moon	x1.2 → x1.4 @ Perigee	>60.0'
20, 21, 22	◖ Third quarter	x0.8 → x0.6 @ Apogee	<55.0'
28, 29, 00	◖ New Moon	x1.2 → x1.4 @ Perigee	>60.0'

Table Notes

(1) Rotary currents within 1 or 2 days of the moon phases shown should be modified as indicated, being about 20% higher or lower than the average values in the rotary current tables or graphs. In addition to these phase corrections, there is an additional 20% correction when the moon is closest to the earth (perigee, P ± 3 days) or farthest from the earth (apogee, A ± 6 days).

(2) The needed information can be found in the Astronomical Data Table included in the official tide books, sometimes on an inside cover. To explain the day ranges we give for apogee and perigee in Note 1, if you have a *Nautical Almanac*, then you can be more specific about the conditions on any specific day. The Almanac includes the age of the moon as well as the horizontal parallax (HP), which is the angular width of the moon observed from earth. When that angle is large (perigee) the moon is closest to the earth, and when small (apogee), the moon is farthest away. The table shows the ranges of HP that can be used to mark these two locations within the orbit for the purpose of tidal current corrections.

We only apply these corrections to the rotary currents and not the tabulated currents, because the latter are specific daily values and have these known factors already accounted for. Rotary current data, on the other hand, is always presented as average values that we must correct manually.

Rotary Current Data Off San Francisco

Notes. *Figure 1, referred to several times below, in the historical NOAA Tide Tables has several labeling errors, so we do not include it. All information needed for current prediction is in the table. Please keep in mind that even though the rotary tidal currents at this location are relatively small, in other US coastal waters they can be well over 1 kt routinely. For more information on rotary currents as well as the valuable near-live HF-radar measured currents available in US coastal waters see: http://davidburchnavigation.blogspot.com/2014/09/rotary-currents.html*

Point Lobos, 8.7 miles WSW. of (former location of San Francisco Lightship), Calif.—The tidal current here is rotary, turning clockwise, as shown in figure 1, in which the average currents have been referred to each hour of the tides at San Francisco (Golden Gate). The predicted tides for this port will be found in the Tide Tables, West Coast of North and South America, issued annually in advance, by the National Ocean Service. The diurnal inequality here is so great that the current is very largely diurnal; that is during the greater part of the month the current changes direction at the rate of about 15° per hour, giving but one strength of flood and one strength of ebb in a day.

The speed of the tidal current here is generally small, as shown in the following table, which represents the average conditions of figure 1.

Time	Speed	Direction	Time	Speed	Direction
Tide Hrs.	Knot	True	Tide Hrs.	Knot	True
HH–3	0.1	060°	LL–3	0.2	170°
HH–2	0.1	070°	LL–2	0.3	180°
HH–1	0.1	085°	LL–1	0.3	210°
HH	0.1	100°	LL	0.3	240°
HH+1	0.1	120°	LL+1	0.3	275°
HH+2	0.1	145°	LL+2	0.4	300°
HH+3	0.2	160°	LL+3	0.4	325°
LH–2	0.3	000°	HL–2	0.2	110°
LH–1	0.3	015°	HL–1	0.2	125°
LH	0.2	030°	HL	0.2	140°
LH+1	0.2	050°	HL+1	0.2	150°
LH+2	0.2	080°	HL+2	0.1	130°

In the column headed "Time," in the above table, the minus (–) sign before the hours indicates that the time refereed to is before the particular tide, while the plus (+) sign indicates that the time is after the tide. Thus, HH–3 in figure 1 and in the table means 3 hours before higher high water, and LL+1 means 1 hour after lower low water.

The current observations at this location indicated a permanent current in a northwesterly direction of about 0.1 knot. This was especially noticeable during the winter months. This permanent current, therefore, increases the speed of the tidal currents that set in the northwesterly direction and decreases the speed of the tidal currents setting in the southeasterly direction.

When there is considerable runoff from San Francisco Bay, the combined tidal and nontidal current at the former lightship location generally attains a speed of 1 1/2 knots in a northwesterly direction. The greatest observed speed was 2.9 knots.

Example

What is the expected rotary tidal current component at the entrance to San Francisco Bay at 0815 on May 16, 2011? Referring to the tide data on the previous page, the lower low (LL) occurs at 0656, which makes the time of interest about LL+3h. Referring to the rotary current table for this location, we find the current at LL+3h to be 0.4 kts in direction 325 T, but this date is one day away from perigee *and* full moon, so this average prediction would be increased by 40%, or 1.4 x 0.4 = 0.6 kts at 325T. (A *Nautical Almanac*, would show May 16, 2011 is moon age 13d (97% illumination) and the HP was 60.4', which is above the guideline that >60.0' can be called perigee.)

Sample tide data from San Francisco, CA

16 May 2011 - 17 May 2011

2011-05-16	05:13 PDT	-1.35 feet	LL
2011-05-16	12:14 PDT	4.72 feet	LH
2011-05-16	16:55 PDT	1.93 feet	HL
2011-05-16	23:17 PDT	6.68 feet	HH
2011-05-17	06:00 PDT	-1.67 feet	LL

Tide Predictions

Selections from downloaded Annual Data (tidesandcurrents.noaa.gov)

StationId: 9444900
Source: NOAA/NOS/CO-OPS
Station Type: Primary
Time Zone: LST_LDT
Datum: MLLW

> This NOAA label is the year of the tides, not a zip code!

NOAA Tide Predictions

Port Townsend, WA,2022
(48 06.7N / 122 45.6W)
Times and Heights of High and Low Waters

April

Day	Time	ft	cm		Time	ft	cm
1 F ●	05:22	8.6	262	**16** Sa ○	04:33	8.4	256
	11:09	1.9	58		10:36	0.8	24
	17:49	7.5	229		17:33	7.7	235
	23:07	2.7	82		22:41	3.5	107
2 Sa	05:42	8.4	256	**17** Su	04:56	8.5	259
	11:43	1.1	34		11:13	-0.4	-12
	18:44	7.7	235		18:31	8.1	247
	23:48	3.7	113		23:23	4.5	137
3 Su	06:01	8.3	253	**18** M	05:22	8.5	259
	12:18	0.5	15		11:53	-1.3	-40
	19:40	7.7	235		19:32	8.4	256

May

Day	Time	ft	cm		Time	ft	cm
1 Su	04:32	8.1	247	**16** M ○	03:49	8.6	262
	11:10	-0.6	-18		10:45	-2.5	-76
	19:05	8.2	250		18:48	8.7	265
	23:30	5.7	174		23:02	6.3	192
2 M	04:51	7.9	241	**17** Tu	04:19	8.7	265
	11:42	-1.0	-30		11:29	-3.2	-98
	19:53	8.4	256		19:44	9.1	277
					23:56	6.8	207
3 Tu	00:19	6.3	192	**18** W	04:52	8.5	259
	05:12	7.7	235		12:15	-3.3	-101
	12:17	-1.1	-34		20:42	9.2	280
	20:42	8.6	262				

June

Day	Time	ft	cm		Time	ft	cm
1 W	00:17	7.0	213	**16** Th	04:23	8.5	259
	11:49	-1.7	-52		12:00	-3.8	-116
	20:33	8.9	271		20:29	9.4	287
2 Th	01:19	7.1	216	**17** F	00:50	7.1	216
	04:34	7.3	223		05:20	8.0	244
	12:50	-1.5	-46		12:50	-3.2	-98
	21:12	8.8	268		21:16	9.3	283
3 F	13:08	-1.2	-37	**18** Sa	02:08	6.6	201
	21:52	8.7	265		06:26	7.3	223
					13:42	-2.3	-70
					22:01	9.2	280

StationId: 9449994
Source: NOAA/NOS/CO-OPS
Station Type: Subordinate
Time Zone: LST_LDT
Datum: MLLW

NOAA Tide Predictions

Aleck Bay, Lopez Island, WA,2022
(48 25.5N / 122 51.2W)
Times and Heights of High and Low Waters

April

Day	Time	ft	cm		Time	ft	cm
1 F ●	05:04	7.5	229	**16** Sa ○	04:15	7.4	226
	11:01	1.7	52		10:28	0.7	21
	17:31	6.6	201		17:15	6.8	207
	22:59	2.4	73		22:33	3.1	94
2 Sa	05:24	7.4	226	**17** Su	04:38	7.4	226
	11:35	1.0	30		11:05	-0.4	-12
	18:26	6.7	204		18:13	7.1	216
	23:40	3.3	101		23:15	3.9	119
3 Su	05:43	7.3	223	**18** M	05:04	7.5	229
	12:10	0.4	12		11:45	-1.2	-37
	19:22	6.8	207		19:14	7.4	226

May

Day	Time	ft	cm		Time	ft	cm
1 Su	04:14	7.1	216	**16** M ○	03:31	7.6	232
	11:02	-0.5	-15		10:37	-2.2	-67
	18:47	7.2	219		18:30	7.7	235
	23:22	5.0	152		22:54	5.5	168
2 M	04:33	7.0	213	**17** Tu	04:01	7.6	232
	11:34	-0.9	-27		11:21	-2.8	-85
	19:35	7.4	226		19:26	8.0	244
					23:48	6.0	183
3 Tu	00:11	5.5	168	**18** W	04:34	7.5	229
	04:54	6.8	207		12:07	-2.9	-88
	12:09	-1.0	-30		20:24	8.1	247
	20:24	7.5	229				

June

Day	Time	ft	cm		Time	ft	cm
1 W	00:09	6.2	189	**16** Th	04:05	7.5	229
	03:52	6.6	201		11:52	-3.3	-101
	11:41	-1.5	-46		20:11	8.3	253
	20:15	7.8	238				
2 Th	01:11	6.2	189	**17** F	00:42	6.2	189
	04:16	6.4	195		05:02	7.1	216
	12:19	-1.3	-40		12:42	-2.8	-85
	20:54	7.8	238		20:58	8.2	250
3 F	13:00	-1.1	-34	**18** Sa	02:00	5.8	177
	21:34	7.7	235		06:08	6.4	195
					13:34	-2.0	-61
					21:43	8.1	247

StationId: 9444555
Source: NOAA/NOS/CO-OPS
Station Type: Subordinate
Time Zone: LST_LDT
Datum: MLLW

NOAA Tide Predictions

Sequim Bay entrance, WA,2022
(48 04.9N / 123 02.6W)
Times and Heights of High and Low Waters

October

Day	Time	ft	cm		Time	ft	cm
1 Sa	02:06	-0.9	-27	**16** Su	02:33	0.1	3
	09:49	7.3	223		11:21	7.8	238
	14:27	6.2	189				
	18:59	7.3	223				
2 Su	03:02	-1.0	-30	**17** M ◗	03:29	0.6	18
	11:25	7.4	226		12:25	7.8	238
	15:52	6.6	201				
	19:35	7.1	216				
3 M ◗	04:06	-0.8	-24	**18** Tu	04:33	1.0	30
	12:46	7.7	235		13:14	7.9	241
	17:57	6.5	198				
	20:46	6.7	204				

November

Day	Time	ft	cm		Time	ft	cm
1 Tu ◐	03:40	-0.8	-24	**16** W ◑	02:39	0.9	27
	11:59	8.3	253		10:55	8.1	247
	19:20	5.8	177				
	20:54	6.0	183				
2 W	04:48	-0.1	-3	**17** Th	03:37	1.5	46
	12:46	8.4	256		11:25	8.1	247
	19:48	4.9	149		19:05	4.2	128
	22:50	5.5	168		21:49	4.8	146
3 Th	05:56	0.7	21	**18** F	04:36	2.2	67
	13:25	8.4	256		11:47	8.0	244
	20:16	3.7	113		19:10	3.4	104
					23:36	4.9	149

December

Day	Time	ft	cm		Time	ft	cm
1 Th	03:15	0.8	24	**16** F ◐	02:37	1.9	58
	10:46	8.7	265		09:57	8.4	256
	18:15	3.6	110		17:49	3.7	113
	22:16	5.0	152		21:29	4.6	140
2 F	04:17	2.1	64	**17** Sa	03:27	2.9	88
	11:21	8.6	262		10:23	8.4	256
	18:51	2.4	73		18:05	2.6	79
					23:39	4.9	149
3 Sa	00:22	5.4	165	**18** Su	04:25	4.0	122
	05:20	3.3	101		10:49	8.4	256
	11:51	8.5	259		18:29	1.4	43
	19:23	1.2	37				

Light List

U.S. Department of
Homeland Security

United States
Coast Guard

LIGHT LIST

Volume VI

PACIFIC COAST AND PACIFIC ISLANDS

Pacific Coast and outlying Pacific Islands

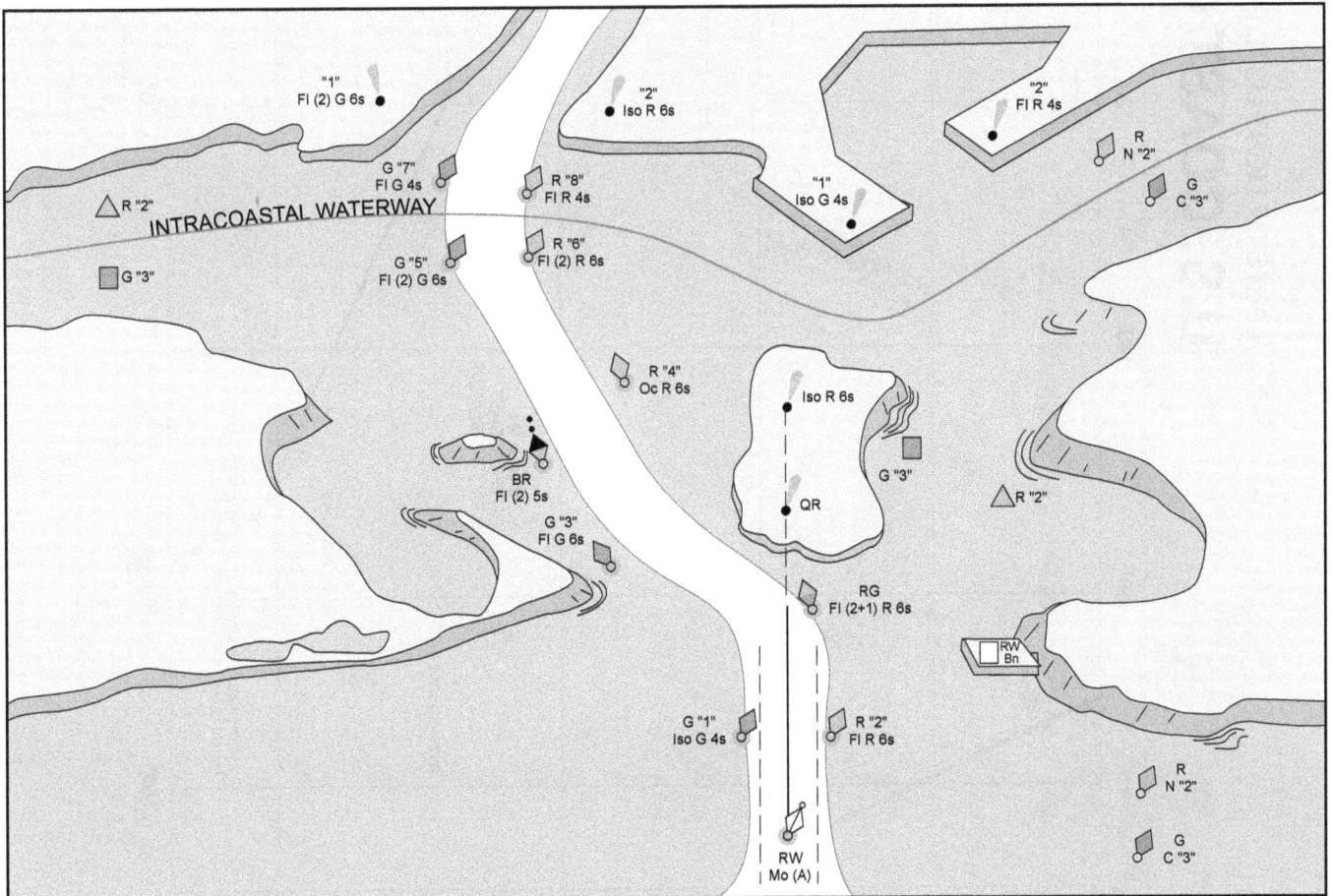

"1"
Fl (2) G 6s

"2"
Iso R 6s

"2"
Fl R 4s

R
N "2"

G "7"
Fl G 4s

"4"
Iso G 4s

R "2" INTRACOASTAL WATERWAY

R "8"
Fl R 4s

G
C "3"

G "3"

G "5"
Fl (2) G 6s

R "6"
Fl (2) R 6s

R "4"
Oc R 6s

Iso R 6s

G "3"

R "2"

BR
Fl (2) 5s

QR

G "3"
Fl G 6s

RG
Fl (2+1) R 6s

RW
Bn

G "1"
Iso G 4s

R "2"
Fl R 6s

R
N "2"

G
C "3"

RW
Mo (A)

Fictitious chart from the Light List used to illustrate standard buoy, daymark, and light placement and labeling.

LIMITS OF LIGHT LISTS PUBLISHED BY
U.S. COAST GUARD

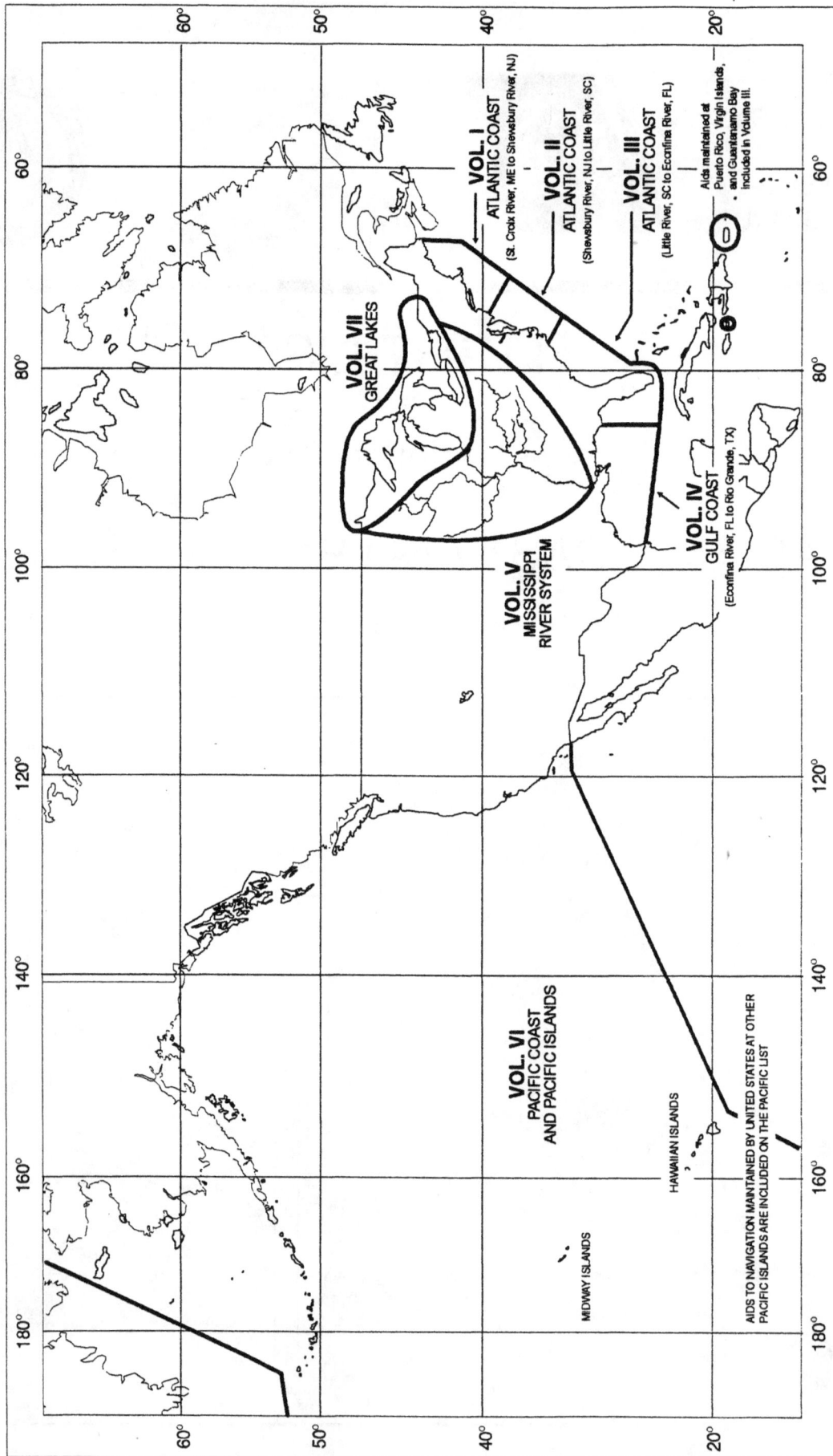

VOL. I
ATLANTIC COAST
(St. Croix River, ME to Shrewsbury River, NJ)

VOL. II
ATLANTIC COAST
(Shrewsbury River, NJ to Little River, SC)

VOL. III
ATLANTIC COAST
(Little River, SC to Econfina River, FL)

Aids maintained at
Puerto Rico, Virgin Islands,
and Guantanamo Bay
included in Volume III.

VOL. VII
GREAT LAKES

VOL. V
MISSISSIPPI
RIVER SYSTEM

VOL. IV
GULF COAST
(Econfina River, FL to Rio Grande, TX)

VOL. VI
PACIFIC COAST
AND PACIFIC ISLANDS

HAWAIIAN ISLANDS

MIDWAY ISLANDS

AIDS TO NAVIGATION MAINTAINED BY UNITED STATES AT OTHER
PACIFIC ISLANDS ARE INCLUDED ON THE PACIFIC LIST

(1) No.	(2) Name and location	(3) Position	(4) Characteristic	(5) Height	(6) Range	(7) Structure	(8) Remarks

WASHINGTON - Thirteenth District

STRAIT OF JUAN DE FUCA (Eastern Part) (Chart 18465)

N/W

Strait of Juan De Fuca

> Excerpts only. Full USCG Light Light Vol. VI is available online.

(1) No.	(2) Name and location	(3) Position	(4) Characteristic	(5) Height	(6) Range	(7) Structure	(8) Remarks
16200	Ideal Cement Range Front Daybeacon	48 10.0 123 57.5				KRW on piles.	Private aid.
16205	Ideal Cement Range Rear Daybeacon 133 yards, 180° from front daybeacon.					KRW on piles.	Private aid.
16210	WHIFFIN SPIT LIGHT (C)	48 21.5 123 42.6	Q W	21	6	White circular tower with green band at top.	HORN: 1 blast ev 30s (3s bl). Operated only on request to Vancouver Coast Guard Radio.
16215	Crescent Bay Bell Buoy 2	48 10.3 123 43.5				Red.	
16221	Race Rocks South Cautionary Lighted Buoy VF (C)	48 14.1 123 31.9	Fl Y 4s			Yellow.	
16222	- Traffic Lane Separation Lighted Buoy PA	48 12.4 123 27.7	Fl Y 4s		6	Yellow.	

STRAIT OF JUAN DE FUCA (Eastern Part) (Chart 18465)

N/W

Strait of Juan De Fuca

(1) No.	(2) Name and location	(3) Position	(4) Characteristic	(5) Height	(6) Range	(7) Structure	(8) Remarks
16265	Trial Islands Light (C)	48 23.7 123 18.2	F W Fl G 5s	93	15	White circular tower. 45	F W with high intensity green flash ev 5s. HORN: 2 blasts ev 60s (3s bl-3s si-3s bl-51s si). Horn points 181° from a white rectangular building close southeastward of lighthouse. Emergency light Fl (6) W 15s.
16270 19685	DISCOVERY ISLAND LIGHT (C)	48 25.5 123 13.5	Fl W 5s	93		White circular tower. 45	Light obscured from 050.5° to 146°. HORN: 1 blast ev 60s (6s bl). Emergency light Fl (6) W 15s.
16275	- Calibration Lighted Bell Buoy	48 14.2 123 21.8	Fl Y 6s		6	Yellow.	
16361	Hein Bank Lighted Isolated Danger Buoy DH	48 21.1 123 02.8	Fl (2) W 5s		6	Black with red band.	
16362	Hein Bank Lighted Buoy 1	48 22.0 123 02.2	Fl G 6s		5	Green.	RACON: K(-•-).
16365	Salmon Bank Lighted Gong Buoy 3	48 25.6 122 58.6	Fl G 4s		4	Green.	
16370	Rosario Strait Traffic Lane Separation Lighted Buoy RA	48 19.8 122 58.6	Fl Y 4s		7	Yellow.	RACON: N (-•)
16375	Smith Island Light	48 19.1 122 50.6	Fl W 15s	97	21	45	Emergency light Iso W 6s.

Light List Index

Luminous Range Diagram

The nominal range given in this Light List is the maximum distance a given light can be seen when the meteorological visibility is 10 nautical miles. If the existing visibility is less than 10 NM, the range at which the light can be seen will be reduced below its nominal range. And, if the visibility is greater than 10 NM, the light can be seen at greater distances. The distance at which a light may be expected to be seen in the prevailing visibility is called its luminous range.

This diagram enables the mariner to determine the approximate luminous range of a light when the nominal range and the prevailing meteorological visibility are known. The diagram is entered from the bottom border using the nominal range listed in column 6 of this book. The intersection of the nominal range with the appropriate visibility curve (or, more often, a point between two curves) yields, by moving horizontally to the left border, the luminous range.

CAUTION

When using this diagram it must be remembered that:

1. The ranges obtained are approximate.

2. The transparency of the atmosphere may vary between observer and light.

3. Glare from background lighting will reduce the range that lights are sighted.

4. The rolling motion of a vessel and/or of a lighted aid may reduce the distance that lights can be detected or identified.

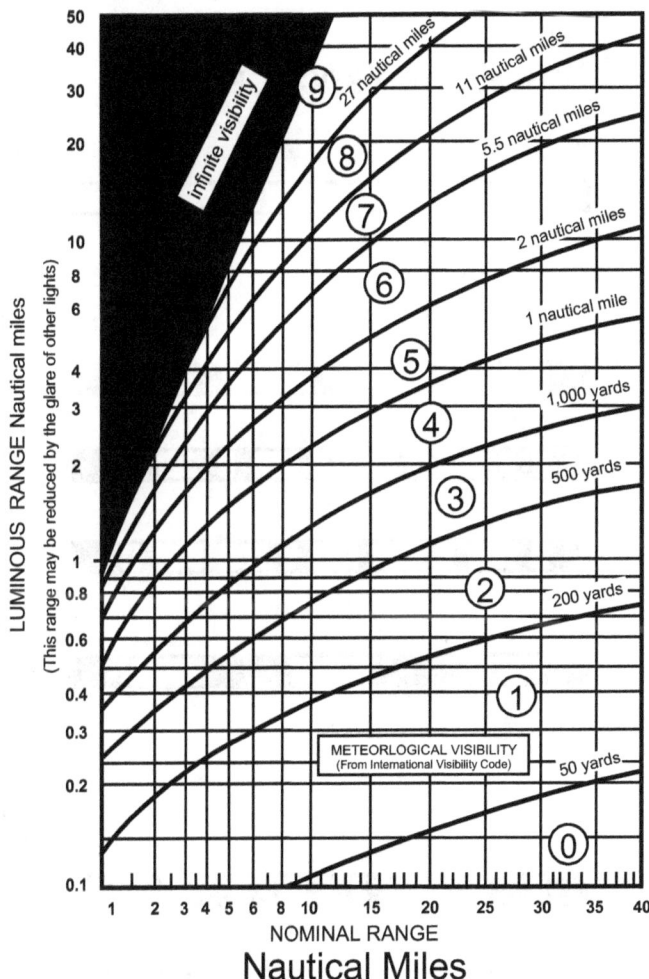

LUMINOUS RANGE Nautical miles
(This range may be reduced by the glare of other lights)

infinite visibility

27 nautical miles
11 nautical miles
5.5 nautical miles
2 nautical miles
1 nautical mile
1,000 yards
500 yards
200 yards
50 yards

METEORLOGICAL VISIBILITY
(From International Visibility Code)

NOMINAL RANGE
Nautical Miles

Starpath Estimate of Luminous Range

Luminous Range =
(Atmospheric Visibility/10) × Nominal Range + 1 nmi

Check a few examples from the table above to see where and how this approximation works.

CHARACTERISTICS OF LIGHTS

Illustration	Type Description	Abbreviation

1. FIXED.
A light showing continuously and steadily.

F

2. OCCULTING.
A light in which the total duration of light in a period is longer than the total duration of darkness and the intervals of darkness (eclipses) are usually of equal duration

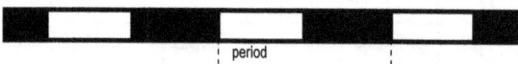

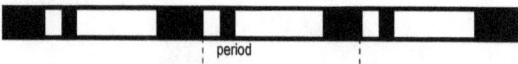

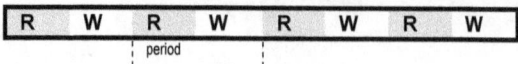

2.1 Single-occulting.
An occulting light in which an eclipse is regularly repeated.

Oc

2.2 Group-occulting.
An occulting light in which a group of eclipses, specified in numbers, is regularly repeated.

Oc (2)

2.3 Composite group-occulting.
A light, similar to a group-occulting light, except that successive groups in a period have different numbers of eclipses.

Oc (2+1)

3. ISOPHASE.
A light in which all durations of light and darkness are equal.

Iso

4. FLASHING.
A light in which the total duration of light in a period is shorter than the total duration of darkness and the appearances of light (flashes) are usually of equal duration.

4.1 Single-flashing.
A flashing light in which a flash is regularly repeated (frequency not exceeding 30 flashes per minute).

Fl

4.2 Group-flashing.
A flashing light in which a group of flashes, specified in number, is regularly repeated.

Fl (2)

4.3 Composite group-flashing.
A light similar to a group flashing light except that successive groups in the period have different numbers of

Fl (2+1)

5. QUICK.
A light in which flashes are produced at a rate of 60 flashes per minute.

5.1 Continuous quick.
A quick light in which a flash is regularly repeated.

Q

5.2 Interrupted quick.
A quick light in which the sequence of flashes is interrupted by regularly repeated eclipses of constant and long duration.

I Q

6. MORSE CODE.
A light in which appearances of light of two clearly different durations (dots and dashes) are grouped to represent a character or characters in the Morse code.

Mo (A)

7. FIXED AND FLASHING.
A light in which a fixed light is combined with a flashing light of higher luminous intensity.

F Fl

8. ALTERNATING.
A light showing different colors alternately

Al RW

Local Notice to Mariners (LNM)

This is a selection of the new format for the Local Notice to Mariners that began in early 2025, after paper charts were discontinued. They no longer refer to chart numbers, and have a simpler layout. Visit navcen.uscg.gov to see other new related online resources offered. Mariners reliance on the LNM has also changed to some extent in that ENC charts are now updated daily.

Another welcome distinction is the new LNM are now referred to by dates in standard format, whereas historically they used week numbers, which always took an extra step to interpret.

The selections below are pieced together to illustrate the types of announcements in each category. The PDF documents themselves are also in a much cleaner layout, with essentially no decorations, and no explanations of each section. It is a more streamlined layout.

Categories of LNM Announcements:

- Federal Discrepancies
- Federal Discrepancies Corrected

- Private Discrepancies
- Private Discrepancies Corrected

- Temporary Changes

- Additional MSI Categories *(Marine Safety Information)*
    - Hazards to Navigation
    - Marine Events
    - Bridges
    - Marine construction (excluding bridges)
    - Naval activity
    - Threatened and Endangered Species Advisory
    - MSIB *(Marine Safety Information Bulletin)*
    - Miscellaneous

Sample of the historic layout (Prior to 2025).	**New layout on the following pages.**

U.S. Department of Homeland Security
United States Coast Guard

LOCAL NOTICE TO MARINERS

District: 13   Week: 10/14

ISSUED BY: COMMANDER, THIRTEENTH COAST GUARD DISTRICT (dpw)
915 Second Avenue, 35th Floor, Rm 3510, Seattle, Washington 98174-1067
Telephone: (206) 220-7280 or 7285 FAX: (206) 220-7265
Email: D13-PF-LNM@uscg.mil
http://www.uscg.mil/d13/dpw/default.asp
http://www.navcen.uscg.gov/?pageName=lnmDistrict&region=13

COMDTPUB P16502.6, Light List Volume VI, 2014 Edition and Coast Pilot Volume 7, 2014.
Coast Pilots, along with corrections, are available at: http://www.nauticalcharts.noaa.gov/nsd/cpdownload.htm.

SECTION I - SPECIAL NOTICES
This section contains information of special concern to the Mariner.

WASHINGTON – STRAIT OF JUAN DE FUCA TO STRAIT OF GEORGIA – SWINOMISH CHANNEL – Reported shoaling in the South Entrance

Shoaling has been reported in the Swinomish Channel, on the north side of the channel between Swinomish Channel South Entrance Daybeacon 13 (LLNR 18826) and Swinomish Channel South Entrance Light 11 (LLNR 18815) in the vicinity of Goat Island. The USACE survey from Nov 2012 shows the channel varying from 8 feet to 14 feet in the vicinity. The southern Swinomish Channel has a history of shoaling, therefore, mariners are advised to transit this waterway at the highest tide possible and exercise good seamanship and voyage planning.

Chart   18427   LNM: 09/14

SECTION II - DISCREPANCIES
This section lists all reported and corrected discrepancies related to Aids to Navigation in this edition. A discrepancy is a change in the status of an aid to navigation that differs from what is published or charted.

DISCREPANCIES (FEDERAL AIDS)

LLNR	Aid Name	Status	Chart No.	BNM Ref.	LNM St	LNM End
690	Columbia River Approach Lighted Whistle Buoy CR	OFF STA/RAC INOP	18521	0017-14	52/13	

Local Notice to Mariners for District 13   11/05/2025

Strait of Juan De Fuca

New Layout of the LNM

Federal Discrepancies

NAME	LLNR	STATUS	AID TYPE	LOCATION
Salmon Bank Lighted Gong Buoy 3	16365	LT EXT	FD	

Additional MSI Categories

TITLE	SUBCATEGORY	DESCRIPTION	LOCATION
Sector Puget Sound, Submerged Land Act (SLA) - Strait of Juan De Fuca/General/Miscellaneous	Miscellaneous	NOAA Fisheries has deployed a subsurface mooring with passive acoustic recorders to monitor marine mammal presence in approximate location: 48-29-30N, 124-47-00W, in 285 m of water. Vessels conducting in-water work are requested to avoid this location by at least 1000 yards to avoid entanglement of gear. For more information, contact Brad Hanson at 206-300-0282.	Lat: 48° 29' 30" Lon: -124° 46' 60"
Sector Puget Sound, Submerged Land Act (SLA) - Strait of Juan De Fuca/General/MSIB	MSIB	MSI Bulletin 005- 25: Advisory For Actions During Heavy Weather in the Puget Sound Captain of the Port Zone. Unexpected heavy weather or rapid changes in weather can significantly increase the likelihood of marine casualties. During times of severe weather, the Coast Guard reminds all maritime stakeholders to exercise increased vigilance and implement appropriate measures to ensure the safety of vessels and protect the environment. 1. Prepare for heavy weather events ahead of time. Ensure crewmembers are designated to check and report weather updates prior to getting underway. Organize training with crew and passengers, conduct heavy weather drills, and review response and potential storm evasion options. 2. Understand your vessel's operating limitations and key factors with respect to weather conditions. 3. All vessel owners and operators are highly encouraged to familiarize themselves with the Heavy Weather Standards of Care from Puget Sound Harbor Safety Committee's Safety Plan, which can be found at https://marexps.com/membership/puget-sound-harbor-safety-committee/#documents. 4. If weather conditions deteriorate, it is imperative that vessels coordinate with the Cooperative Vessel Traffic Service (CVTS) regarding recommendations for harbors of safe refuge, anchorage, or other arrangements as per the specific standards of care. To coordinate efforts, contact the CVTS via channel 5A or 14 depending on vessel location or the watch supervisor at (206) 217-6152.	Lat: 48° 13' 34" Lon: -122° 54' 03"
General/Naval Activity/Naval Gunnery Exercises	Naval Activity	The NAS Whidbey Island Small Arms Safety Range located off the western shore of Whidbey Island will be active on the following schedule: 30 OCT 25 0800 to 1500 03 NOV 25 0800 to 1500 06 NOV 25 0800 to 2300 07 NOV 25 0800 to 1500 12 NOV 25 0800 to 2300 13 NOV 25 0800 to 1500 14 NOV 25 0800 to 2300 Red flashing lights (at nighttime) mark the onshore Northern and southern firing boundaries out to 2000 yards from the shoreline during live fire operations. For more information contact the Safety Officer at 360-257-3825 or VHF-FM channel 82A (1082).	
Sector Pudget Sound, Submerged Land Act (SLA) - StraitofJuanDeFuca/General/Threatened And Endangered Species Advisory (TESS Advisory)/Marine Wildlife Migration	Threatened And Endangered Species Advisory (TESS Advisory)	As of 01 Jun 2025, the Enhancing Cetacean Habitat and Observation (ECHO) Program voluntary route alteration is in effect for all tugs transiting the Canadian inshore area of the Strait of Juan de Fuca. If it is safe and operationally feasible to do so, tugs are requested to move south of the known killer whale feeding area and navigate either through the outbound shipping lane or the inbound route alteration zone, while maintaining a buffer distance of 1,000 meters from the Traffic Separation Scheme. The inbound route alteration zone is 1,500 meters wide and occurs in the area between 123-52-21.192 W, 48-18-37.332 N and 124-31-33.378 W, 48-28-53.316 N. The ECHO Program voluntary route alteration initiative aims to reduce underwater noise in known southern resident killer whale feeding areas along the northern edge of the Strait of Juan de Fuca. This initiative will remain in effect 24 hours a day through 30 Nov 2025. For more detailed information related to the ECHO program, visit the following internet address: https://www.portvancouver.com/environment/healthy-ecosystem/echo.	

Strait Of Georgia

Private Discrepancies

NAME	LLNR	STATUS	AID TYPE
Birch Bay Mooring Basin Light 2	19912	DAYMK IMCH*	PA
Birch Bay Mooring Basin Daybeacon 3	19913	DAYMK IMCH	PA

*IMCH = Improper characteristic

Ediz Hook

Federal Discrepancies Corrected

NAME	LLNR	AID TYPE	STATUS	CORRECTION DATE
Ediz Hook Light	16280	FD	RELIGHTED	2025-10-22

Haro Strait

Additional MSI Categories

TITLE	SUBCATEGORY	DESCRIPTION	LOCATION
Strait of Juan De Fuca - Haro Strait/General/Marine Events/Regatta (Race)	Marine Events	08-09 NOV 2025, 0700-1800 each day. The race starts at Lydia Shoal and goes counter- clockwise around San Juan County, past Orcas Island and out to Stewart Island then into Roche Harbor, the next day boats leave Roche Harbor and continue along San Juan Island and Lopez back along Rosario Strait to the Lydia Shoal finish.	

Quillayute River

Additional MSI Categories

TITLE	SUBCATEGORY	DESCRIPTION	LOCATION
Sector Pudget Sound, Submerged Land Act (SLA) - Quillayute River/General/Hazards To Navigation/Obstructions	Hazards To Navigation	There is a large, submerged log stuck in Quillayute River navigational channel approximately 100 yards downriver of the Quileute Marina entrance. The log may be marked with an orange or red float. Mariners should use extreme caution.	Lat: 47° 54' 35" Lon: -124° 38' 21"
Sector Puget Sound, Submerged Land Act (SLA) - Quillayute River/General/Marine Construction (Excluding Bridges)/Dredging	Marine Construction (Excluding Bridges)	Duwamish Services will be conducting dredging for USACE in the Quillayute River Inner Channel and Boat Harbor for approximately 30 days. Dredging will occur 7 days per week (Monday-Sunday). 24-hours per day, weather permitting, from a floating hydraulic dredge and a tender vessel and work skiff. If dredge equipment obstructs the channel, it will be moved upon approach of a vessel to allow for safe vessel passage. Mariners should take care when transiting the area, travel at reasonable speeds, and be aware of marker buoys indicating the location of the submerged hydraulic dredge discharge pipe. The dredge crew will monitor VHF channels 16 and 69 during active dredging operations. For more information, contact Tyler Southworth at (509) 856-7700	

Online NOAA Chart Catalog

Electronic Charts (ENC)	Coast Pilot	Help

Place Name ⌄   [   ] ⌄   Submit   All Bands ⌄

Available Product Information

NOAA ENCs (ENC):
Vector files of chart features
and available in S-57 format.

NOAA ENCs support marine
navigation by providing the
official Electronic Navigational
Chart used in ECDIS and in
electronic charting systems.

NOAA ENCs are updated weekly with
Notice to Mariner corrections.

Map Selection Information

Chart: US4WA1II	
Title:	Northern Puget Sound
Scale:	1 : 45,000
Edition:	1
Update:	0
Published:	2025-05-24

Available Products

ENC

Continue Clicking...
Charts at current location: 1 of 5

48.1841 , -122.8765

Status of New NOAA ENCs

Chart catalogs are now online only, or built into a nav app, such as qtVlm. These two samples are linked from starpath.com/getcharts. Top is the active catalog as of Nov, 2025; bottom is the status of the rescheming program, with green done, red in progress, and outlines are planned.

Excerpts from Coast Pilot

UNITED STATES
Coast Pilot®

NOAA

10

Oregon, Washington, Hawaii and Pacific Islands

2025 (6th) Edition

> Chart 18465 Tr is covered in Chapter 7 of Volume 10. The following are excerpted parts of Chapter 7 (just a small part of the full chapter) to practice use of this important resource. Paragraphs are numbered in the original books. Answers are referenced with these paragraph numbers. An Index to terms used is at the end of the excerpt. All Coast Pilots are online in full.

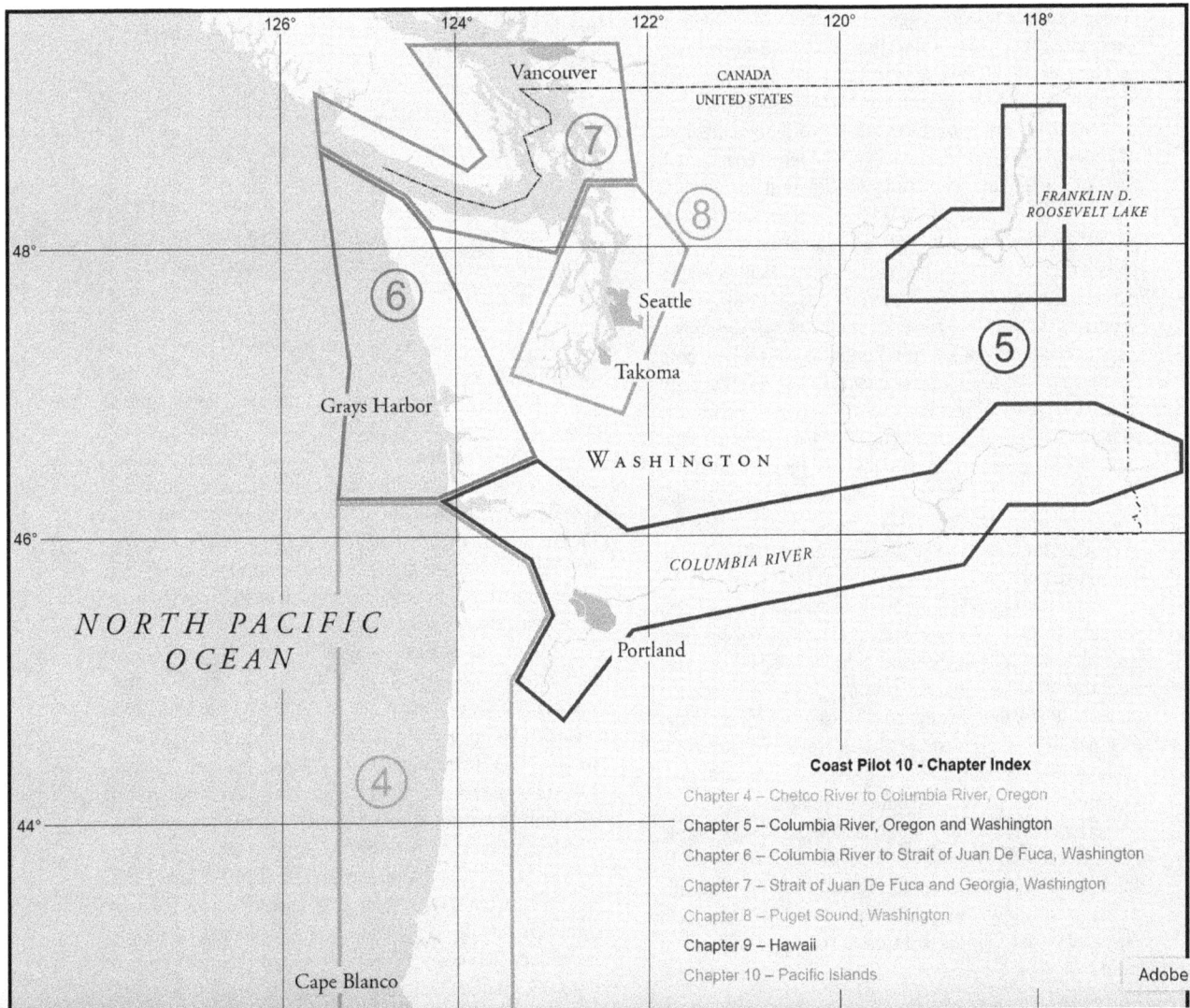

Coast Pilot 10 - Chapter Index

Adobe InDe

Regions covered by Chapters in US Coast Pilot Volume 10.

Strait of Juan De Fuca and Georgia, Washington

(1)　　This chapter includes the Strait of Juan de Fuca, Sequim Bay, Port Discovery, the San Juan Islands and its various passages and straits, Deception Pass, Fidalgo Island, Skagit and Similk Bays, Swinomish Channel, Fidalgo, Padilla, and Bellingham Bays, Lummi Bay, Semiahmoo Bay and Drayton Harbor and the Strait of Georgia as far north as Burrard Inlet. The more important U.S. harbors described are Neah Bay, Port Angeles, Friday Harbor, La Connor, Anacortes, Bellingham and Blaine Harbor. Deep-draft vessels use the harbors at Port Angeles, Anacortes, and Bellingham, the principal cities in the area. The Canadian coasts are only briefly described. (See **Pub. 154, Sailing Directions (Enroute) for British Columbia**, published by the National Geospatial-Intelligence Agency, and the **Sailing Directions PAC 201, Juan de Fuca Strait and Strait of Georgia**, published by the Canadian Hydrographic Service, for detailed information on Canadian waters.)

(2)　　**Strait of Juan de Fuca** separates the south shore of Vancouver Island, Canada, from the north coast of the State of Washington. The entrance to the strait lies between parallels 48°23'N., and 48°36'N., on the meridian of 124°45'W. This important body of water is the connecting channel between the ocean and the interisland passages extending south to Puget Sound and north to the inland waters of British Columbia and southeastern Alaska.

(3)　　The commerce of this region is extensive, both foreign and domestic. Vast quantities of lumber, fish, grain and general merchandise are exported, while the manufacturing and shipbuilding industries are important. Several transcontinental railroads have their terminals on Puget Sound. There are many steamer lines, foreign and domestic, operating from this area to places across the Pacific or through the Panama Canal, in addition to the coastal vessels.

(4)　　At its entrance and for 50 miles east to Race Rocks, the strait is about 11 miles wide and then widens to about 16 miles for 30 miles east to Whidbey Island, its east boundary. The waters as a rule are deep until near the shore with few outlying dangers, most of which are in the east part. The shores on both sides are heavily wooded, rising rapidly to elevations of considerable height, and, except in a few places, are bold and rugged.

(5)　　The navigation of these waters is relatively simple in clear weather. The aids to navigation are numerous. In thick weather, because of strong and irregular currents, extreme caution and vigilance must be exercised. Navigators not familiar with these waters should take a pilot.

(6)

COLREGS Demarcation Lines

(7)　　The International Regulations for Preventing Collisions at Sea, 1972 (72 COLREGS) apply on all the waters of the Strait of Juan de Fuca, Haro Strait, and Strait of Georgia. (See **33 CFR 80.1385** and **80.1390**, chapter 2.)

(8)

Traffic Separation Scheme

(9)　　There are traffic separation schemes in the approaches and within the Strait of Juan de Fuca, Puget Sound, Haro Strait, Boundary Pass and the Strait of Georgia. See **33 CFR 167.1** through **167.15**, chapter 2, for general regulations on the schemes. Limits and regulations detailing specific schemes can also be found in chapter 2 (reference the following table.)

(10)

Traffic Separation Scheme Regulations	
Strait of Juan de Fuca (approaches to)	33 CFR 167.1300 through 167.1303
Strait of Juan de Fuca	33 CFR 167.1310 through 167.1315
Puget Sound	33 CFR 167.1320 through 167.1323
Haro Strait, Boundary Pass, Strait of Georgia	33 CFR 167.1330 through 167.1332

(11)　　A V-AIS marks the precautionary area west-northwest of Cape Flattery and a lighted buoy marks the precautionary area between Race Rocks and Port Angeles and is equipped with a RACON. These ATONS assist in the separation of inbound and outbound vessels transiting the Strait of Juan de Fuca and eliminating, as much as possible, the cross-vessel traffic that can occur between the entrance to the Strait of Juan de Fuca at Cape Flattery and the pilot stations at Port Angeles and Victoria, British Columbia. It is recommended that all vessels navigate so as to leave these buoys to port.

(12)　　Vessels so desiring may while transiting the Strait of Juan de Fuca contact the Puget Sound Vessel Traffic Service by calling SEATTLE TRAFFIC on VHF-FM channel 5A to receive desired information on known traffic, aids to navigation discrepancies and locally hazardous weather conditions. In Admiralty Inlet, south of a line between Nodule Point on Marrowstone Island and Bush Point on Whidbey Island, vessels should use VHF-FM channel 14 to contact SEATTLE TRAFFIC. VHF-FM channel 13 should be used to make passing arrangements in U.S. waters and is Seattle Traffic's secondary frequency; however, because channel 13 is not used in Canadian waters as the primary bridge-to-bridge

(18)

Washington State Requirements—Reporting Oil Spills and Vessel Emergencies

All vessels must report oil spills or potential oil spills to both Washington State (800–258–5990) and the National Response Center (800–424–8802). Tank vessels and cargo and passenger ships 300 gross tons or larger must make notifications to Washington State for vessel emergencies, including a loss or serious degradation of propulsion, steering, means of navigation, electrical generating capability and seakeeping capability constituting a substantial threat of pollution affecting Washington State natural resources. In addition to any notifications to the USCG, the owner or operator must notify the state of any vessel emergency that results in the discharge or substantial threat of a discharge of oil to state waters or that may affect the natural resources of the state within one hour of the onset of the emergency.

Tug Escorts for Laden Tankers

Any laden oil tanker, whether enrolled or registered, proceeding east of a line extending from Discovery Island Light (British Columbia, CN) south to New Dungeness Light (Washington State, US) must be escorted by a tug or tugs with an aggregate shaft horsepower equivalent to five percent of the deadweight tons of that tanker. For additional details see Washington state law at 88.16 Revised Code of Washington (RCW).

Emergency Response Tug at Neah Bay

An industry-funded emergency response tug is located at Neah Bay at the entrance to the Strait of Juan de Fuca. The tug is available 24 hours a day and can be underway within twenty minutes of a decision to deploy. The purpose of the tug is to assist vessels having propulsion and steering failures or that are directed by either the U.S. or Canadian Coast Guards to obtain towing assistance. Among other capabilities, the tug is intended to be able to make up to, stop, hold, and tow a drifting or disabled vessel of 180,000 metric dead weight tons in severe weather conditions. The tug can be contacted through the USCG VTS or the Puget Sound Marine Exchange.

Washington State Vessel Inspections

The Washington State Department of Ecology regulates cargo and passenger vessels and tank vessels operating in Washington waters. A cargo vessel is any self-propelled vessel in commerce that is 300 gross tons or more. A passenger vessel is any vessel 300 gross tons or more with a fuel capacity of at least 6,000 gallons that carries passengers for compensation. A tank vessel is a ship that is constructed or adapted to carry, or that carries, oil in bulk as cargo or cargo residue. Washington State Ecology inspectors may conduct vessel inspections on regulated cargo, passenger, and fishing vessels when in Washington waters. Additional information—
www.ecology.wa.gov/regulations-permits/guidance-technical-assistance/guidance-for-oil-industry/vessel-information.

Oil Transfer Requirements

Safe bunkering procedures must be followed during fueling operations. For vessels 300 gross tons or greater, Washington State Ecology inspectors may conduct inspections of these regulated oil transfers on vessels receiving fuel for propulsion within Washington waters. Details can be found in state regulations at Washington Administrative Code (WAC) 317-40. Additional information—
www.ecology.wa.gov/regulations-permits/guidance-technical-assistance/requirements-for-bunkering.

Tank vessels delivering oil in bulk to a non-recreational vessel or facility within Washington waters must meet state oil transfer requirements. They may also be subject to Washington State oil transfer inspections for these regulated oil transfers. Details can be found in WAC 173-184. Additional information—
www.ecology.wa.gov/regulations-permits/compliance-enforcement/oil-transfers.

For a transfer of more than 100 gallons of bulk oil to a facility or non-recreational vessel, the delivering vessel must submit an Advance Notice of Transfer (ANT) report to Ecology. This ANT must be submitted 24 hours prior to the transfer for facilities or within the timeframe required by local USCG Captain of the Port. The ANT report can be made either: online using the state website at: *https://secureaccess.wa.gov/ecy/ants*, by e-mail to *OilTransferNotifications@ecy.wa.gov*, or by fax to 360–407–7288 or 800–664–9184.

Contingency Plan Requirements

Tank vessels and cargo and passenger ships 300 gross tons or larger transiting Washington waters must either have a Washington State Department of Ecology approved oil spill contingency plan or be a member of a non-profit cooperative that provides oil spill response capabilities consistent with their Washington State approved contingency plan. The non-profit cooperative for the Columbia River is the Maritime Fire & Safety Association (MFSA) and for Puget Sound and Grays Harbor is Washington State Maritime Cooperative. Also available is the National Response Corporation, a multiple vessel plan. Additional information—
www.ecology.wa.gov/regulations-permits/plans-policies/contingency-planning-for-oil-industry.

radiotelephone channel, vessels are encouraged to use channel 5A to make passing arrangements in the Strait of Juan de Fuca. Preliminary calls to SEATTLE TRAFFIC on VHF-FM channel 16 are not required or desired. (See Traffic Separation Schemes, chapter 1, for additional information.)

(13) The Canadian Government recommends that ships conduct themselves in accordance with the navigational procedures set forth in the Ship Routing Regulations when navigating in or near the traffic separation scheme in Canadian waters. Mariners are advised that the Canadian Ship Routing Regulations are based upon the International Maritime Organization's "General Principles of Ships' Routing," except for a relaxation that permits vessels engaged in fishing to proceed in any direction in or near traffic lanes and on the high seas. (Canadian Ship Routing Regulations are published in the Annual Edition of Canadian Notices to Mariners.)

(14) Complete details of the traffic separation schemes and the vessel traffic management and information system for the coastal waters of southern British Columbia are given in the following:

(15) Pub. No. 154, Sailing Directions Enroute, British Columbia, published by the National Geospatial-Intelligence Agency;

(16) Sailing Directions PAC 201, Juan de Fuca Strait and Strait of Georgia, published by the Canadian Hydrographic Service, and

(17) Annual Edition of Canadian Notices to Mariners, published by the Canadian Coast Guard.

(19) **Vessel Traffic Service**

(20) The U.S. Coast Guard operates **Puget Sound Vessel Traffic Service (PSVTS)** in the U.S. waters of the Strait of Juan de Fuca and the Strait of Georgia, Rosario Strait, Puget Sound, Hood Canal, Possession Sound, the San Juan Islands Archipelago and navigable waters adjacent to these areas; the system is mandatory. Vessel operating procedures and designated radiotelephone frequencies are published in **33 CFR 161**, chapter 2, and/or the **Puget Sound Vessel Traffic Service User Manual**, available online at *uscg.mil/d13/psvts*. Mariners should consult these sources for applicable rules and reporting requirements. The PSVTS is a full-service VTS providing Information Service, Traffic Organization Service and Navigation Assistance Services to vessels operating in the VTS area. The system is designed to prevent collisions and groundings and to protect the navigable waters concerned from environmental harm resulting from such collisions and groundings.

(21) A **Cooperative Vessel Traffic Service (CVTS)** has been established in the Strait of Juan de Fuca region, based on an agreement between the United States and Canada. Operated by the U.S. Coast Guard and the Canadian Coast Guard, the system is intended to enhance safe and expeditious vessel movement and to minimize risk of pollution to the marine environment; the system

is mandatory. Regulations which apply to the CVTS can be found in **33 CFR 161.1** through **161.23** and **161.55**, chapter 2. The CVTS exchange lines delineating the service boundaries and frequency change lines between Vessel Traffic Center management authorities are detailed in the **Puget Sound VTS User's Manual** which can be found at *www.pacificarea.uscg.mil/VTSPugetSound/*.

(22) Mariners are advised that **Ferry Routes** may differ from the established Vessel Traffic Services, Traffic Separation Schemes and Cooperative Vessel Traffic Management Systems for the entire Strait of Juan de Fuca and Puget Sound area.

(23) In accordance with the Cooperative Vessel Traffic Service, the United States and Canada, in cooperation with industry and the British Columbia Coast Pilots have established a **Special Operating Area (SOA)** at the intersection of Haro Strait and Boundary Pass in the vicinity of Turn Point Light (48°41'20"N., 123°14'15"W.). This area enhances order and predictability and the efficient and safe movement of goods and services and further reduces the risk of accidents with respect to vessels transiting the boundary waters of Haro Strait and Boundary Passage in the vicinity of Turn Point on Stuart Island, Washington. Complete information on this special operating area can be found in the **Puget Sound Vessel Traffic Service User's Manual**.

(24)

Regulated navigation area

(25) Due to heavy vessel concentrations, the waters of the Strait of Juan de Fuca, the San Juan Islands, the Strait of Georgia and Puget Sound, and all adjacent waters, are a regulated navigation area. (See **33 CFR 165.1** through **165.13** and **165.1301**, chapter 2, for regulations.)

(26)

Caution

(27) Since logging is one of the main industries of the region, free-floating logs and submerged deadheads or sinkers are a constant source of danger in the Strait of Juan de Fuca and Puget Sound. The danger is increased during freshets and after storms and unusually high tides. **Deadheads** or **sinkers** are logs that have become adrift from rafts or booms, have become waterlogged and float in a vertical position with one end just awash, rising and falling with the tide.

(28)

Currents, Cape Flattery to Race Rocks

(29) The currents may attain velocities of 2 to 4 knots, varying with the range of tide, and are influenced by strong winds. East of Race Rocks, in the wider portion of the strait, the velocity is considerably less. At Race Rocks and Discovery Island the velocity may be 6 knots or more.

(30) The **flood current** entering the Strait of Juan de Fuca sets with considerable velocity over Duncan and Duntze Rocks, but, instead of running in the direction of the channel, it has a continued set toward the Vancouver Island shore which is experienced as far as Race Rocks.

(39)

METEOROLOGICAL TABLE – COASTAL AREA OFF SEATTLE, WA
Between 48°N to 50°N and 122°W to 129°W

WEATHER ELEMENTS	JAN	FEB	MAR	APR	MAY	JUN	JUL	AUG	SEP	OCT	NOV	DEC	YEARS OF RECORD
Wind > 33 knots [1]	3.6	2.8	2.3	1.2	0.8	0.6	0.3	0.3	0.5	1.7	3.1	3.4	1.6
Wave Height > 9 feet [1]	17.4	18.0	16.8	15.0	6.7	6.1	1.9	2.1	4.7	16.0	24.0	30.5	12.3
Visibility < 2 nautical miles [1]	11.4	10.4	8.1	7.1	6.6	6.7	9.2	14.0	12.0	13.2	11.7	12.1	10.3
Precipitation [1]	24.4	24.4	19.6	16.7	13.5	10.8	7.5	5.8	9.2	16.6	24.0	24.9	15.6
Temperature > 69° F	0.0	0.0	0.0	0.1	0.5	1.6	3.0	2.8	1.2	0.3	0.0	0.0	0.9
Mean Temperature (°F)	44.0	45.3	46.1	48.7	52.8	56.3	58.8	59.3	58.2	53.7	48.3	45.5	52.1
Temperature < 33° F [1]	3.3	0.8	0.2	0.0	0.0	0.0	0.0	0.0	0.0	0.0	0.6	0.9	0.4
Mean RH (%)	84	84	82	82	82	82	84	85	84	84	83	84	83
Overcast or Obscured [1]	46.3	43.3	34.5	32.8	32.7	33.1	32.6	32.9	30.6	36.5	38.4	41.3	35.8
Mean Cloud Cover (8ths)	6.2	6.0	5.5	5.5	5.4	5.5	5.1	5.0	4.7	5.4	5.9	6.0	5.5
Mean SLP (mbs)	1014	1015	1014	1016	1017	1017	1018	1017	1017	1016	1014	1014	1016
Ext. Max. SLP (mbs)	1041	1057	1041	1060	1044	1042	1048	1040	1050	1041	1043	1048	1060
Ext. Min. SLP (mbs)	951	974	967	977	987	988	993	990	973	967	966	964	951
Prevailing Wind Direction	SE	SE	SE	NW	NW	NW	NW	NW	NW	SE	SE	SE	NW
Thunder and Lightning [1]	0.3	0.2	0.2	0.1	0.1	0.1	0.1	0.2	0.3	0.3	0.3	0.2	0.2

[1] Percentage Frequency

The flood current velocity is greater on the north shore of the strait than on the south.

(31)　　The **ebb current** is felt most along the south shore of the strait, and between New Dungeness Light and Crescent Bay there is a decided set south and west, especially during large tides. With the wind and swell against the current, a short choppy sea is raised near the entrance to the strait.

(32)　　The current movement is complicated by a large daily inequality. See the Tidal Current prediction service at *tidesandcurrents.noaa.gov* for specific information about times, directions, and velocities of the current at numerous locations throughout the area. Links to a user guide for this service can be found in chapter 1 of this book.

(33)　　**Tide rips** occur off the prominent points and in the vicinity of the banks. These are particularly heavy off Cape Flattery, Race Rocks, Dungeness Spit and Point Wilson, at times becoming dangerous to small vessels.

(34)

Weather, Straits of Juan De Fuca and Georgia

(35)　　Winds are strongest from October through March. This results from the numerous winter storms that move through these waters; this is also an area where storms tend to intensify. As low-pressure systems approach the coast, winds strengthen and back to the southeast quadrant, sometimes reaching gale force. After the storm passes, winds veer to the southwest or northwest. Gales usually last less than 1 day, whereas the interval between storms normally varies from 1 to 5 days or up to 2 weeks when a strong high-pressure system settles in. These systems can also present local wind problems in the Georgia Strait. The mountainous terrain of this region plays an important part in determining the direction and speed of the wind. There are normally two wind seasons; winter lasts from October through March, while a summer regime covers the other 6 months.

(36)　　From October through March, winds at the Pacific entrance to the Strait of Juan de Fuca blow mostly out of the southeast through southwest. Gales blow on 4 to 6 days per month. They can come from any direction; however, southeast winds are consistently the strongest, averaging about 18 knots. Strong southeast winds raise dangerous confused seas off Cape Flattery, when they meet the long, rolling southwest swells that frequent these waters. The frequent strong winds from a south quarter make the Vancouver coast between Cape Cook and Port San Juan a dangerous lee shore. When gales blow from the southwest through west, it is usually safer inside the Strait than out. In general, winds are strongest and gales more frequent in the west end of the Strait. In the open water of the middle of the Strait, winter winds blow mostly out of the east through southeast. Gales occur on about 2 to 4 days per month in the east half. The south shore is protected from the southeast gales; Port Angeles provides good shelter. An approaching storm often sets up strong east winds in the central part of the Strait. This, in turn, sets up a drainage of air from the Georgia Strait, so that winds near the east entrance are frequently from the north through northeast. As the storm moves inland, it produces a reversal of this flow. Winds blow from the west through most of the strait, backing to the southwest in the east. Winds near the west entrance have reached 65 knots with gusts to 90 knots. In the strait, 50-knot winds and 80-knot gusts have been reported.

(37)　　Summer winds at sea blow mainly from the southwest through northwest around the subtropical Pacific high. Heating of the North American continent helps draw air into the Strait of Juan de Fuca. This sea breeze reinforces the prevailing flow and results in winds up to 30 knots in the late afternoon. The land breeze opposes the normal flow, and calms are often the rule in early morning. Southwest through west winds are most frequent in the Strait of Juan de Fuca.

(39) See page 272

(38)   In few parts of the world is the vigilance of the mariner more called upon than when entering the Strait of Juan de Fuca from the Pacific in fog. Sea fog is the most common type, and it is at its worst from about July through October. Local land fog extends the visibility hazard into the winter. Fog is most frequent at the west end of the Strait. Here, visibilities drop to less than 0.75 mile (1.4km) on about 55 days annually, compared to about 35 days in the east end. Dense fog sometimes hangs over the ocean entrance to the Strait for days at a time; this is most likely during calms or light breezes. It gives the appearance of a wall, and ships entering often run into clear, bright weather before they pass Tatoosh Island. Often the fog is carried east on the west sea breeze. When this happens, the fog usually penetrates farther east along the south shore. It is much more likely to reach Port Angeles or Port Townsend than Victoria. In spring, the east penetration of an infrequent fog is usually limited to Crescent or Freshwater Bays. Often when thick weather prevails in the Strait of Juan de Fuca, skies are clear north of Race Rocks.

(39)   See Page 272.

(40)
Pilotage, Strait of Juan de Fuca and Puget Sound

(41)   Pilotage is compulsory for all foreign vessels and U.S. vessels engaged in foreign trade. Pilotage is optional for U.S. vessels engaged in the coastwise trade with a federally licensed pilot on board.

(42)   Puget Sound Pilots serve all U.S. ports and places east of 123°24'W., including Port Angeles, Puget Sound, and adjacent inland waters. The office address is Puget Sound Pilots, 2003 Western Avenue, Suite 200, Seattle, WA 98121; telephone, 206–448–4455 (24 hours), 206–728–6400; Fax 206–448–3405. Pilot station address is 305 Ediz Hook Road, P.O. Box 788, Port Angeles, WA 98362; telephone, 800–221–0234, 360–457–7944; fax 360–452–8566.

(43)   Port Angeles has been designated as the pilotage station for all vessels enroute to or from the sea. The pilot station is located on Ediz Hook about 0.7 mile west of Ediz Hook Light. There are two pilot boats; both are 22 meters in length with white hulls and orange houses. The standard day and night signals are displayed. The pilot station and pilot boats are equipped with radar to locate and track vessels; radio communication can be made by calling "Puget Sound Pilots" on VHF-FM channel 13.

(44)   Pilotage should be arranged between 0800 and 1700 at least 24 hours in advance of inbound ETA through the vessel's agent, by direct telephone communication with Puget Sound Pilots at the previously mentioned telephone numbers or the Marine Exchange of Puget Sound (telephone: 206–443–3830 or Telex 6734358 "Matex"). If subsequent conditions make it necessary, an amended estimated time of arrival should be made. Inbound vessels are requested to reaffirm their estimated time of arrival to the pilot boarding station when they are

(45)   Loaded petroleum tankers requiring a pilot should proceed to position 48°09'54"N.,123°24'19"W., (1.5 miles north of the east end of Ediz Hook); all other vessels to position 48°09'24"N.,123°24'00"W., (1.0 mile north of the east end of Ediz Hook). A pilot ladder should be rigged in compliance with SOLAS regulations on the leeward side about 1 meter above the water. When approaching the boarding area, vessels are requested to monitor VHF-FM channel 13 and maintain a steady course and speed of about 6 knots when the pilot boat comes alongside.

(46)
Towage

(47)   Tugs are stationed at Port Angeles. Arrangements are usually made in advance through ships' agents.

(48)
Quarantine, customs, immigration and agricultural quarantine.

(49)   (See chapter 3, Vessel Arrival Inspections, and Appendix A for addresses.)

(50)   Quarantine is enforced in accordance with regulations of the U.S. Public Health Service. (See Public Health Service, chapter 1.)

(51)
Strait of Juan de Fuca (Canada)

(52)
Strait of Juan de Fuca (Canada)

(53)   Carmanah Point is described in the previous chapter. **Bonilla Point**, the north entrance point at the west end of the strait, is about 1.8 miles east-southeast from Carmanah Light. Inland of Bonilla Point, which slopes gradually to the sea, the mountains attain heights of over 3,500 feet and are heavily wooded. A reef extends 0.5 mile off the point, and the shores should be given a berth of at least 1.5 miles.

(54)   From Bonilla Point the coast trends in a southeast direction for 9.5 miles to Owen Point. It is nearly straight, rocky, and bluff, with high mountains rising immediately behind it; all are heavily wooded.

(55)   **Port San Juan** offers the first anchorage on the north shore within the entrance to the Strait of Juan de Fuca. The port is conspicuous from seaward, appearing as a deep gap between two mountain ranges.

(56)   The entrance between **Owen Point** and **San Juan Point**, 1.7 miles wide and 3.5 miles long, is 13 miles northeast of Cape Flattery Light. It is marked by a lighted whistle buoy.

(57)   The port is open to southwest winds, and a heavy sea rolls in when a moderate gale is blowing from that direction. Though it is possible that a vessel with good ground tackle could ride out a gale if anchored in the most sheltered part, it is recommended that with any indication of southwest gales a vessel should weigh anchor immediately and, if the vessel's draft is 16 feet

(58)   Anchorage may be had in 6 to 9 fathoms anywhere in Port San Juan; a good position is in 5½ fathoms about 1 mile from the beach at the head of the port.

(59)   **Cerantes Rocks**, about 300 yards southwest from San Juan Point, include several high pinnacle rocks with a few trees growing on them. About 800 yards north of these rocks and 300 yards from shore is another reef partly uncovered.

(60)   **Port Renfrew** is a settlement on the southeast side of Port San Juan, about 2 miles northeast of San Juan Point. A T-head pier has depths of 15 feet alongside.

(61)   From Port San Juan the coast trends southeast for 23.5 miles to Sheringham Point. This stretch of coast presents no prominent features. The country is thickly wooded, and the land rises to a considerable elevation. The points, some of which are bare on their extremities, are not prominent nor are they easily identified, except from close inshore.

(62)   A Canadian Armed Forces **firing** and **practice exercise area** is established in the vicinity of Sheringham Point and San Simon Point about 8 miles to the west. (See Annual Edition of Canadian Notices to Mariners for area limits, types of practices, warning signals, etc.)

(63)   Between Port San Juan and Race Rocks, fish traps and broken piles are reported to extend 0.5 mile offshore in places.

(64)
Sheringham Point to Discovery Island

(65)   **Sheringham Point** is marked by a light. Victoria marine radio station VAK is at Sheringham Point.

(66)   From Sheringham Point the coast continues in a series of bays and inlets for 16.5 miles to Race Rocks.

(67)   **Beechey Head**, 11.5 miles east-southeast of Sheringham Point, is bold, wooded and steep-to. Vessels bound up the strait and passing outside Race Rocks should give Beechey Head a berth of 2 miles.

(68)   **Race Rocks**, 5 miles east of Beechey Head, are a cluster of bare low rocks from 0.5 mile to almost 1.5 miles from shore. Foul ground extends for 0.5 mile in all directions from the light; dangerous overfalls and races occur during bad weather. A light and sound signal are on the largest rock of the group, and a lighted buoy marks the southeast rock of the group. The tidal currents in Race Passage and in the vicinity of Race Rocks attain a velocity of 4 to 6 knots at times, and dangerous tide rips are formed.

(69)   **Firing practice** and **exercise areas** of the Canadian Armed Forces are east of Race Rocks in the approaches to Esquimalt and Victoria Harbors. (See the Annual Edition of Canadian Notices to Mariners.)

(70)   Foul ground, due to dumping of heavy steel wire mesh material, is 3.2 miles west from Race Rocks Light.

(71)   East of Race Rocks the Strait of Juan de Fuca expands to a width of about 16 miles and extends for 30 miles east-northeast to the entrance to Admiralty Inlet on the south and Rosario Strait on the north.

(72)   A 25-fathom bank lies 8.5 miles southeast of Race Rocks along the steamer track from Race Rocks Light to Point Wilson Light. The west edge of this bank is sometimes sharply defined by a line of ripples with glassy calm water to the east.

(73)   **Bentinck Island**, 1 mile northwest of Race Rocks Light, is fringed with kelp on its south and east sides. **Pedder Bay, Parry Bay** and **Royal Roads**, separated by William Head and **Albert Head**, form the coast between Bentinck Island and the west entrance to Esquimalt Harbor.

(74)   A **027°43'–207°43' measured nautical mile** has been established on the northwest shore of Parry Bay. Range beacons, consisting of fluorescent orange diamond-shaped daymarks, mark the northeast and southwest ends of the measured course.

(75)   A **prohibited area** has been established in Parry Bay by the Canadian Government. No vessel may anchor in the area without permission.

(76)   **William Head** is a comparatively low promontory extending about 0.5 mile northeast of **Ned Point**. Close west of William Head is **Quarantine Cove**, on the east shore of which are the conspicuous red brick buildings of the former quarantine station, now used as a penitentiary. Unauthorized vessels should not approach William Head within 200 yards.

(77)   Anchorage affording protection from west weather may be had in 7 fathoms about 0.5 mile north of William Head and about 1,200 yards from the mainland.

(78)   **Constance Bank**, 6.8 miles east of William Head Light, has general depths of 8 to 13 fathoms. It is about 2 miles long and 1 mile wide, within the 20-fathom curve. The bottom is rocky, and tide rips form in this vicinity. Vessels should not attempt to anchor on the bank.

(79)   **Albert Head** is 3.3 miles northeast of William Head. **Fisgard Island**, on the west side of the entrance to Esquimalt Harbor, is marked by a light. Its red sector covers **Scroggs Rocks** off the east entrance point. Scroggs Rocks are marked by a light.

(80)   **Esquimalt Harbor**, about 3 miles north-northeast of Albert Head, affords safe and ample anchorage and can be entered at any time. The entrance channel has general depths of 8 fathoms. Depths within the entrance gradually decrease for 1.5 miles north to **Cole Island**, above which the head of the harbor dries.

(81)   **Victoria Harbor**, landlocked and well protected, is about 2 miles east-southeast of Esquimalt Harbor and can accommodate large vessels. A U.S. Immigration station is in Victoria.

(82)   Victoria Harbor is entered between **Macaulay Point** on the west and the breakwater extending from **Ogden Point** on the east; the breakwater is marked by a light. Vessels requiring a pilot are requested to notify **"Pilots Victoria"** by radio station **VAK** at least 6 hours in advance of their estimated time of arrival. The harbor extends for more than 0.5 mile north to **Shoal Point** on the east side, and thence trends east to **James Bay**. From the north part of James Bay, the upper harbor, which is

crossed by three bridges, extends about 0.8 mile north-northwest to **Selkirk Water**, the west extremity of which is connected to **Portage Inlet**.

(83)   **Brotchie Ledge**, the only outlying danger, about 200 yards long within the 5-fathom curve, lies 0.6 mile south of Ogden Point. The ledge has a least depth of 12 feet and is marked by a light.

(84)   **Clover Point**, 2 miles east-southeast of the entrance to Victoria Harbor, is low, bare of trees, and steep-to. Strong tide rips form off the point.

(85)   **Trial Islands**, 4 miles east of Victoria Harbor, are bare and rocky; from most directions the two islands appear as one. The islands are marked by a light. The south and larger island is 80 feet high, and from **Staines Point**, its south extremity, a rocky ledge that uncovers 2 feet extends about 100 yards. Severe tide rips form off Staines Point, especially on the flood tidal current, which attains a velocity of 3 to 6 knots during large tides. The point should be given a wide berth.

(86)   **Discovery Island**, 2 miles east-northeast of **Gonzales Point**, lies off the junction of Haro Strait and the Strait of Juan de Fuca. The island is wooded, and near its southeast tip, **Pandora Hill** attains a height of about 125 feet. The island is marked by a light on the east side. The shores on all sides of the island are fringed with rocks in some places extending as far as 600 yards offshore.

(87)
Strait of Juan de Fuca (east end)

(88)
Strait of Juan de Fuca (east end)

(89)   **Hein Bank**, with a least depth of 2½ fathoms, lies 8.5 miles southeast of Discovery Island; it is about 2 miles long in a north direction, within the 10-fathom curve, and 0.8 mile wide. The shoalest part of the bank is covered with thick kelp in the summer. It is marked by a lighted buoy.

(90)   **Smith Island**, 5 miles west of Whidbey Island and 8 miles east-southeast of Hein Bank, is irregular in shape and about 0.5 mile long. The east end is low but rises abruptly to an elevation of 55 feet at its west end, terminating in a white perpendicular cliff composed of sand and gravel. A rocky bank, covered with kelp, extends about 2 miles west of the island over depths of 3 to 6 fathoms. A rock that bares at lowest tides is about 0.3 mile west of Smith Island. Strong currents set in and around the shoal area, especially on the flood, and deep-draft vessels should keep well outside the 10-fathom curve to avoid being set into danger. **Smith Island Light** (48°19'14"N., 122°49'51"W.), 55 feet above the water, is shown from a 50-foot skeleton tower on a multi-pile structure with a white and black dayboard. The light is obsured from 068° to 084°.

(91)   A **restricted area** of an air-to-surface weapon range is west of Smith Island. (See **33 CFR 334.1180**, chapter 2, for limits and regulations.)

(92)   **Minor Island**, small, low, and rocky, lies 1 mile northeast of Smith Island and at lowest tide is connected with it by a gravel and boulder spit.

(93)   The northernmost part of the western shore of **Whidbey Island** forms the east end of the Strait of Juan de Fuca. This part of the island has a uniform sandy shore backed by low and rolling upland of farm and wooded areas. A marina at Oak Harbor, on the east side of the island, has electricity, gasoline, diesel fuel and pumpout facility.

(94)   **Naval restricted areas** are adjacent to the northernmost part of the west shore of Whidbey Island. (See **33 CFR 334.1200**, chapter 2, for limits and regulations.)

(95)   The aerolight (48°20.9'N., 122°40.2'W.) at Ault Field is conspicuous.

(96)
Neah Bay

(97)   On the south side of the Strait of Juan de Fuca the coast trends east for 4 miles from Cape Flattery to **Koitlah Point**, the west point of Neah Bay. The shores are rugged, and the country is heavily timbered.

(98)   **Neah Bay**, about 5 miles east of Cape Flattery, is used extensively by small vessels as a harbor of refuge in foul weather. Its proximity to Cape Flattery and ease of access at any time make the anchorage very useful. It is protected from all but east weather.

(99)   **Baada (Baadah) Point**, the east entrance point to Neah Bay, is rocky and grass covered for some distance back from the shore. **Waadah Island**, 0.3 mile north of Baada Point, is 0.5 mile long, high, and wooded. A light marks the north and south end of the island. A stone breakwater extends from the west side of the bay to about the middle of Waadah Island. A reef and foul ground extend 0.2 mile from the southwest side of the island. A reef that bares, marked by a lighted bell buoy, extends 500 yards northwest from **Dtokoah Point**, southeast of the entrance.

(100)   The buildings of **Neah Bay Coast Guard Station**, 0.4 mile southwest of Baada Point, are prominent from the entrance.

(101)   The entrance to the bay is between Waadah Island and Baada Point. A depth of 17 feet can be carried into the bay. Anchorage is in 20 to 35 feet, mud bottom.

(102)   The west shore of Neah Bay is high and precipitous and bordered by craggy rock outcroppings. The shore east of the village of Neah Bay is a low sand beach to Baada Point.

(103)   The village of **Neah Bay**, on the southwest shore of the bay, is the site of considerable sport fishing.

(104)   The Makah Indian T-head pier with a 300-foot face, and the ruins of a T-head pier no longer visible, are about 375 and 500 yards southwest of Baada Point. Caution is advised in the vicinity of the pier in ruins, as submerged piles may exist. The Coast Guard pier is 0.5 mile southwest of Baada Point.

(105)   Two cooperative fish piers, 1 mile and 1.2 miles southwest of Baada Point, have facilities for icing and supplying fishing boats. Limited berthage, electricity, gasoline, diesel fuel, water and ice are available. Both piers have reported depths of 12 feet off the ends. There are many small-craft floats extending along the south shore of the bay. A marina is about 1 mile southwest of Baada Point on the south shore and has 200 slips; gasoline, diesel fuel, water, electricity, pump-out and a launching ramp are available.

(106)   A paved highway extends along the Strait of Juan de Fuca to Port Angeles; telephone service is available.

(107)
Seal Rock to Twin Rivers

(108)   From Neah Bay to Clallam Bay, the coast for more than 14 miles is rugged and the back country high and heavily wooded.

(109)   **Seal Rock** and **Sail Rock**, about 2 miles east of Neah Bay and about 600 yards offshore, are very prominent. Seal Rock, the westerly of the two, is 100 feet high with a flat top showing east, light in color. Sail Rock, 0.2 mile east of Seal Rock, is lower and more pointed. Covered rocks extend from Seal Rock to shore, and there are patches of kelp in this area.

(110)   A marina is along the shore near Sail Rock. Berths, gasoline, water, ice provisions, and a 3-ton lift are available. Mariners are advised to exercise caution in approaching the marinas because of the numerous rocks and ledges. The floats at the marina bare at low water. **Sail River** empties near Seal and Sail Rocks. **Sekiu River**, about 6.5 miles southeast of Sail River, has some logging operations. The bridge over the river shows prominently through the trees.

(111)   **Clallam Bay**, about 15 miles southeast of Neah Bay, is a broad open bight about 2 miles long and 1 mile wide. It affords anchorage in 6 to 10 fathoms, sandy bottom, and is used to some extent in south or thick weather.

(112)   **Slip Point**, the east point of the bight, is high and wooded; there is a light-colored streak like a landslip down its face, which is visible for a long distance. A reef, extending 0.2 mile west of the point, is marked by a bell buoy.

(113)   **Sekiu** is a resort and sport fishing town on the west end of Clallam Bay and south of Sekiu Point. The town has berths, gasoline, water, ice, launching ramps and limited marine supplies. A marine railway that can handle craft to 24 feet long is at the town. **Clallam Bay**, a small town on the east side of Clallam Bay, has no waterfront facilities.

(114)   In entering Clallam Bay, give Slip Point a berth of more than 0.2 mile to avoid the reef projecting west of it. Storm-bound vessels generally anchor abreast the rocky point near the middle of the long semicircular beach on the south shore of the bay.

(115)   **Pillar Point**, 6.7 miles east-southeast of Slip Point, is bold, 700 feet high, wooded up to its summit, with a dark

pillar-shaped rock more than 100 feet high lying close under its east face. The rock shows prominently from west. Good anchorage may be had in 9 to 12 fathoms, sticky bottom, about 0.8 mile southeast of Pillar Point. This anchorage offers good shelter from the heavy west swell but gives no protection from the brisk east and northeast winds that prevail in winter.

(116)   **Twin Rivers** are two small streams that flow into the strait about 7 miles east of Pillar Point. An earthfilled barge-loading facility, 0.3 mile west of West Twin River, has a reported depth of 15 feet alongside. The facility is owned by a cement company and used for barging clay to Seattle.

(117)
Low Point to Angeles Point

(118)   Shoal water makes out a considerable distance from **Low Point** (48°09.6'N., 123°49.5'W.), 5 miles east of Twin Rivers, and vessels should not approach this point closer than 0.8 mile. Many boulders that uncover are west of the point. A salmon pen, about 2.4 miles west of the point and 0.6 mile from the nearest shore, is marked by two private lighted buoys.

(119)   **Agate Bay**, 3.5 miles east of Low Point, is clear and deep; 10 fathoms can be carried to within 0.2 mile of the shore.

(120)   **Crescent Bay**, 4.2 miles east of Low Point, is a small semicircular bight 1 mile in diameter. The east part is shoal, and near the west shore the remains of a wharf should be avoided. This is not a good landing place in north weather. The anchorage is of limited extent and suitable only for small vessels. **Crescent Rock**, covered ¼ fathom and marked by a buoy, is 0.4 mile north of the west entrance point of Crescent Bay. The rock extends 0.4 mile in east direction, with a narrow channel between it and the point. The channel has a reported depth of 10 fathoms and is not recommended without local knowledge. A reef extends about 400 yards northwest from **Tongue Point**, the east entrance point of Crescent Bay. A shoal, covered 1¼ fathoms, is about 0.3 mile west of Tongue Point. Except for crabs and fish, the 1¼-fathom shoal is a marine sanctuary for other shellfish and sealife. A wreck is off the entrance about 0.3 miles north of Tongue Point.

(121)   **Observatory Point** is 3 miles east of Tongue Point. Between these points is a wooded ridge which, because of the lower land behind it, makes this area appear as an island when raised from east or west. The ridge attains an elevation of 1,135 feet and is known as **Striped Peak**. A rock, 20 feet high, is close off Observatory Point; the rock and the point are almost joined at low water.

(122)   **Freshwater Bay**, about 4 miles east of Crescent Bay, is a broad open bight, affording anchorage in 6 to 10 fathoms. The bay and adjacent waters are designated as an **emergency explosives anchorage**. (See **33 CFR 110.1** and **110.230 (a)(1)** and **(b)**, chapter 2, for limits and regulations.) A park with a launching ramp is along the southwest shore of Freshwater Bay.

(123)   **Angeles Point**, on the east side of Freshwater Bay, is low, sandy, and covered with alders. The **Elwha River** empties into the strait at this point.

(124)   A microwave tower, marked by aircraft warning lights and a good landmark by day and night, is on Angeles Point.

(125)
Caution

(126)   The U.S. Navy advises that the precautionary area, located within a 1-mile radius centered around a point in about 48°15'36"N., 123°15'48"W., approximately 9 miles north-northeast of Ediz Hook, is used by naval vessels to conduct equipment calibration tests. Surface vessels or submerged submarines will occasionally be maneuvering in circles in this area for several hours or days. When these operations are in progress, the test facility located on the east end of Ediz Hook will be manned and reference lights consisting of a lazy "T" bar, 1 sec flashing yellow, 2/sec flashing red, and a high intensity spot will be lit. The group of lights is visible from the north side of Ediz Hook with the "T" bar to the west and spot light to the east. The naval vessels will be participating in the Seattle Vessel Traffic System on VHF-FM channel 5A. The Navy Test Facility Port Angeles will monitor VHF-FM channels 16 and 69. Mariners transiting this area are requested to proceed with caution.

(127)   A **Vessel Traffic Service** has been established in the Strait of Juan de Fuca, east of Port Angeles, and in the adjacent waters. (See **33 CFR 161.1** through **161.55**, chapter 2, for regulations, and the beginning of this chapter for additional information.)

(128)
Port Angeles

(129)   **Port Angeles**, 6.5 miles east of Freshwater Bay and 56 miles from Cape Flattery, is entered between **Ediz Hook**, a low and narrow sandspit 3 miles long, and the main shore to the south. The harbor, about 2.5 miles long, is easy of access by the largest vessels, which frequently use it when refueling, making topside repairs, waiting for orders or a tug and when weather-bound.

(130)   The harbor is protected from all except east winds, which occasionally blow during the winter. During southeast winter gales, the wind is not usually felt but some swells roll in. The depths are greatest on the north shore and decrease from 30 to 15 fathoms in the middle of the harbor; from the middle, the depths decrease regularly to the south shore, where the 3-fathom curve in some places in the east part is nearly 0.2 mile from the beach. A rock covered 5 fathoms is at 48°07'22"N., 123°13'18"W. A shoal with a least depth of 2¼ fathoms is 330 yards northwest of the northwest corner of the easternmost pier on the waterfront; a buoy is 200 yards east of the shoal.

(131)   Extra caution in navigating the waters inside Ediz Hook should be exercised because of the large number of submerged deadheads or sinkers in the area. Deadheads or sinkers are logs that have become adrift from rafts or booms, have become waterlogged and float in a vertical position with one end just awash, rising and falling with the tide.

(132)
Anchorage

(133)   Puget Sound Vessel Traffic Service requires advance notification of watch supervisor for all vessels using Port Angeles anchorage; telephone 206–217–6050. The best anchorage is off the wharves, in 7 to 12 fathoms, sticky bottom.

(134)   A **non-anchorage area** has been established in the east part of Port Angeles Harbor. (See **33 CFR 110.1** and **110.230**, chapter 2, for limits and regulations.)

(135)   Extensive log booming grounds in the north part of the harbor extend more than 1 mile from the west shore. Care must be taken when anchoring at night to avoid the rafted logs; the booming grounds are charted.

(136)   **Ediz Hook Light** (48°08'24"N., 123°24'09"W.), 50 feet above the water, is shown from a skeleton tower, 0.3 mile west of the east extremity of Ediz Hook; a mariner-radio-activated sound signal is at the light, initiated by keying the microphone five times on VHF-FM channel 81A. A 170-foot Coast Guard VTS radar tower is about 0.1 mile west-southwest of the light. Shoals extend to about 75 yards east of the east extremity of Ediz Hook. A lighted buoy is about 150 yards east of the outer limits of the shoals. A Coast Guard radio station (NOW) is at the air station. A shoal, with a least depth of 7 fathoms and marked by a lighted buoy, is about 3.4 miles west-northwest of Ediz Hook Light. An aquaculture site, marked by private lights, is off the south side of Ediz Hook about 800 yards west-southwest of the light.

(137)   **Port Angeles** is on the south shore of the harbor. Logs, lumber, plywood, newsprint, pulp, shakes and shingles and petroleum products are the principal commodities handled.

(138)
Pilotage, Port Angeles

(139)   Pilotage is compulsory for all vessels except those under enrollment or engaged exclusively in the coasting trade on the west coast of the continental United States (including Alaska) and/or British Columbia. Pilotage for Port Angeles is provided by the Puget Sound Pilots. They monitor VHF-FM channel 13. (See Pilotage, Strait of Juan de Fuca and Puget Sound, indexed as such, early this chapter.) The pilot station is about 0.7 mile west from Ediz Hook Light. A pier for berthage of the pilot boats is on the south side of Ediz Hook, adjacent to the pilot station.

(140)
Towage

(141)   Tugs to 1,200 hp are stationed at Port Angeles, and tugs to 5,000 hp are available from Seattle with advance notice.

(142)
Quarantine, customs, immigration and agricultural quarantine

(143)   (See chapter 3, Vessel Arrival Inspections, and Appendix A for addresses.)

(144)   **Quarantine** is enforced in accordance with regulations of the U.S. Public Health Service. (See Public Health Service, chapter 1.)

(145)   Port Angeles is a **customs port of entry**.

(146)
Coast Guard

(147)   Port Angeles Coast Guard Air Station/Sector Field is on Ediz Hook, about 0.3 mile west of the east extremity.

(148)
Harbor regulations

(149)   The Port of Port Angeles Terminal Manager's office is in Port Angeles at the foot of Cedar Street.

(150)
Wharves

(151)   The major piers described, both private and port operated, extend along the south and west sides of the harbor. The alongside depths of the facilities described are reported depths—for information on the latest depths contact the port authorities or the private operators.

(152)
Port-operated facilities

(153)   Port Terminal No. 1 (48°07'30"N., 123°26'24"W.): 956-foot berthing space on north side with an additional 425 feet to dolphins; 610 foot berthing space on south side, 42 feet at the end; deck height, 17 feet; 17,000 square feet covered storage; 96,000 square feet open storage; shipment of general cargo, lumber, logs, pulp and other forest products; berthing space for top side repair of large ocean going vessels.

(154)   Port of Port Angeles, Terminal No. 3 (W of Port Terminal 1): 480-foot berthing space; 41 to 45 feet alongside; deck height, 17 feet; receipt and shipment of general cargo, shipment of logs and lumber.

(155)
Privately operated facilities

(156)   Black Ball Ferry Transport (48°07'21"N., 123°25'45"W.): Terminus of passenger and automobile ferry connecting Port Angeles and Victoria, BC; ferry makes two trips daily from March to May and October to January. From May to October it makes 4 trips daily. Visit *northolympic.com* for the current schedule. Operated by Black Ball Transport, Inc.

(157)   Diashowa America, Port Angeles Mill Dock (48°07'57"N., 123°27'33"W.): 640-foot total berthing space with dolphins; 28 feet alongside; deck height, 10 feet; shipment of lumber; owned and operated by Merrill and Ring, Inc. **Note:** Vessels moor portside-to at this wharf; a tug is recommended for both docking and undocking.

(158)   Diashowa America, Port Angeles Barge Dock (48°08'08"N., 123°27'37"W.): 570-foot berthing space with dolphins; 36 to 40 feet alongside; deck height, 17½ feet; approximately 28,000 square feet covered storage; receipt of fuel oil for plant consumption; shipment of paper products; owned by Diashowa; operated by Diashowa America and BP Marine Americas. A 25-foot shoal is charted about 100 feet east of the face of the Wharf; a tug is recommended when undocking.

(159)   In addition to the facilities mentioned, there are several small piers and wharves at which tugs and other floating equipment moor. Many log dumps are in the harbor.

(160)
Supplies

(161)   Water, ice and marine supplies are available. Groceries are nearby. Diesel oil and gasoline are available at the port boat haven. Bunkering is available by barge.

(162)
Repairs

(163)   Port Angeles has several companies and facilities to perform major topside repairs to large oceangoing vessels; the nearest drydocking facilities are in Seattle/Tacoma or Bellingham.

(164)
Small-craft facilities

(165)   **Port Angeles Boat Haven**, operated by the port, is a large, well-equipped small-craft basin in the southwest part of the harbor that can accommodate a large fleet of fishing boats and pleasure craft. The basin is marked by lights. In 2007, the controlling depth in the entrance and basin was 16 feet with 12 feet alongside the berths. About 660 berths, electricity, gasoline, diesel fuel, water, ice, a pump-out station, launching ramps, marine supplies and winter wet storage are available. A boatyard at the east end of the basin has a marine railway that can handle craft to 100 tons; a 225-ton lift is also available. Hull and engine repairs can be made at the yard, and electronic repair work can be arranged. The **harbormaster** controls the moorings in the basin (360–457–4505).

(166)   A **121°16'-301°16'** 200-yard **measured course** is in the southwest part of the harbor close north of Port Angeles Boat Haven.

(167)
Communications

(168)   Port Angeles is served by U.S. Highway 101. It is connected by ferry to Victoria, BC. The airport is 2.5 miles west of the city.

(169)
Dungeness Bay to Partridge Bank

(170)   From Port Angeles the coast trends east for 13 miles to the end of **Dungeness Spit**, which borders the west side of **Dungeness Bay**. This bay affords shelter in west winds, but is open east; in north weather, the protection afforded is only fair. It is a dangerous place in winter gales, especially from the southeast. The bay is formed by a sandspit extending northeast 4 miles and forming, in

addition to Dungeness Bay, a small lagoon at the head of the harbor that can be entered by light-draft vessels with local knowledge.

(171)   A **075°–255° measured nautical mile** has been established on the strait side of Dungeness Spit; the range markers are in the small lagoon at the head of the harbor.

(172)   **New Dungeness Light** (48°10'54"N., 123°06'37"W.), 67 feet above the water, is shown from a 63-foot white conical tower on a dwelling on the outer end of the spit.

(173)   From the end of the spit a shoal extends northeast for 0.8 mile from the light. This has been reported as extending farther north, and it should be passed with caution. A lighted buoy marks the shoal but it may be submerged during periods of strong current; vessels should not pass between the buoy and the light. A shoal makes out about 1 mile from the south side of the bay.

(174)   The best anchorage is in 5 to 9 fathoms, sticky bottom, about 1 mile southeast of the light, clear of the cable area.

(175)   **Dungeness** is a small town on the south shore of the bay. The ruins of a former wharf extend about 1,000 yards out across the flats.

(176)   **Sequim Bay**, 6 miles southeast of Dungeness Bay, is a landlocked bay 3.8 mile long. The bay is separated from the Straits by **Travis Spit**, a sandspit that extends west from the northeast corner of the bay almost to the west shore. A narrow channel marked by daybeacons and a light at the entrance leads around Travis Spit and west of a shoal area called The Middle Ground into the bay. Depths in the marked channel are about 9 feet; local knowledge is advised. The area between the light at the entrance and Gibson Spit on the west shore reportedly bares at minus tide and several groundings are known to occur; caution is advised. Strong currents that tend to follow the channel have also been reported. Anchorage inside Sequim Bay can be had anywhere in 6 to 21 fathoms, muddy bottom.

(177)   A marina is located on the west side of the bay just north of **Pitship Point**. Lights mark the breakwater entrance. Depths in the entrance are reported to be 12 feet, with 7 feet alongside the piers. Services include transient berths, electricity, gasoline, diesel fuel, water, ice, launching ramp and a pump-out station. The harbormaster controls moorage in the basin and can be contacted at 360–417–3440; VHF-FM is not monitored. A marine research center of the Battelle Memorial Institute, is on the west side of the entrance to the harbor abreast the sandspit. Some log rafts are made up in the bay. **Sequim Bay State Park** is at the southwest end of the bay. A seasonal mooring float is at the park.

(178)   **Protection Island**, a prominent feature in approaching Discovery Bay, is 200 feet high near its western extremity, 1.5 miles long and sparsely wooded; its north shore consists of bare, light bluffs. The east end and south shore are clear of dangers, but off **Kanem Point**, its southwest end, a shoal extends southwest for over 0.2 mile, and depths of 5 fathoms and less are found 0.5 mile west of the point. **Dallas Bank** extends north from Protection Island; the 10-fathom curve lies about

2.5 miles from the north point. North of the 10-fathom curve the bank drops off abruptly to depths of over 20 fathoms. **Miller Peninsula**, about 6 miles long and 3 to 5 miles wide, separates Sequim Bay and Discovery Bay.

(179)   **Discovery Bay** is 2 miles south-southeast of Protection Island. The bay trends in a southeast direction for about 8 miles. The entrance is masked from seaward by Protection Island, which protects it from northwest winds. Strong southeast gales have been observed and can have winds higher than outside the bay. There are no outlying dangers, and the depths are great. There is good anchorage with excellent holding ground at the head of the bay in 20 fathoms. **Cape George** is at the east entrance point of Discovery Bay. A private marina is also located at Cape George. The nearest marinas to Discovery Bay providing electricity and fuel are in Sequim Bay and Port Townsend.

(180)   **Diamond Point** is the west point at the entrance to Discovery Bay. A wharf in ruins is just inside the point.

(181)   The shore from Cape George for 3 miles to **McCurdy Point** consists of high, bare, clay bluffs, wooded on top, attaining a height of 400 feet near the northeast end. A shoal covered 11 feet extends 0.6 mile northwest of McCurdy Point; it is marked by a buoy. Vessels are cautioned not to pass between the buoy and the point.

(182)   From McCurdy Point, the shore trends east for 3.5 miles to **Point Wilson**, the west point at the entrance to Admiralty Inlet, and consists of high, bare, clay bluffs, sparsely wooded on top, decreasing in height near McCurdy Point, and ending abruptly close west to Point Wilson.

(183)   **Point Wilson Light** (48°08'39"N., 122°45'17"W.), 51 feet above the water, is shown from a white octagonal tower with a black top on a white building with a red roof, on the east extremity of the low point.

(184)   Shoals extend 0.5 mile northwest of Point Wilson to the 5-fathom curve over irregular bottom; these are generally indicated by kelp. The east edge of the shoals rises rather abruptly from deep water. Heavy tide rips extend north of these shoals, being especially heavy with a west wind and ebb current. A lighted buoy marking the shoals is about 0.7 mile northwest of Point Wilson Light.

(185)   In approaching Point Wilson in thick or foggy weather, soundings should be taken continuously.

(186)   **Point Partridge**, the Westernmost point of Whidbey Island, has a yellow face and is prominent from the north or south; it is rounding and not easily identified from the west. **Point Partridge Light** (48°13'29"N., 122°46'10"W.), 105 feet above the water, is shown from a skeleton tower on the west extremity of the point. A rocky ledge, marked by a lighted bell buoy, extends 0.5 mile west from the point. In the summer, the ledge is usually marked by kelp.

(187)   The west shore of Whidbey Island, between Admiralty Head and Point Partridge, is mostly a sandy beach rising sharply to bluffs 100 to 250 feet high, backed by pine trees. The shoreline is generally strewn by logs.

(188)   **Admiralty Head**, 80 feet high, on Whidbey Island, is the east entrance point of Admiralty Inlet and the southeast extremity of a succession of light bare bluffs that extend north of Point Partridge, where they attain their highest elevation. About 0.5 mile north of Admiralty Head an abandoned lighthouse tower 39 feet high stands on top of a bluff.

(189)   From Point Partridge the northwest coast of Whidbey Island extends north-northeast for 11.5 miles to Deception Pass. It is free of offlying dangers but should not be approached closer than 1 mile.

(190)   A **Small Arms Safety Zone** operated by Naval Air Station Whidbey Island is located about 5 miles north-northeast of Point Partridge. The zone is in operation 7 days a week; red flashing lights and flags are displayed during live exercises. Mariners should exercise extreme caution when transiting the area.

(191)   **Partridge Bank**, within the 10-fathom curve, is about 3 miles long and 1.5 miles wide; the southeast end reaches within 2 miles of Point Partridge. The north and east sides fall off abruptly to 20 and 30 fathoms. The shallowest part, 2½ fathoms, is near the north side about midway between the ends; it is marked by a buoy. A lighted bell buoy is about 0.6 mile south-southeast of the 2½ fathom spot. A considerable part of the bank is covered with kelp, which is usually drawn under by currents. The kelp generally extends to the 7-fathom curve, except toward the east end where the shoal narrows, and no kelp exists beyond a depth of 4 fathoms; kelp density varies by season.

(192)
San Juan Islands

(193)   The waters of the **San Juan Islands** embrace the passages and bays north of the east end of the Strait of Juan de Fuca. These passages are used extensively by pleasure craft, especially in July, August and September. Some tugs and barges use the larger passes. Automobile ferries, operated by the State of Washington, are on regular round-trip runs from Anacortes through Thatcher Pass, Cayou Channel, Wasp Passage, San Juan Channel and Spieden Channel and across Haro Strait to Sidney, BC. The island ferry landings are at Upright Head, Lopez Island; on the east side of the entrance to Blind Bay, Shaw Island; Orcas, Orcas Island; and Friday Harbor, San Juan Island. Oceangoing vessels normally use Haro and Rosario Straits and do not run the channels and passes in the San Juan Islands. Many resorts and communities have supplies and moorage available for the numerous pleasure craft cruising in these waters. Well-sheltered anchorages are numerous.

(194)   The directions that follow are intended for use only in clear weather; in thick weather or at night strangers should take a pilot for large vessels. Small craft should not attempt navigation under these conditions without local knowledge. Sailing craft should not attempt the passages against the current unless the wind is fair and fresh. A reliable auxiliary engine for sailboats is an absolute necessity. The tidal currents have great velocity in places, causing heavy tide rips that are dangerous. Because of the variable direction and velocity of the currents, compass courses are of little value, and, where followed, allowance must be made for the set of the current.

(195)   **Haro Strait** and **Boundary Pass** form the westernmost of the three main channels leading from the Strait of Juan de Fuca to the southeast end of the Strait of Georgia; it is the one most generally used. Vessels bound from the west to ports in Alaska or British Columbia should use the Haro Strait/Boundary Pass channel, as it is the widest channel and is well marked. Vessels bound north from Puget Sound may use Rosario Strait or Haro Strait; the use of San Juan Channel by deep-draft vessels is not recommended.

(196)   A **Vessel Traffic Service** has been established in the Strait of Juan de Fuca, east of Port Angeles, and in the adjacent waters. (See **33 CFR 161.1** through **161.55**, chapter 2, for regulations, and the beginning of this chapter for additional information.)

(197)   Haro Strait extends north from the south end of San Juan Island for about 18 miles to Turn Point Light on Stuart Island, thence Boundary Pass leads northeast for 13 miles to its junction with the Strait of Georgia between East Point, the east end of Saturna Island, BC, and the west end of Patos Island, the small United States island; both of which are marked by lights. These waterways have widths from 1.5 to 5 miles, and the depths are generally great.

(198)   No difficulty will be experienced in navigating Haro Strait and Boundary Pass in clear weather; strangers should take a pilot in thick weather.

(199)   The east shore of the passage will be described in detail, with only a brief general description of the west shore. More complete detail of the west shore is contained in Pub. 154, Sailing Directions (Enroute) for British Columbia, published by the National Geospatial-Intelligence Agency Hydrographic/Topographic Center, and the Sailing Directions, British Columbia Coast (South Portion) Vol. 1, published by the Canadian Hydrographic Service.

(200)   The International Boundary between the United States and Canada passes through Haro Strait and Boundary Pass.

(201)   In accordance with the Cooperative Vessel Traffic Service, the United States and Canada, in cooperation with industry and the British Columbia Coast Pilots, have established a **Special Operating Area** at the intersection of Haro Strait and Boundary Pass in the vicinity of Turn Point Light (48°41'18"N., 123°14'12"W.). This special area will help reduce the risk of incidents between both commercial and recreational vessels transiting the boundary waters of Haro Strait and Boundary Pass. For the boundaries and rules regarding the **Special Operating Area**, see **Cooperative Vessel Traffic Service (CVTS)** at the beginning of this chapter.

(202)

Tidal currents

(203)   In Haro Strait and Boundary Pass, the flood current sets north; the ebb current sets in the opposite direction. The ebb usually runs longer and has a greater velocity. At the north entrance to Boundary Pass, the flood sets east along the north and south sides of Sucia Islands and across Alden Bank; the velocity is about 1 to 2 knots. The Current has moderate velocity between Sucia and Orcas Islands. There is a large, daily inequality in the current. See the Tidal Current prediction service at *tidesandcurrents.noaa.gov* for specific information about times, directions, and velocities of the current at numerous locations throughout the area. Links to a user guide for this service can be found in chapter 1 of this book. Heavy, dangerous tide rips occur between East Point on Saturna Island and Patos Island and for two miles north in the Strait of Georgia. Tide rips also occur on the ebb between Henry Island and Turn Point, as well as around Turn Point where the ebb may attain a velocity of 6 knots during large tides. The flood current sets east from Discovery Island across the south end of Haro Strait until close to San Juan Island. This east set is especially noticeable during the first half of the flood. Heavy tide rips occur north of Middle Bank as well as on the Bank and around Discovery Island.

(204)   **Middle Bank**, with a least depth of 10 fathoms, is in the south approach to Haro Strait. The bank is about 3.5 miles long, and the least depth is in its northeast part and 5.7 miles southwest of Cattle Point Light on the southernmost tip of San Juan Island. Heavy tide rips, dangerous to small craft, form in the vicinity of this bank in bad weather.

(205)   **Beaumont Shoal**, covered 9 fathoms, lies 3 miles northwest of the northwest corner of Middle Bank and is marked by a lighted buoy. A second small bank with a least depth of 7 fathoms lies 1 mile to the north. In bad weather, heavy tide rips form over these banks.

(206)   **San Juan Island**, the largest of the group, is about 13 miles long, rugged, and partly wooded. **Mount Dallas**, the highest of several hills on the island, rises abruptly from the middle of the west side to a height of 1,080 feet. In most places the shores are free of outlying dangers. The north end of the island is indented by several small bays that, with the exception of Roche Harbor, are shoal and of no commercial importance.

(207)   From **Eagle Point**, the west shore of San Juan Island trends northwest and forms the east side of Haro Strait. This shore is steep-to and rocky, and beyond 400 yards offshore it is free of danger; however, the depths off this shore are too great for anchoring.

(208)   **Kanaka Bay**, a small cove used by fishing boats, is 2.5 miles northwest of Eagle Point.

(209)   **Lime Kiln Light** (48°30'57"N., 123°09'09"W.), 45 feet above the water, is shown from a 31-foot white octagonal tower with a black cupola and red roof, attached to a square white building on the west side of San Juan Island. Two dwellings are about 150 yards southeast of the light. Rocks awash lie close inshore about 1 mile southeast of the light.

(210)   **Smallpox Bay** and **Andrews Bay**, 1.5 miles northwest of Lime Kiln Light, offer protection for small craft from north and east weather.

(211)

Local magnetic disturbance

(212)   Differences from the normal variation of as much as 4° have been observed in the vicinity of **Bellevue Point**, 1 mile north of Lime Kiln Light.

(213)   During the June–October fishing season, many purse seiners operate in this area. At night these vessels anchor close inshore, generally between Cattle Point and Pile Point.

(214)   **Hanbury Point** (48°34.7'N., 123°10.3'W.), 3.8 miles north of Lime Kiln Light, is the north entrance point to **Mitchell Bay**, one of a series of well-sheltered bays on the northwest coast of the island. A small islet 3 feet high is in the center of the bay about 350 yards southeast of the entrance. A rock about 100 yards west of the islet uncovers 6 feet. The only safe passage into the bay is north of the islet. **Snug Harbor**, a resort and yacht haven on the south side of Mitchell Bay, has about 70 berths with electricity, gasoline, water, ice and limited marine supplies. A launching ramp is available; engine repairs can be made to small craft. **Mosquito Pass**, available only to small craft with local knowledge, leads north from Hanbury Point to **Garrison Bay**, **Westcott Bay** and Roche Harbor.

(215)   A large aquaculture facility, covered 3 feet and consisting of clam beds and suspended oyster racks, is in the middle of Westcott Bay about 1 mile above the entrance. Mariners should use caution in the area.

(216)   **Henry Island** is close west of the north point of San Juan Island, from which it is separated by Mosquito Pass and Roche Harbor.

(217)   **Kellett Bluff**, at the south end of Henry Island, is steep and rocky and prominent from either south or north. It is marked by a light. **Open Bay**, east of Kellett Bluff, offers good holding ground and protection for small boats from west, north and east weather.

(218)   **Roche Harbor** has its main entrance between the north end of Henry Island and the west end of **Pearl Island**, which is marked by a light. Sandspits covered 17 and 18 feet extend into the channel from the islands on each side of the entrance. Entrance to the harbor can also be made from the south through Mosquito Pass between Henry Island and Bazalgette Point. The harbor has depths of 4 to 9 fathoms. It affords good anchorage and in the summer is used extensively by yachts. The harbormaster can be contacted on VHF-FM channel 78A.

(219)   A large resort is on the east side of Roche Harbor. The resort operates a wharf with shed, floats with berths for over 450 craft, including over 150 transient berths, a hotel, cabins, a general store and restaurant. Electricity, gasoline, diesel fuel, water, ice, a launching ramp, pump-out station and marine supplies are available. The site

Coast Pilot Volume 10, Chapter 7 Index

Refers to numbered paragraph

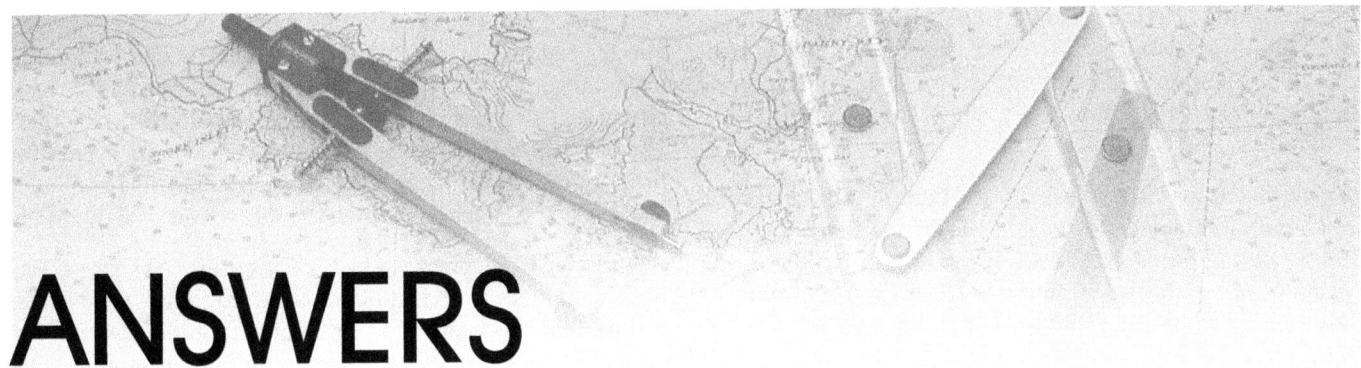

ANSWERS

CHAPTER 1 – THE ROLE OF NAVIGATION

1-1. (A) Determining a best guess for your position based on continuing measurement of Course, Distance and Time.

1-2. (B) By reference to nearby landmarks and buoys.

1-3. (B) "The Rules do not apply to kayaks, rowboats or jet skis." is a false statement.

1-4. (D) Magnetic bearing, if the value is referenced to Magnetic North.

1-5. (B) The Navigation Rules.

1-6. (C) A fix.

1-7. 6,000 ft [exact is 1852 m, which is also exactly 1852 × (100/2.54) × (1/12), which is 6076.12… ft].

1-8. (D) Good seamanship calls for us to be prepared to navigate in any condition.

1-9. (C) There is no single definition; it depends on the circumstances.

1-10. We traveled 20 miles according to our vessel's odometer, which I wrote into the book we use for keeping records of our voyage.

1-11. You can buy an instrument that tells you where you are, but you cannot buy one that tells you the safest and most efficient way to get to where you want to go.

1-12. (B) For safe navigation I need up to date nautical charts (ENC or NCC) and at least three books (*Coast Pilot*, *Navigation Rules*, then at least either: *Chart No. 1*, tide and current predictions, *Light List*, depending on the route.)

1-13. One example is rounding an island with near shore dangers. We set a radar range ring around our vessel that we watch on the screen compared to the shoreline, and not let it touch as we proceed, which guarantees we are that far off. We know we are safe, but we do not know where we are. Or use a maximum or minimum compass danger bearing to be certain you do not enter into dangerous waters. Or just watch the depth sounder (corrected for tide and draft) to be sure you stay in water deep enough to pass known hazards. There are many more such instances. We do not care if the GPS is right or wrong, we know we are safe.

1.14. (A) Red. (B) Green.

1.15. Boy.

CHAPTER 2 – NAUTICAL CHARTS AND CHART READING

2-1. (A) 185.2 meters, exactly. (B) 600 approximately—it is very useful in marine navigation to memorize that 1 nmi is about 6,000 feet. (C) A "cable," although this is strictly one tenth of a "sea mile," which is defined as a distance equal to 1' of latitude. In most practical applications, a nautical mile and a sea mile are the same. Sea miles are used in the UK, but rarely in the US. Such definitions are included in the Navigation Glossary which is part of Bowditch. (D) 34 miles tall by 47 miles wide. ie top lat is 48° 30' and bottom is 47° 56', so difference is 34' = 34 nmi. To get width, simplest is to just set dividers to, say, 5 miles and walk it off, then add in the last bit.

2-2. 6.30 nmi @ 058T = 038M.

2-3. Yellow.

2-4. "R." Anything in quotes on a charted buoy or light symbol is printed right on the aid to navigation itself.

2-5. 15.34 nmi @ 264 T.

2-6. (A) 200 yards NE of the buoy falls on the 20 fathom contour line. Notice how the shelf drops steeply to 50 fathoms in just another 100 yards or so. Read contour depth labels about 3 miles west of the buoy. (B) 8±2 fathoms.

2-7. 8.84 nmi @ 199 M.

2-8. 42.3 nmi as follows: Buoy S to Buoy 1 = 8.0 nmi; Buoy 1 to E. end Protection Is = 2.5 nmi; E. end to Buoy SA = 5 nmi; Buoy SA to Minor Is Lt = 8.0 nmi; Minor Is Lt to Buoy DH = 9.3 nmi; Buoy DH to Buoy R = 5.4 nmi; Buoy R to Buoy S = 4.1 nmi.

2-9. (A) Black and Red (black top and bottom with horizontal red band). (B) Isolated Danger — the area is shallow, a rock lies at 2.25 fathoms. Kelp beds are often a key to detecting shallows where such rocks might be. (C) LL#16361, confirms it is an isolated danger mark, and adds that nominal range is 6 nmi. We did not know this from the chart alone. See later exercises on light predictions.

2-10. (A) 0.5 nmi. (B) 0.25 nmi.

2-11. (A) 1 nmi. (B) 2.15 nmi.

2-12. 250 M.

2-13. 9 nmi.

2-14. 340 M.

2-15. (A) 48° 12.4' N, 123° 27.7' W. (B) LL#16222, 48° 12.4' N, 123° 27.7' W which is as it should be. You will find if you check others that they will most all be right on this chart, but this is not guaranteed for all charts. Here we are dealing with latest editions of LL and chart. If they differ, generally the LL is correct if most recent.

2-16. (A) 4.01 nmi @ 004.2 T, this is a computed result, you cannot measure this close from a chart. (B) Sand, Shells, and Pebbles. (C) Mud. (D) "swirls" probably means rips on the surface, but this is more of a charting error in that the term is no longer defined in any of the standard references. (E) +0.01' = + 0.01 nmi = 60 feet.

2-17. 48° 16.27' N, 122° 58.7' W.

2-18. No. Light list gives obstructed area, inside of which Trial Island lies. Notice the obstruction area clearly marked on your chart with black dashed lines. You may want to see if these bearings on the chart agree with those given in the Light List. [In Glossary see "light sectors"]

2-19. (A) 2. (B) 50.

2-20. USWA20M. 1:10,000

2-21. US3WA46M. 1:150,000

2-22. Can be submerged. At mean high water, the water level goes right up to where the dashed line begins.

2-23. (A) 0.72 nmi offshore at 7.75 fathoms. (Note: This one covers at 9.75 fathoms.) (B) 1.2 nmi offshore just inside the 10 fathom contour. (C) 1.4 nmi offshore but note the "PA" which means position approximate. This, too, is just inside the 10 fathom contour line. (D) The fourth wreck is symbolized not by a graphic symbol on your chart, but by an abbreviation, "Wk." It is in about 7 fathoms of water, 1 mile offshore.

2-24. The 5 rocks marked as plus signs with dots in each corner are just barely awash at zero tide height. These are the most dangerous kind of rock — every vessel from ship to kayak can hit these just under the surface at some time or other. The one rock marked by an asterisk covers and uncovers with the tide (rock awash), but it is further specified that it will be 7 feet above the water level when the tide equals exactly 0 feet.

2-25. Refer to Figure 2-25 in the Exercises. (A) 55 feet. Notice the number in ( ) just below the word Smith. (B) We can deduce that this is about 52' by subtracting the height of the structure from the height of the light, both given as heights above MHW. Thus 97-45 = 52 feet. See LL#16375. (C) The Coast Pilot details this even further. It states the elevation is 55 feet at the west end of the island, tapering down to east end. See (CP 90).

2-26. (A) National Wildlife Refuge. (B) Area B1 - note the two sections lie near Port Angeles, and East of Victoria. See box in upper left corner of chart.

(C) None. See note just below Lake Crescent.

(D) Small Arms Safety Zone. See Note E.

2-27. (A) 013 T. (B) 5.84 nmi.

2-28. (A) The rock is just inside the 3 fathom depth contour line. (B) Covers and uncovers, particularly dangerous. (C) Likely to be breaking wavelets and ripples, foreshore (green area will be exposed. Variations arise with stronger conditions of wind, current.

2-29. "You are not the only one to scratch your head over that charting abbreviation. The answer is 'East CORner of HOuse.' This landmark probably has a very old date of origin. Also, when it was established it was probably the predominate, or only, feature of the area. Upon close inspection, that stretch of coast has many such landmarks, from cavern entrances on cliffs, slide areas on mountains, to a chimney on a yellow house.

Please remember that a landmark that may not be seen close in to shore maybe very visible out in the middle of the Straits."—Jim Gardner, CDR, NOAA Corps, Chief, Pacific Hydrographic Branch.

Note (1) "Ho" is not in the gov edition of Chart No.1 but "Lt Ho" and "Cus Ho," etc. are... had we just flipped pages through Section E of *Chart No 1* on landmarks, we might discover this. It is simply an oversight. But a good hint that other examples might occur as well.

Note (2) that the abbreviation was all in CAPs, which means the landmark is conspicuous. Normal abbreviation for house is Ho but this one is HO.

Note (3), the symbol marking this landmark is one that is often used for a tower, and it is pictorially more like a tower, rather than a square or such for the corner of a house, but if you check section E, you will see that this is indeed the symbol to mark the precise location of any landmark, not just towers.

2-30. (A) WP1 - WP2: Course 074 M, D = 10.2 nmi. (B) WP2 - WP3: Course 064 M, D = 15.2 nmi. (C) WP3 - WP4: Course 080 M, D = 13.5 nmi.

2-31. Bell, gong, and whistle are on buoys, usually wave activated in all visibility, and have no standard characteristic Bells have one tone, gongs have multiple tones. Horns are usually on fixed structures, only heard in the fog, or can be triggered by keying a VHF radio. Horns have a charted characteristic sound pattern. Whistles have been described as a moaning sound, as compressed air is forced into bell chamber that fades in and out.

2-32. 4 miles.

2-33. 8 miles.

2-34. LARGER. The 1:10,000 harbor chart is a large scale chart. A specific island would appear larger on a large scale chart than on a small scale chart.

2-35. Large scale charts would be better.

2-36. See starpath.com/NCC for a portal to NCC info.

2-37. No. We can create NCC for any region we like, at any scale we like, and even whatever paper size we want, although there are logical paper sizes to consider.

2-38. (A) Charts are updated daily.

2-39. (A) Red and White buoy, with the letters NA painted on it, and a white light flashing the Morse code for the letter A (dit-dah, 'short long'), and with a whistle. (B) Buoy with flashing green light, period 4 seconds, with a bell. (C) Green buoy, with numbers 31 painted on it, green light flashes on every 4 seconds, with a gong. (D) Red light always on (fixed), 25 ft above MHW, with an 8 painted on it. (E) Flashing light (usually white when not specified) 4 seconds period, 30 ft above MHW, nominal range of 8 nautical miles, with a 2 pained on the structure.

2-40. (B) Is usually sequential, but may occasionally be missing numbers of the sequence.

2-41. The lower is the nearer set.

2-42. We must look over our shoulder and follow their alignment outbound.

2-43. Either side, as it is a safe water buoy; also called a mid-channel marker.

2-44. Prohibited area.

2-45. (A) Course. (B) Heading. (C) Range and Bearing. (D) Course Over Ground. (E) Course Made Good. (F) Track.

2-46. (A) Direction you want to go. (B) Direction the boat is pointed toward. (C) Direction to a landmark or other vessel. (D) the instantaneous value of your CMG read from the GPS. (E) Direction from one position to a later position, regardless of the track between them. (F) The record or trail of your past positions.

2-47. An isolated danger.

2-48. (A) Navigable water to their named side.

2-49. (C) Navigable water to the west.

2-50. (A) Navigable water to the south. A quick look at the chart will often answer questions like this as well, but knowing or looking up the definition could sometimes be very helpful.

2-51. The brightness of a navigation light expressed as clear-weather visible range in nautical miles. Clear is defined as visibility of 10 nmi.

2-52. See *Chart No. 1* section K for a description as "submerged pile, stake, snag, or stump (with exact position). The risk of running a vessel onto a log stuck into the mud bottom is sinking. It could tear the bottom out of the boat. (CP 27) Deadhead is also used to describe a water soaked log that is floating vertically in the water, sometimes just barely visible. These are a common hazard in Pacific NW waters, often warned of on USCG VHF broadcasts.

CHAPTER 3 – OTHER NAVIGATION AIDS

Answers in the Coast Pilot (CP) are marked with the paragraph number in the excerpted text.

3-1. The elevation at west end of the island is 55 ft. Note there is further discussion of its elevation given. (CP 90)

3-2. Look up Low Point (CP 118) and go to the 18465 Tr to see it is Lyre River.

3-3. Yes. "Aircraft warning lights" How would we find out what these might be? (CP 124)

3-4. There is a small offshore islet that has an elevation of 20 feet, but this islet is too small to show outlined. (CP 121)

3-5. From the front section of the Coast Pilot (look under nav rules in the index) learn that the International Rules (called COLREGS) apply to all local and connecting waters. This is a unique regulation considering that most such inland waterways around the US use the Inland Rules. (CP 7)

3-6. During freshets, after storms, or unusually high tides. (CP 27)

3-7. July to October. (CP 38) There are more weather statistics presented throughout the Coast Pilot.

3-8. 4 to 6 knots. (CP 68)

3-9. It can be submerged in strong current—pulled under. (CP 173)

3-10. (A) Geo. Range = 1.17 x [SQRT(9) + SQRT(118)] = 16.2 nmi, Nom. Range = 15 nmi on the paper chart (or RNC of it), and 19 nmi according to the Light List. Usually the LL will be the newest information so we use 19 nmi as the Nominal range, which means the light is bright enough to show over the full geo range, but the geo range is the limiting factor. Answer is Visual Range = 16.2 nmi.

| 16225 | Race Rocks Light (C) | 48-17-52.914N 123-31-53.165W | Fl W 10s | 118 | 19 | Cylindrical tower with white and black horizontal bands. | HORN: 3 blast ev 60s (2s bl-3s si-2s bl-3s si-2s bl-48s si). Horn points 155°. |

(B) Geo. Range = 1.17 x [SQRT(9) + SQRT(67)] = 13.1 nmi, Nom. Range = 22 nmi, therefore Visual Range = 13.1 nmi.

| 16335 | New Dungeness Light | 48-10-54.298N 123-06-37.001W | Fl W 5s 0.1s fl 4.9s ec. | 67 | 18 | White conical tower on dwelling. 67 |

(C) No! New Dungeness Lt. is charted 4 nmi brighter than the Light List, and Race Rocks light is charted 4 nmi dimmer than the Light List. We have to assume that the Light List data are more accurate as they are updated weekly. Using electronic navigational charts (ENC) on the other hand, we would find these two sets of data stay in sync as both are updated weekly. Remember, too, that we are using a training chart locked into 1998. The present charted values of these lights match the Light List data.

Note: if you are using ENC charts, and keeping them updated, then the light descriptions on chart and LL should stay in sync, because the charts are updated weekly. However, using updated ENC and an annual printed LL, you may well find that the chart data is newer than your printed LL, which is in part why NOAA and the USCG are moving away from annual publications of nav data.

3-11. (A) 16 nmi. (B) 4.2 nmi. (C) 1.3 nmi.

These answers are approximate since they must be interpolated from a logarithmic scale. Furthermore, in practice you never know the actual visibility very accurately, so approximate answers are all you can hope for.

3-12. (A) 15.3 nmi. (B) 3.6 nmi. (C) 1.65 nmi. We see the agreement is fine.

3-13. geo range = 1.17 x [sqrt(49) + sqrt(118)] = 1.17 x (7 + 10.9) = 20.9.

Also note that the luminous range result of 10 from the diagram is essentially the same as 9.25 from the estimate, since

luminous range is rarely known well because we do not know the visibility very well. 20 % accuracy should be considered good.

In clear weather we compare this geo range to the nominal range of 15 nmi, to conclude that the visible range is dominated by the nominal range. In visibility of 5.5 nmi, the nominal range of 15 is reduced to the luminous range of 10 nmi, which is then the visible range we expect.

3-14. NOAA charts (ENC and NCC) are updated daily. Nav apps like qtVlm let you check for updates and download as needed with a button click. Likewise, the digital *Light List* online is updated daily, so these two should agree. If an aid is missing or not working as expected, we would check the LNM. If no help there, then we can call the USCG, nav aids department and report it. If a *Light List* aid is not on the chart, you can report it to NOAA using item 2.2 at starpath.com/getcharts, called their Assist program.

3-15. 9 ft. (CP 176)

3-16. You are "bobbing the light" which means you are at about the geographic range. So we look at the geo range from both observation heights. The Pt Wilson light is at 51 ft. Cabin top: Geo range = 1.17 x [SQRT(51) + SQRT(15)] = 12.9 nmi. From the cockpit: Geo range = 1.17 x [SQRT(51) + SQRT(8)] = 11.7 nmi. So the light is more than 11.7 nmi off but less than 12.9 . This technique works best for lights that are bright and low, i.e., for ones with a geographic range that is smaller than its nominal range—the more smaller, the more better.

3-17. (A) In clear weather this is limited by its height, which is about 200 feet (see Coast Pilot), so 1.17 x [SQRT(200) + SQRT (9)] = 20.0 miles, which would be a theoretical value for the tip to be just on the horizon. But the reality is you would not see it (unlit) from that far off—about 17 or so with binoculars would be a practical estimate. (B) The answer is 4 miles, since this is precisely the definition of atmospheric visibility, i.e., how far you can see unlighted objects in daylight.

3-18. Using our estimate of luminous range: (5/10) × 5 + 1 = 3.5 nmi.

3-19. (A) One approach to this is to just skim through the Light List and look at a lot of buoys to see what they average. Typical values are 4 to 6 nmi, with a few at 3 and 7. Thus we can call 5 nmi an average buoy nominal range. However, these days many are now know. Sadly, this valuable data is so far not in NOAA ENC. We have been pleading with NOAA for some years now to add it. (B) Heights of buoys vary quite a bit, but 12 ft might be an average for the typical lighted buoy. So from an eye height of 9 ft we have a geographic range of about 1.17 x [sqrt(9) + sqrt(12)] = 7.6, which shows that it is the light brightness that is usually the limit, which would be about 5 miles. In practice this would likely take binoculars to spot them on this limit on a clear night.

3-20. You are "bobbing the light" (see 3-16) which means you are at about the geographic range. So we look at the geo range from both observation heights. The light in view is at 27 ft. Cabin top: Geo range = 1.17 x [SQRT(27) + SQRT(12)] = 10.1 nmi. From the cockpit: Geo range = 1.17 x [SQRT(27) + SQRT(7)] = 9.2 nmi. So the light is more than 9.2 nmi off but less than 10.1.

3-21. (B) Radar because it can be used for both collision avoidance and positional navigation.

3-22. Navigation Rules, tide predictions, current predictions, Coast Pilot, and Light List. We need to make the tide and current predictions ourselves as NOAA no longer publishes these.

3-23 (A) red lights (B) Every day. See LNM for the times of day on given dates.

3-24. This is the locally famous Round the County yacht race, descried online.

3-25. 14% of the time, from weather table, (CP 39).

3-26. 3 to 6 kts. (CP 85).

CHAPTER 4 – COMPASS USE

4-1. (A) Variation is 19° 45' E in 1998. (B) The 1998 chart forecasts a deviation in 2015 of 18° 03' E. We find this by taking the annual decrease of 6', multiplied by the 17 years which will pass. Thus 17 x 6' = 102'. Subtract this from the 1998 variation and we have our answer. Note: Variation can either increase or decrease annually. The rate is typically just a few minutes per year, but over large time periods, the rate of change and even direction of change can also vary.

Looking at what actually happened at this location in 2015, the charted variation in 2015 was 17° 15'E with an annual decrease of 11'. The 2015 chart notes say this variation data is from 2011, implying it is based on the 2010 World Magnetic Model (WMM) predictions from 2010. These are updated every 5 years, on the 5th year.

4-2. Construct the TVMDC table.

T 330 T

V 20° E

M ?

D 00°

C ?

Rule is + E going up, - E going down. We go down to get M = 330 - 20 = 310, and Deviation 0, means M = C = 310 C.

4-3. The inner ring is magnetic bearings marked off in compass points, 11.25° = 1 point. This bearing system and feature of nautical charts is rarely, if ever, used these days.

4-4. (A) 135°. (B) 247 and 1/2°. (C) 056 and 1/4°.

The compass points system divides the circle into 32 parts, so each pt is 360/32 = 11.25°. Each of these points has a name: starting at the top, 0 pts = N, 1 pt to the right is NxE, 2 pts is NNE, 3 is NNExE, 4 is NE, etc., on around the circle.

WSW is halfway between W (270) and SW (225) or (270+225)/2 = 247.5. NExE is 1 point to the East of NE, the phrase "by" means "1 pt in the direction of." Hence part (C) NExE means go to NE then 1 pt in direction E or NE which is 4 pts, plus 1 is 5 points, or 5x11.25 = 056 1/4°. NExN would be 1pt to the N of NE or 4-1 = 3 pts = 3x11.25 = 033 3/4°. There is little virtue in knowing this, but it is considered part of maritime tradition.

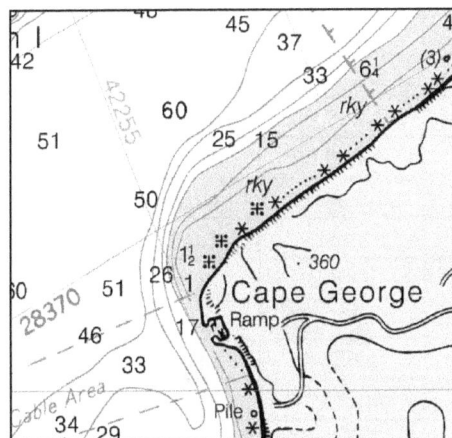

Figure 3-24a. *Region of interest on Training chart 18465 Tr from 1998. These were likely found on a high tide as they are all covered at MHW. We need a larger chart scale to see precise locations. All of these charts can be viewed online.*

Figure 3-24b. *Region of interest on 2015 edition of 18465. The new rocks are shown in place now. The precise locations are being checked in this exercise. Also review the meaning of that type of rock symbol. That is, what precisely does the 2 fathoms and 2 3/4 fathoms measure?*

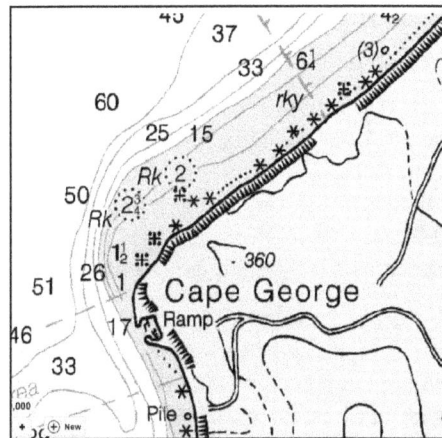

4-5. You should work the complete TVMDC and get all the answers in order to answer the specific questions. (A) 260 M. (B) 280 T. (C) 263 C. (D) Distance 13.6 nmi.

4-6. Another question where working the complete TVMDC helps ensure correct answers are selected. (A) 16.5 nmi. (B) 341 M. (C) 001 T. (D) 338 C.

4.7. See Table below.

4.7	A	B	C	D	E	F	G	H	I
True	280	035	007	266	114	138	345	049	012
var	16W	21E	21E	10W	21E	4E	21W	21E	17E
Mag	296	014	346	276	093	134	006	028	355
dev	0	5E	8W	0	5W	4W	0	0	4E
Comp	296	009	354	276	098	138	006	028	351

4-8. (A) No. (B) 15 fathoms. (C) 48° 16.78' N, 122° 58.82' W. (D) Course: 143 M, D = 9.63 nmi.

4-9. (A) 48° 09.2' N, 122° 53.35' W. (B) 2.3 nmi. (C) 47 fathoms. (D) 5.15 nmi @ 070 M.

4-10. (A) 48° 10.8' N, 122° 51.02' W.

4-11. The bearing to the tank will be 160 M. Distance is 13.6 nmi. Half that is 6.8 nmi. Mark that spot on your rhumb line, and read the bearing.

4-12. (A) WP4 to WP3 offers several options affirming your half-way point. Just before halfway on this leg, the tank on Protection Island aligns with the AERO light on Diamond Pt, bearing 164M. Either of these alone would be useful landmarks. A natural range, bearing 146M, runs between the tip of Violet and Beckett Points right at the mid point. You're in 13 fathoms of water just north of the Dallas Bank—a good way to know you are not on the bank.

(B) The halfway mark from WP3-WP2 is 7.6 miles along that leg. Not so much onshore to rely on. Slightly past halfway, an unnamed point aligns with Lost Mt, bearing 139M. Green Pt. will be slightly ahead, bearing 163M. The Coast Pilot lacks details for this section. The western most "stack" at the foot of a small dock bears 214M. Remember you can check your depth here as well. You are inside or near a depth area of 27 to 30 fathoms.

(C) At 5.1 miles, (halfway between WP2 and WP1 the tower at Angeles Pt. bears 103 M, the tower west of Observatory Pt. bears 227 M. The mouth of Colville Creek is about 2 miles off, bearing 174M, which should be discernible as it forms a notable valley in the elevation contours. See apps.nationalmap.gov/viewer

4-13. (A) Setting 36° north of due west. (B) Must be early summer if the setting sun is north. During fall and winter sunrise and sunset is south of due east and west; spring and summer it is north of due east and west.

4-14. (A) 48° 11.4' N, 123° 00' W. (B) You are just on the edge of the inbound lanes. (C) 60 ± 3 fathoms. (D) From this angle, one might have difficulty choosing the precise point to call the "north tip". If we wait until we can see Protection Island falling SE toward Violet Pt, we could have a clearer bearing. Is the radar range to the foreshore or to where the charted solid part of the island actually begins? The relative bearing of 045 is added to your heading of 075 to give you 120 M as a bearing to the north tip off your starboard beam. To be entirely accurate underway, one must hold this course steadily while taking an exact bearing to an exact point. With winds and currents present, precise work requires more concentration.

4-15. (A) 48° 12.1' N, 123° 40.4' W. (B) 0.3 nmi. (C) 2.4 nmi @ 190 M. (D) Disused submarine cable.

4-16. (A) 48° 19.05' N, 123° 47.37' W. (B) 284 M. (C) 076 M.

4-17. (A) The correcting direction is C to M using deviation or M to T using variation. If deviation is east, then it is added to C to get M, If variation is east, then it is added to M to get T. The rule is meant to remind us that if the correction is west, we subtract it when correcting. (B) Can Dead Men Vote Twice (at elections, for add east correcting), or going the other way: TV makes dull companion (add whiskey, for add west uncorrecting.)

4-18.

	A	B
T	330	330
V	15 W	15 W
M	345	345
D	0	4 E
C	345	341

4-19. (A) Interpolated deviation values are shown in Deviation Table 1 Answers.

Deviation Table 1 Answers		
Compass	Deviation	Magnetic
000°	10.5° E	010.5
015°	13.7° E	028.7
030°	16.8° E	046.8
045°	20.0° E	065.0
060°	17.2° E	077.2
075°	14.3° E	089.3
090°	11.5° E	101.5
105°	7.3° E	112.3
120°	3.0° E	123.0
135°	1.2° W	133.8
150°	2.6° W	147.4
165°	4.1° W	160.9

180°	5.5° W	174.5
195°	6.3° W	188.7
210°	7.2° W	202.8
225°	8.0° W	217.0
240°	9.5° W	230.5
255°	11.0° W	244.0
270°	12.5° W	257.5
285°	10.6° W	274.4
300°	8.7° W	291.3
315°	6.8° W	308.2
330°	1.0° W	329.0
345°	4.7° E	349.7

i.e., dev(167)=4.1+((5.5-4.1)/(174.5-160.9))*(167-160.9)

	4-19 (B)			4-19 (C)			
	a	b	c	d	e	f	g
T	340	032	152	321	034	296	259
V	15W	15W	15W	15W	15W	15W	15W
M	355	047	167	336	049	311	274
D	6.2E	16.8E	4.7W	0.9E	17.2E	6.0W	10.6W
C	349	030	172	335	032	317	285

(D) We guess steel because the deviations on opposite headings are not equal and opposite, which imply a more complex disturbance to the magnetic field common on steels vessels.

CHAPTER 5 – DEAD RECKONING

5-1. (A) 3.33 h. (B) 12.9 h.

(C) 2.3 h. (D) 0.63 h.

(E) 1.083 h. (F) 2 h 27 m.

(G) 12 h 47 m 24 s. (H) 2 h 5 m 24 s.

(I) 0 h 22 m 48 s. (J) 1 h 43 m 48 s.

(K) 1212 today. (L) 1840 today.

(M) 0307 tomorrow. (N) 1342 today.

(O) 1453 yesterday. (P) 0507 tomorrow.

[Hint on N, 1425-0043 goes to 1385-0043 after borrowing 1hr and adding it to the minutes. Hint on O, From the initial problem, 1232 - 2139, we can see the answer is negative, meaning backwards in time, or yesterday. To get the answer, add 24 h to get 3632 - 2139, but we still need to fix min, so borrow 1hr and add 60 min to get 3592-2139, and you get the answer, which is a time to be marked "yesterday."]

5-2. (A) 8.3 kts. (B) 120 nmi.

5-3. 0.625 kts.

5-4. 9h 15m.

5-5. (A) 22h, (B) 7h 8m + 2h + 15h = 24h 08m.

5-6. 6.1 kts.

5-7. 3.3 kts.

5-8. 4.1 kts.

5-9. (A) 8m 34s, (B) 10m 34s means S = 5.7 kts, off by 1.3 kts, (C) 7.0 divided by 5.7 = 1.23, or 23% high. (D) 4.0 / 1.23 = 3.2 knots.

5-10. (A) 8.75 ft per sec = 5.25 kts. (B) One approach: 1 sec. out of 4 sec. is 25%, and 25% of 5.25 is 1.3 knots. In short, the longer the measured time, the smaller the per cent error. Assuming a time uncertainty of 1 sec., a measurement time of 10 sec. gives a 10% error. The way around this is to make several measurements and average the results. Then your error in timing could be less than 1 sec., and your speed measurement would be more accurate. [More on this: if we measure something that is 4 seconds long and this has an error in it of 1 second, then the measurement is in error by 1 out of 4, or 25%. We then assume that anything we deduce from this measurement, such as a speed, will also be in error by 25%. This is valid reasoning if there are no other uncertainties involved. If the length we used to compute the speed also had an error in it, then we need to combine the two sources of error, but that is a bit more involved. The topic of combining typical navigation errors is discussed in detail in the book Emergency Navigation. In an emergency you may have little but DR to go by, in which case it is crucial to do realistic evaluations of errors.]

5-11. T = (18/6) x 1.5 = 4.5 h.

5-12. T = 48m x 1.5 + 1h 20m = 2h 32m.

5-13.(A) D = 6 nmi, C = 064 T, T = 0.92 hours or 55 minutes. (B) D = 12.4 nmi, C = 017 T, T = 2.48 h or 2 h 29 m. (C) D = 9.3 nmi, C = 280 T, T = 1.29 h or 1h 17 m. (D) D = 16.4 nmi, C = 179 T, T = 3.41 h or 3 h 25 m. (E) 1950 PM or 7:50 PM - Sum of times = 8.1 hours = 8 h 6 m. Add this to departure time of 11:44 am. Double-check your work.

5-14. (A) C = 300 T, D = 25.75 nmi. (B) T = 3.67 h = 3h 40m. (C) With a perfectly constant NW wind (315 T) the laylines emanating from Brotchie Ledge run due south and due east. When you are tacking against this wind, your course will be either due north (port tack) or due west (starboard tack). It does not matter at all what route you take (i.e. does not depend on when you tack or how many times you tack), the distance will be the same: D = 35.17 nmi, T = 35.17/7 = 5.02h, which is 1.35h longer. If you take 5.02/3.67 you get about 1.4 which is nearly the 1.5 we use as a rough estimate of how long tacking takes compared to reaching. (In actual sailing of cruising yachts, it will indeed be closer to 1.5 than 1.4 anyway, even in good conditions.) (D) The simplest route is one tack due west for 22.27 nmi then tack and sail due north to the mark for 12.90 miles. Note you just miss the Dungeness Spit this way, but it is still outside of the buoy. This, however, is usually not the smartest route when tacking a long way, since it takes us the farthest off the original rhumbline. If the wind changes at all during the passage you have a 50% chance of suffering the maximum penalty in distance made good.

Show that the following route will also get you there in the same amount of time, although it uses 7 tacks:

11.2 miles to the W, then tack and

5.7 N, etc...

5.0 W

3.0 N

2.0 W

2.5 N

4.1 W

1.65 N.

5-15. (A) 48° 09.64', 123° 43.71', just inside of Crescent Bay. (B) 34.0 miles. (C) 0.59 miles (plot the vectors or the trick given in the text that 6° = 10%, so 3° = 5%, 1° = 10/6 or 1.7%, so 1° error over 34 miles = 0.017 x 34 = 0.58 miles. If you plot by just 1° degree wrong on the course you will miss the mouth of the bay. (D) 34/3 = 11.33 miles per leg. So 11.33/3.2 + 11.33/6.7 +11.33/8.1 = 6.63h = 6h 38m.

5-16. One approach: choose a minimum speed with good steerage, say 3 kts. Compute how far you would go in 10 minutes at 3 kts: d = 3 x 10/60 = 0.5 miles, then consider this the circumference of the circle, and since c = pi x diameter, we get a circle diameter of 0.5/pi = 0.16 miles = 0.16 x 6000 = 960 ft = 320 yd.

To execute something like this, we might divide 360 by 15 to get 24 steps around the compass, 000, 015, 030, 045, etc, and then say that we are going to hold each course for 10min/24 = 0.417 min = 25 seconds. Then watching a stop watch, head off at 000 for 25 seconds, turn to 015 for 25 seconds, etc and you should trace out a circle of about 320 yards diameter, probably it bit larger, in about 10 minutes, maybe a bit longer.

5-17. 3h 38m. Solution: From magic circle we get: T(minutes) = 60 x 22.9/6.3 = 218.1 min then 218.1/60 = 3.635h = 3h + .635 x 60 = 3h 38m.

5-18. (A) 48° 22.30' N, 123° 17.84' W. (B) 48° 22.25' N, 123° 17.70' W. (C) ~0.11 nmi = 220 yds. (D) The message is, we get smaller errors with closer targets.

5-19. First note that although depth sounding navigation is a very powerful tool, this chart is barely, if at all, useable for

this in this region. Generally we need a larger scale chart for these maneuvers. With those limitations in mind, this exercise illustrates several points in this type of navigation. (A) Water goes blue at 10-fathom line which is easy to trace on the chart. The 20-fathom line should be safe to the buoy. We are on a steep edge, which should be easy to follow.(B) About 105 M. (C) About 4.3 miles to get there, so look for log = 711.3 or so. (D) The depth of 20 changing to a southerly run is essentially a fix — we have found the point on earth that does this specific thing — so if log reads right, it means there was no current. Had there been current with us, we would have got there on a smaller log reading, or if against us it would have been bigger.

For example, if we were going 4 kts we would get there in about an hour, but if there were 2 kts against us, we would be running through the water at 4 kts logging miles but only making 2 kts to the mark... it would take us twice as long and we would log about 8 miles.

If we slip into 10 fathoms and follow that south, we would pass the buoy at about 0.4 miles off.

(E) This is hard to answer. If it is dead calm, the buoy makes no noise, it is wave activated. With waves, from 0.4 off it will depend on wind direction most likely. If we are downwind we might hear it, if the buoy is downwind we most likely would not.

(F) Most likely a strong current set to the SE.

(G) Quick look to the chart to account for the depth, then head west at full power. We must have crossed a prominent current line, but might get back out of it. There would seem to be no risk in this direction as we are either going to get back onto the bank or pass below it. We will get some idea of where we are by watching the depth profile as we head west. At some point we will enter shallower water, or get out of the current either way. Then we can head north and go back to where we started from or anchor in the region where the contour turned south.

5-20. Distance you have traveled is 4.6 nmi. Using the bearing to the light as your course, from the 26 fathom point just west of the buoy, staying on course that distance, you end up precisely on the 30 fathom curve. Thus, your depth sounder is working fine.

5-21. (A) 025 M. (B) 5125.6. (C) 276 M. (D) 036. (E) 5129.9. (F) 1 nmi.

5-22. (A) 039 M. (B) 288 M. (C) 8.3 nmi. (D) 5155.7.

5-23. (A) 127 M. (B) 11:34.

5-24. (A) 48° 22.2' N, 123° 13.1' W. (B) 2.3 nmi. (C) 122 M. (D) 15:30 - 12:00 = 3 h 30 m = 3.5 h. Drift = 2.3 nmi / 3.5 h = 0.7 kts. Set = 142 T, i.e. current would be about .7 kts to the southeast. (E) No. For this to be the true current, even assuming that there were no other sources of error in the DR, you would have to assume that this current was constant in direction and speed over the entire DR track. Looking at the shape of the coastline along this course, it is unlikely that this is true in this case. The current moves on along widely different curve lines in and out of Haro, Rosario and Juan de Fuca Strait, with numerous variables. So, the affects of the current in this exercise are cumulative. The final result is from averaging the current speed and direction during the overall trip.

CHAPTER 6 – PILOTING

6-1. (A) 48° 21.81' N, 123° 18.52' W (B) 48° 21.69' N, 123° 16.29' W. (C) 0.23 nmi = 460 yds. Compare to 5-18.

6-2. From a point about 0.2 nmi north of VK the bearing to Cadboro Pt light is 266T, variation is 20E, so the magnetic danger bearing is 246 M. As long as bearing is less than that you will not get set down into the rocks. So "no more than 246 M."

6-3. (A) 4 nmi. Note this is doubling the bow angle, so it can be computed accurately; distance off = distance run. (B) 2.43 nmi. (C) 45 fathoms is the closest sounding.

6-4. (A) 35°. (B) 70°. (C) 4 nmi. (D) distance off = distance run. (E) yes

6-5. (A) 42°. (B) 338°. (C) 1.7 nmi.

6-6. Should get the same result as 6-5.

6-7. (A) 320 M. (B) 2.8 nmi. (C) 48° 19.73' N, 123° 49.18' W. (D) The continuous quick flashing (Q 21 ft 6 M) at the entrance to Sooke Basin.

6-8. Small Angle Rule says 6° is 10%, so 3° is 5%, and 0.05 x20 = 1.0 nmi.

6-9. About 9 miles. (6° is 10% = 4.5 nmi x 2 = 9 nmi.)

6-10. H = 118 ft, Hs = 1.25°, D = 1 nmi x H / (100 x Hs) = 1.18/1.25 = 0.94 nmi.

6-11. H = 480 ft, Hs = 2.75°, D = 4.80 / 2.75 = 1.75 nmi.

6-12. (A) 352 M. (B) 1.7 nmi. (C) 1.3 nmi.

6-13. 48° 27.9' N, 123° 08.3' W.

6-14. 48° 24.1' N, 122° 54.6' W.

6-15. H = 940 ft, Hs = 2.33°, D = 9.40/2.33 = 4 nmi. Fix = 4 miles off the point along bearing line 218 M, so your position is 48° 10.9' N, 123° 49.1' W.

6-16. (A) 1.5 miles. (B) 0.8 miles. (C) 1.8 miles. Plot the two bearings and compute the distance run. Graphically match the distance run on the course line to the two bearing lines. There is only one point on each line where the distance on the course line will fit. Each point is an EP (estimated position). "A" measure the distance from 1255 EP to the Buoy R. "B" and "C" are solved by calculating the distance the current will carry the vessel in the elapsed time and constructing vectors

from the 1255 EP in the direction of the current with lengths calculated above. You now have 1255 EPs for the given current conditions. See Video Index at starpath.com/18465tr.

6-17. (A) 1.8 miles. (B) 1.0 miles. (C) 1.95 miles.

Notes: Using the Problem 5-14 graphic diagram, construct the 007° leeway course lines of identical length and plot the current vectors from Problem 5-14 to obtain new EPs. Measure the distance from the new EPs to Buoy R.

6-18. (A) 48° 11.5' N, 123° 10.4' W; (B) 1.0 miles.

Notes: In (A), plot initial EP. Plot the three course legs from the initial EP. Plot the initial 180° bearing on Ediz Hook Light from the last EP. Plot the bearing on New Dungeness Lt. The intersection of the advanced bearing and the second bearing on is your RFIX. For (B), back plot from the RFIX.

6-19. (A) 48° 16.5' N, 122° 53.5' W, just crawling up onto Partridge Bank, headed toward the 4 fathom shoaling. (B) about 4 fathoms. (C) 10 minutes ahead, at 1420. (D) If this data is all right, we can't be much farther north, but we could be maybe half a mile south, but the initial depths as we entered the Eastern Bank actually would rule that out... in short it is a pretty good fix. We will prove it precisely when we hit the 4 fathom shoaling. See video solutions in the Course Video Index at starpath.com/18465tr.

6-20. 2 fathom = 12 feet, so depth at that location at low water would be 14 feet.

6-21. About 9 miles. (6° is 10% = 4.5 nmi × 2 = 9 nmi).

CHAPTER 7 – ELECTRONIC NAVIGATION

7-1. (A) You run into land! Straight into the mud of Dungeness Bay. For the true story see davidburchnavigation.blog-spot.com/2014/12/how-big-well-run-high-tech-race-boat.html. (B) First of all, do not use automatic waypoint advancement. In most cases this is more dangerous than helpful. The waypoints are the place the navigator should touch base with the navigation. Secondly, add real observations to each leg of the trip that will confirm where you are. In this example, when the navigator came on deck, someone stated that they did not realize they could see Smith Island light so brightly from this far off. In reality they were looking at the New Dungeness Light, and just had time to swing around some 180° and get out from behind the spit before hitting ground.

7-2. (A) Use buoy locations: S and SA for the first lanes to cross and then R and RA for the second. S by the way stands for Seattle, R for Rosario. The buoys go on along these water ways as RA, RB, RB etc...SA, SB(missing), SC, SD on to T for Tacoma, TA, TB, etc. The lanes are 0.5 miles wide and the separation zone is 0.30 wide, hence the XTEs of interest are 0.65 into the lane, 0.15 into separation zone. (B) Store all of these midchannel buoys as waypoints and from these make up the routes that cross any one of them, R to RA, S to SA, RA to SA, etc...

7-3. (B) Vertical accuracy about half as good as horizontal. This has been studied in depth by those interested in aircraft navigation by GPS. It is also true with WAAS assistance. Both are better then, but vertical accuracy still roughly half as good as horizontal.

7-4. (A) Fix at 1300 = 48° 17.8'N, 123° 46.5' W, (B) Fix at 1400 = 48° 17.8'N, 123° 40.1' W, (C) Sailed 5.7 nmi due E in 60min but made good only 4.26 nmi, so current sets due W at 5.7-4.26 = 1.44 kt.

7-5. Intersection of the two circles of position gives 48° 16.91'N, 123° 41.23'W.

7-6. (A) Assumed simultaneous ranges gives a fix of 48° 19.01'N, 123° 43.12'W. (B) 12 kts for 3 min is 0.6 nmi in direction 300T. Advancing the 1410 COP to 1413, the new intersection and proper fix is 48° 19.42'N, 123° 43.82'W. (C) The correct fix (solution B) is 0.61 nmi from the incorrect fix (solution A) in the direction of 131 T.

7-7. (B) ± 20 ft.

7-8. (C) Wide Area Augmentation System.

7-9. (D) You have sailed into a region or moved the instrument in such a way that part of the sky is now blocked from view of its antenna.

7-10. (A) The cigarette lighter socket and wiring. (This question arises from personal experience.)

7-11. In this installation the chartplotter uses GPS-derived COG for its direction reference, not a magnetic-based reference; therefore, the chartplotter's direction will be affected by current.

7-12. (B) One range and one bearing is fastest. It can be read directly from the radar screen in seconds.

7-13. (C) Two ranges is most accurate, because the largest uncertainty comes in the calibration of the heading used for bearings. This however is the slowest fix if done by manual plotting, but still relatively fast if solved by ECS.

7-14. You can use an ECS on a home computer to set up and fine tune your desired route taking into account tides and currents on the date of sailing, then print out a route plan to take on the boat. This shows all courses, distances, ETAs at assumed speeds, along with the Lat-Lons of your waypoints which can then be entered into the boat GPS you will use.

7-15. Set up range rings on the vessel icon that match the range rings on the radar display and then you can easily identify the land masses seen on the radar, regardless of your heading.

7-16. AIS signals include vessel class and name, location, COG, SOG, call sign, destination, and ETA.

7-17. (C) is not true. AIS Class B vessels broadcast position every 30 seconds provided they are faster than 2 kts. If slower, they broadcast position every 3 minutes. Let us emphasize that AIS is not to be considered a replacement for the capabilities of traditional marine radar. Not at all.

7-18. AIS Class A (large ships plus certain smaller commercial vessels) broadcasts on VHF frequencies with 12.5 watts of power; AIS Class B broadcasts on VHF with 2 watts power. Clearly there will be a significant difference in the useful range of these two classes. VHF is not purely line-of-sight transmission, so as a general estimate, AIS Class A can be received some 20 miles or more distant, while AIS Class B can be received some 4 or 5 miles distant.

7-19. Differences between ENC and RNC include:

(1) RNC are identical to the printed chart, whereas ENC are vector representations of the paper chart information.

(2) RNC have chart symbol information printed right on the chart, whereas using ENC we must often right click or otherwise request the metadata describing the symbol.

(3) Essentially all echart programs can display the RNC, whereas only selected programs display both (though this is changing with time as more have a vector chart option)

(4) RNC are large files sizes; ENC are relatively small files.

(5) In principle the ENC can include much more information about individual features.

(6) Chances of finding a charting error is somewhat higher in the ENC as they include any errors that the RNC include plus new ones that might get introduced during the digitizing process.

(7) RNC have a fixed layout, whereas with ENC the user can control colors, fonts, depth contours shown, etc.

(8) The zoom display levels in ENC are sometimes in coarser steps than in effect for RNC images.

(9) ... and more.

CHAPTER 8 – TIDES AND CURRENTS

8-1. 2 fathom = 12ft, so 12 + 2 = 14 ft water depth.

8-2. (A)
	HH	0456	8.5 ft
	LL	1113	-0.4 ft
	LH	1831	8.1 ft
	HL	2323	4.5 ft

(B)
	HL	0050	7.1 ft
	LH	0520	8.0 ft
	LL	1250	-3.2 ft
	HH	2116	9.3 ft

8-3. (A) Evening high tide is at 1826 PDT at 6.7 ft. (B) Charted depth (on 18465 Tr) = 5.5 fathoms = 33 ft + 6.7 ft = 39.7 ft.

8-4. (A) 90ft = 15 fathoms which is the depth about 2.4 miles offshore -- the halfway point between the 14- and 16-fathom soundings is right on the bearing line.

(B) Water depth = depth read plus draft = 90+1 = 91. Of this 91, 13 = tide, so actual charted depth would be 91-13 = 78 ft = 13 fathoms. This depth is located 1.9 miles offshore along the measured bearing to the house.

8-5. From tide predictions we have -3.3 ft at 1215 and +9.2 ft at 2042. To simplify the Rule of Twelfths we approximate this as -3 ft at 1200 and +9 ft at 2000. Then our range is 12 ft, so 1/12th is just 1 ft. Our time step will be (20-12)/6 = 1h 20m. Thus we have at 1200 -3ft and 2000 +9 ft, then at 1320 we have -2 ft and 1840 we have +8 ft. At 1440 we have 0 ft and at 1720 we have +6 ft. And in the middle of the cycle we have +3 ft. With a range of 12 ft, the corrections are ±1 ft, ±2 ft, and ±3 ft. Figure 8-5 shows the Rule of Twelfths approximation (inset and dots) overlaid on the NOAA plot.

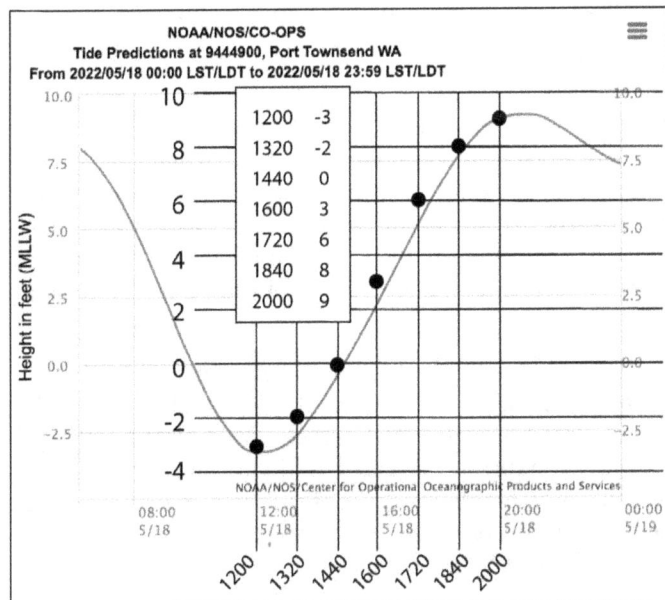

Figure 8-5. *Rule of Twelfths tide estimates overlaid onto the NOAA plot of tide height vs time. The insert shows the Rule values based on rounded tides and times.*

A rougher, but faster rule is: tide is the same for an hour either side of high and low water, and half the duration is half the range. Intermediate points can then be estimated.

8-6. Approximately 23 fathoms, as the location given is approximately half-way between the charted 21- and 25- fathom soundings.

8-7. (A) Port Townsend, LL 1113, -0.4 ft; HH is 0456, 8. 5ft. (B) Aleck Bay, LL is at 1105, -0.4 ft; HH is 0438, 7.4 ft.

8-8. (A) 18471. (B) 9 ft. (CP 176) (C) 0949 to 1859, plus about an hour extra on each end. (D) Seems to have one low water and then high water all day. It is not uncommon to see unique tidal behavior in some bays. Across the Strait from here in Victoria Harbor they typically have diurnal tides, whereas most of the area has mixed semi-diurnal tides.

8-9. Clearance heights are given in feet above MHW. The chart says MHW for Port Townsend is 7.7 ft. The clearance under the bridge would be 58 ft when the tide is 7.7 ft. The tide is now at 10 ft, which is 2.3 ft above MHW (10 - 7.7). Clearance is actually 55.7 ft at this time (58 - 2.3).

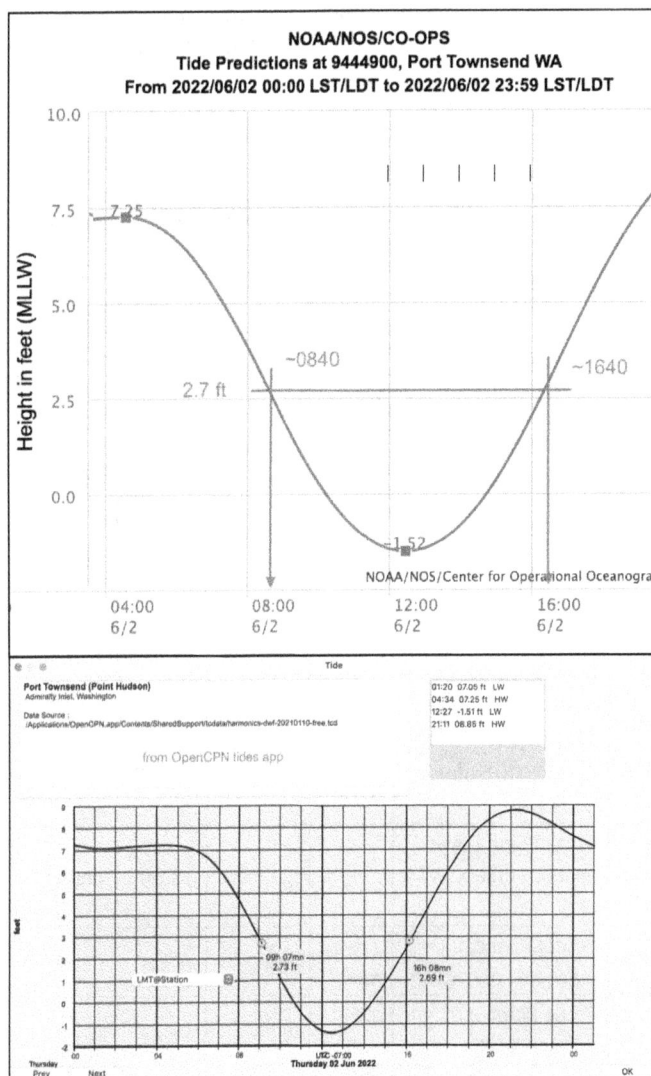

Figure 8-10. *Finding tide times range to plan for bridge clearance. Top is the NOAA plot; bottom is from OpenCPN.*

8-10. Wanting 1 ft safety margin, you need at least 5 more feet of clearance than is available at MHW (tide of 7.7 ft). Thus we need the tide to be 2.7 ft or lower. The tides on June 2 are 7.3 at 0434, then -1.5 at 1227, then back up to 8.8 at 2112. Thus the center of the window is at 1227, and need to figure when the tide rises to 2.7 ft on either side of that, which we can estimate with the Rule of Twelfths or more easily from a plot such as the NOAA version and the OpenCPN version shown in Figure 8-10. Note that the two have the same tides data but slightly different formulas for curves between tides.

8-11. (A) Lowest Normal Tide is the average of the single lowest tide of each year for a station over the standard 19-year lunar cycle (a total of 19 data points); Mean Lower Low Water is the average of the lowest daily low water mark for a station over the same period (a total of 19 x 365 data points). Hence, sounding datum for charts using LNT will always read a shallower depth than the sounding datum for the same location on a chart using MLLW; conversely, tidal differences computed for charts using LNT will be correspondingly greater. In the Strait of Juan de Fuca, for example, LNT is about 2.5 ft. lower than MLLW, so tabulated tide heights are about 2.5 ft. greater in Canadian Tide Tables than in American — if they happen to report for the same place using these two separate datums, which as a rule they do not. One way to detect this difference is to look at the mean tide level at nearby stations that use different datums. The overall depth of water is the same. Note too, that this distinction has essentially no practical significance since the chart and tidal datums are always coordinated. The only way you could possibly get into difficulties here would be to use mixed resources, that is tides from one datum and charts from another.

8-12. (A) Tide & Current stations within 5 miles of Iceberg Pt are shown in Table 8-12 and Figure 8-12.

(B) From the Table 8-12 we see that Richardson is the closest tide station but just barely. See plot in Figure 8-12.

8-13. (A) PUG1632. Smith Island, 5.5 mi WNW of (43 ft). Located 2.65 nmi @ 097.7. (B) PUG1630. Kanem Point, 1.5 mi SW of Protection Island (22 ft).

8-14. (A) 0906 and 1630. (B) 1230 at 1.1 kts. (C) PDT. It changes to PST in Nov. (D) Statute miles. Some are nautical (written nmi or nm) and others statute (mi). This one is statute.

8-15. (A) Peak currents and slack times (F=flood; E=ebb).

03:06 slack
04:30 0.5F
06:24 slack
10:24 -3.2E
14:06 slack
16:54 2.5F
21:06 slack

(B) *Mean* Ebb direction is toward 090 T. *Mean* flood direction is toward 286 T.

8-16. Referring to Figure 8-16, (A) The trip is 15 nmi, so at 5 kts with no current it would take 3 hr. This would then be about 1.5 hr down to the bottom of the island (Halfway Point) and then 1.5 hr up to the destination, with no current.

(B) If we assume the San Juan Channel station is a good representation of current along the whole west side—an assumption to simplify the analysis, although more stations do exist on both sides of this island—then the favorable flood north starts at about 1300 (1248) and peaks at about 1600. We also see that there is strong current of 4.3 kts peak. If we just average half that amount then our engine speed of 5 kts goes to 7 kts SMG, and this half of the 15 mi run takes just about an hour.

Thus for the very best current ride north, we would hit the halfway point at 1530 and in an hour we would be at the End point at 1630 or earlier. In the real world, this is a little optimistic as the current forecast right in the narrow point of the channel is higher than outside of that, but we see that getting to the halfway point any time between about 1400 and 1700 would give us a huge current boost up that side.

ID	Station	Range	Bearing	Lat N	Lon W
T1	Richardson, Lopez Island, San Juan Channel	1.5 nmi	350°	48°27'	122°54'
T2	Aleck Bay, Lopez Island	1.6 nmi	083°	48°26'	122°51'
T3	Telegraph Bay	3.8 nmi	070°		
C1	Cattle Point, 1.2 miles southeast of	2.3 nmi	290°	48°26'	122°57'
C2	Iceberg Point, 2.1 miles SSW of	2.5 nmi	201°	48°23'	122°55'
C3	Colville Island, 1 mile SSE of	3.3 nmi	112°	48°24'	122°49'
C4	SAN JUAN CHANNEL (south entrance)	3.3 nmi	315°	48°28'	122°57'
C5	Kings Point, Lopez Island, 1 mile NNW of	4.4 nmi	326°	48°29'	122°57'
C6	Point Colville, 1.4 miles east of	4.5 nmi	092°	48°25'	122°47'
C7	Cattle Point, 2.8 miles SSW of	4.4 nmi	252°	48°24'	123°00'
C8	Lopez Pass	4.6 nmi	040°	48°29'	122°49'

Table 8-12. Tide (Tx) and Current (Cx) Stations near Iceberg Pt.

The east side, riding the ebb south, has similar strong currents. The ebb starts at about 0600 and peaks at about 1030. Again, we can assume that a current boosted travel time will be about 1 hr. On this side the best run would be 1000 to 1100, but that gets us there too early to meet the flood. We have to compromise.

If we start down at 1300 in 1.7 kts we arrive halfway at 1400 in 0.3 kts, for an average current boost of 1.0 kts. Then start up the west side at 1400 in 2.1 kts and arrive at 1500 in 3.6 kts, for an average current boost of 2.9 kts. Thus you have SMG of 5+1 = 6 coming down and 5+2.9 =7.9 going up. Your average up and down would be about SMG = 7.0 kts. This can be experimented with, but some time around 1300 seems optimum, based on this simple analysis.

(C) From part (B), we assume an average SMG of about 7 kts for the trip counting the current, or 15/7 = 2.5h. We saved about half an hour choosing an opportune time.

8-17. It always ebbs. Very rarely ever any flood direction current.

8-18. (A) Cape Cod Canal, east end (COD0901). (B) Semidiurnal. (C) Floods and ebbs are about the same strength throughout the year in this semidiurnal pattern. See data in the annual print out for any year.

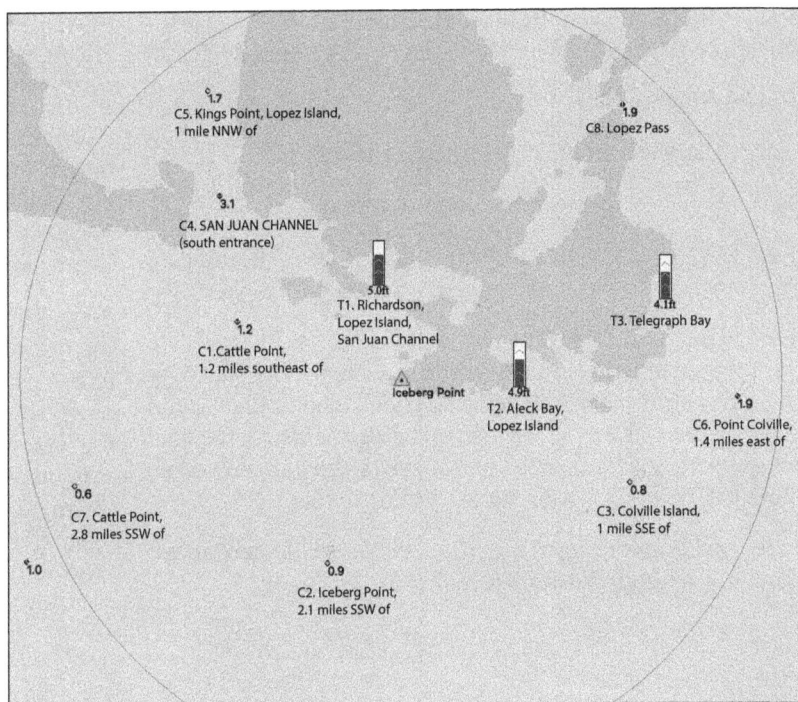

Figure 8-12. *Finding tide and current stations using OpenCPN.*

8-19. (A) Mobile River Entrance (ACT8741). (B) Diurnal. (C) Ebbs are 2 to 3 times larger than the floods, which is common at a river entrance as the river flow contributes to the ebbs and distracts from the floods. This is often true of larger estuaries with many river inlets.

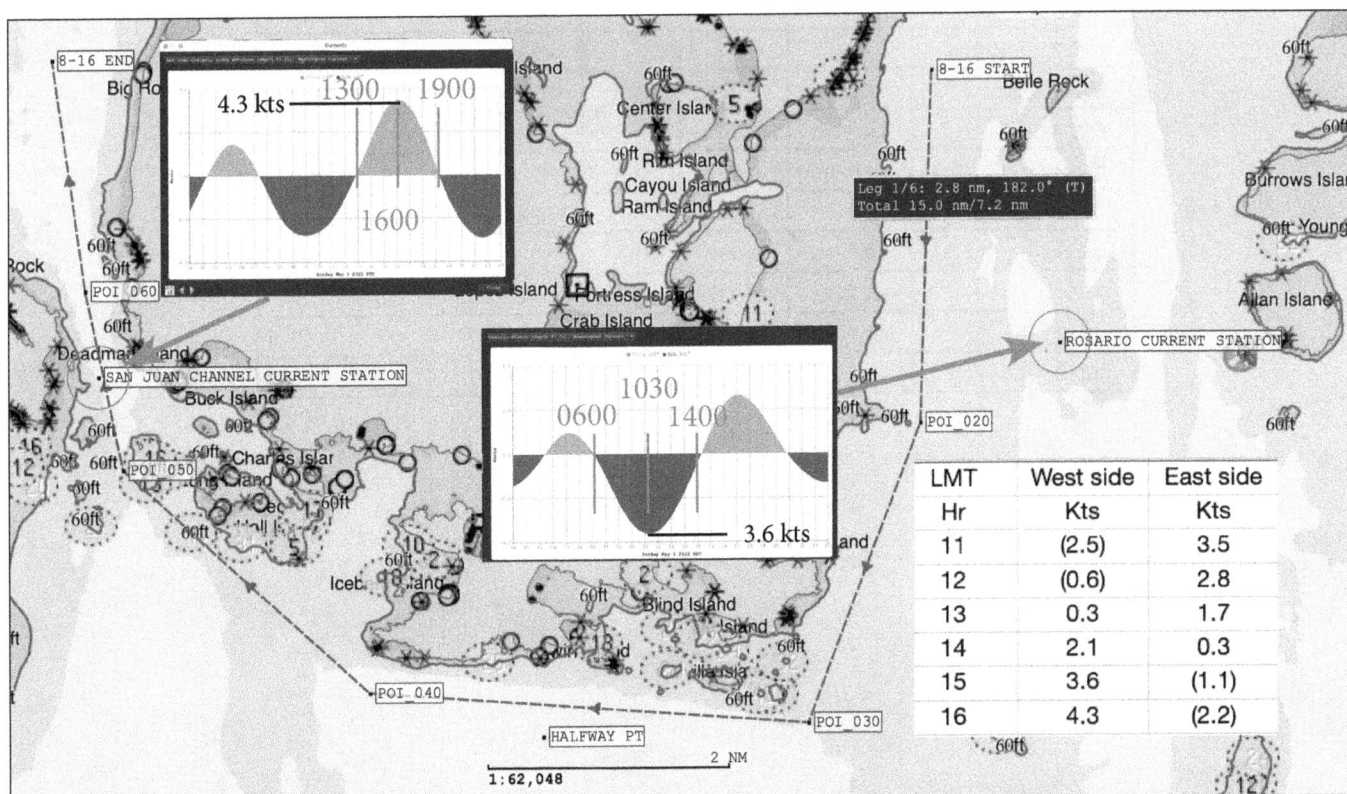

LMT	West side	East side
Hr	Kts	Kts
11	(2.5)	3.5
12	(0.6)	2.8
13	0.3	1.7
14	2.1	0.3
15	3.6	(1.1)
16	4.3	(2.2)

Figure 8-16. *Route with currents displayed in qtVlm and then annotated. Similar plots can be made in OpenCPN or other programs. The current graphs and hourly values can also be obtained at the NOAA site. Currents in parenthesis are opposing currents.*

8-20. The lat-lon is on the tide data page. The station is just outside of Travis Spit, exposed to the Strait of Juan de Fuca.

8-21. See Figure 8-21.

8-22. (A) 0.3 kts at 240 T. (B) 0.1 kts at 100 T.

8-23. (A) LL + 2 to 3 hr. (B) 0.4 kts at 300 to 325T.

8-24. (A) March 19, both full moon and perigee. (B) June 23 or 24, with 3rd quarter and apogee on successive days.

8-25. LL at the Golden Gate is at 0515, so 0815 is LL+3 which, from the rotary current table we get 0.4 kts at 325T. But May 16 is 1 day away from both perigee and full moon which would enhance this to 1.4 x 0.4 = 0.6 kts. (Recall this is only the tidal component; with any wind present over the past day or so there will be wind-driven current adding to this.)

8-26. 2.9 kts according to the NOAA current tables footnote—though in exceptional cases it could be even larger.

8-27. Answers comparing NOAA Table 3 with the 50-90 Rule are shown in Table 8-27. We see that the 50-90 Rule works very well and is easy to apply.

8-28. April 16 and May 16 are full moons in 2022. There are others, of course, but these are the only ones we know of from our limited current predictions, indicated by a full moon symbol. Note the new moon (all black, April 1) and the half moons (Sept 3 and 17)

8-29. The Sept 3 moon has the right side lit; the 17th has the left side lit. In the Northern Hemisphere, the right side lit means the sun is west of the moon. The moon moves east away from the sun, and the farther the moon is from the sun the larger it becomes. A full moon is directly opposite to the sun; one rises when the other sets. Thus right side lit means waxing; left side means waning, sun is east of the moon and the moon is getting closer to it each night. This is reversed in the Southern Hemisphere.

Table 8-27							
Current Data		**NOAA Table 3-A**				**50-90 Rule**	
PDT	*Current*	*Intervals*	*Cycle*	*Factor*	*Current*	*Current*	*Factor*
0443	0.0				0.0	0.0	
0543		1h 00m	3h 34m	0.45	1.0	1.2	0.5
0630		1h 47m	3h 34m	0.75	1.7	1.6	0.7
0717		2h 34m	3h 34m	0.9	2.1	2.1	0.9
0817	2.3				2.3	2.3	
0917		2h 14m	3h 14m	0.9	2.1	2.1	0.9
0954		1h 37m	3h 14m	0.72	1.7	1.6	0.7
1031		1h 00m	3h 14m	0.6	1.4		0.5
1131	0.0				0.0	0.0	
1231		1h 41m	2h 41m	0.8	-1.4	-0.9	0.5
1251		1h 21m	2h 41m	0.7	-1.2	-1.2	0.7
1312		1h 00m	2h 41m	0.6	-1.0	-1.5	0.9
1412	-1.7				-1.7	-1.7	

CHAPTER 9 – NAVIGATION IN CURRENTS

9-1. Set 080° T, Drift 1.0 kts

9-2. (A) 9.1 nmi at 141 T - 20 = 121M. (B) 9.1/5.5 = 1.65 hr = 1 hr 39m. (C) New Dungeness Light (PUG16325); the current is ebbing toward 273T, which is against us. It will slow us down. (D) The ebb peaked at 1.6 kts at 0948 local time. It is now 1015, 27 min past the peak ebb of 1.6 kts, so it will be a bit slower. The time of next slack is 1454, about 5 hr later, so the one third period time, (1454-1015)/3, is 1h 40m. The Rule tells us that in the first third of the period the speed drops to 0.9 x the peak or 0.9x1.6=1.4 kts, but that is not till 0948+0140=1128. So in the first hour (1015 to 1115) we expect the current to be something like 1.5 kts in direction 273, which is plenty accurate enough, in that these current predictions could be off 20% and ±20 min or so. (E) ECS plot in Figure 9-2a gives CTS = 130T = 110M, with a resulting SMG = 4.4 kts. Figure 9-2b shows computed solutions. (F) 9.1 / 4.4 = 2.07h = 2h 4m, then + 1015, to get there at 1219. (G) Nearest station is Kanem Pt, which is slack at 1230 coming

down from a peak of 1.6 ebb at 0930. This is a 3-hr interval, implying that at 1130 the current was about 0.8 kts, and about 0.4 at 1200. In short the current is much weaker, so if we were watching our GPS track on the screen we would have been steering more like 141 on the last third of this leg.

9-3. (A) 6.45 @ 122 T (B) 8.77 @ 112 T

9-4. (A) 2/6 × 60° = 20°. CMG is about 200 + 20 = 220 M. (B) Larger. (C) CMG = 218.4, SMG = 6.32.

9-5. 2/6 of 40° = 13V. CMG is about 200 -13 = 187 M. The factor of 40° is used because the current is not on the beam, but quartering.

9-6. 1.5/5 × 60° = 0.3 × 60 = 18°. Head in about 18 or 20°.

9-7. (A) Beating in a southerly, the wind is on your bow. Current set is 2/6 × 40° = about 13°. With a leeway of 10° you slip another 10° to leeward for a total of about 23 or say 25°. If your compass reads 205, you are actually making good a course more like 205 + 25 or 230 M. (B) With no current set or leeway slip, you would look at your compass of 205, know you tack through 90°, and reasonably guess your compass should read 205 – 90 = 115 after you come about to starboard tack. And if you did indeed tack through 90° (which you would know if you have tacked very often in these conditions and watched the compass), this would be right and that is what the compass would read. But we also know (or reasonably estimate) that we are slipping 25° downwind, so even when our compass reads 115 we are actually making good 115 – 25 or about 090. Hence we wait till the buoy bears about 090 then tack. When we tack the compass will read 115, and it will look like we are sailing well to weather of the buoy, as if we went too far tacking. But the wind and current will set us down the same 25° and we will make good a course straight toward the buoy.

Generally in these circumstances it is good practice to throw in another 5° for safety. In this case wait till the buoy bears 085 then tack. If you are too high, as soon as you notice

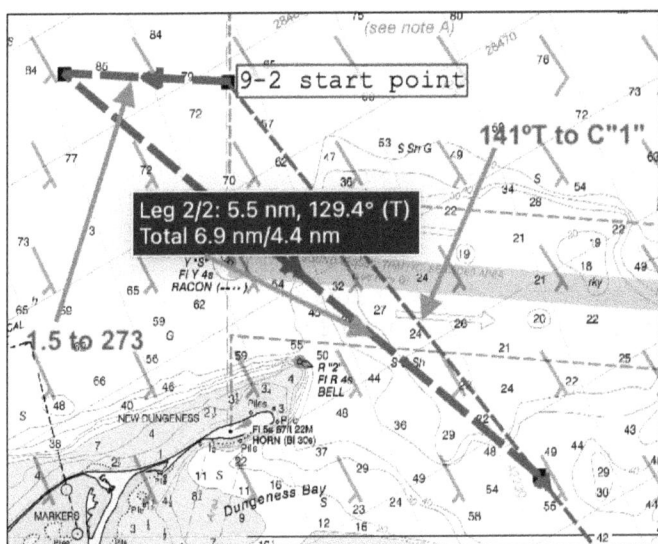

Figure 9-2a. *Plotted solution to find CTS. Drift with the current 1hr, then draw a line length equal to knotmeter speed that takes you back to the desired track. See text for details.*

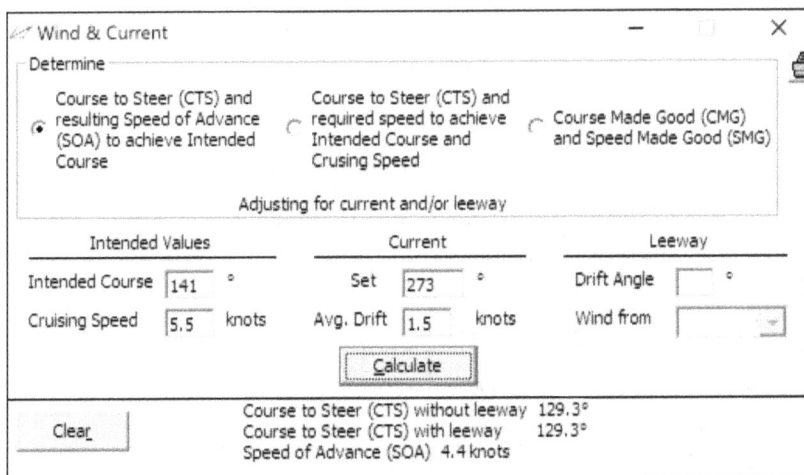

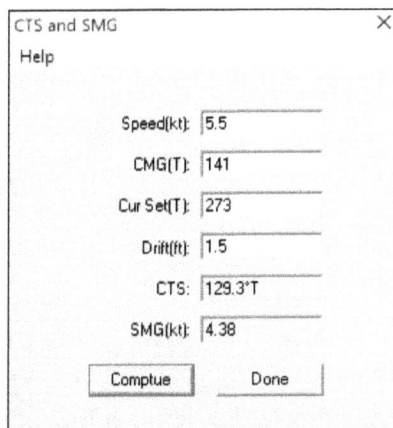

Figure 9-2b *Computed CTS solutions.* **Top** *is from the StarPilot app available in several formats.* **Left** *is from the free app called Celestial Tools available at starpath.com. Both do extensive piloting computations, not just celestial.*

it you can fall off. But if you underestimate it, you may not be able to pinch up enough to get around it. If you don't make it you h ve to tack twice more to get around.

9-8. Selecting two distant objects (such as the tree and a peak behind it) establishes a natural range, and as you walk across the field you maintain the range relationship to make progress on a straight range line. This is the same way you cross a current to check that you are not being set.

9-9. The back bearing shifted from 160 to 135 so you are being set left by about 25°. Sketch a diagram with these headings to see how this comes about. Hence point to the right about 25° or come to course 340 + 25 = 005 M. Then continue to watch the back bearings for a while to see if your correction was about right.

9-10. You can expect the current to be different, sometimes dramatically so, upon crossing a tide rip. However, if you are in a low powered boat, you can usually assume there is indeed a current flowing *through it* so you will, if being pulled in, get pushed out the other side.

9-11. Some answers (shaded numbers) are given to the tenth for best comparison with solutions obtained, but in practice we are lucky to get these answers to within a few tenths, primarily because we do not know the input data well enough. In fact, it is rare to need more than we can get from the simple 40-60 approximation. In practical work we steer by COG from the GPS, but it is nevertheless beneficial to check that the current prediction are correct for future planning.

9-12. (A) Slack to slack (A to G in the Resources diagram) gives 63% of the peak, or average is 0.63 × 1.7 = 1.1 kts Flood. (B) E to G in the diagram is 48%, or 0.48 × 1.7 = 0.8 kts Flood.

Table 9-12. Answers

#	S	H	Set*	Drift	CMG	SMG	Set**	40-60
1	6.0	200	150	2.0	188	7.4	11.9	13.3
2	5.0	100	315	1.5	087	3.9	12.9	12.0
3	7.5	350	260	1.8	337	7.7	13.5	14.4
4	6.0	215	150	2.0	200	7.1	14.8	13.3
5	5.0	110	315	1.5	100	3.7	9.9	12.0
6	7.5	004	260	1.8	350	7.3	13.9	14.4
7	7.4	180	293	3.1	205	6.8	25.0	25.4
8	6.2	130	014	2.1	110	5.6	20.0	20.6
9	6.2	130	049	2.4	110	7.0	20.0	23.4

* Direction current flows toward.
** Difference between H and CMG

(C) F to G gives 25% or 0.25 × 1.7 = 0.4 Flood for about 1h and then A to C for 48%, or 0.48 × 1.4 = 0.7 kts Ebb for 3h. Then we can say that in 1h we went +0.4 miles in the flood direction, then we went 0.7 × 3h = -2.1 miles in the ebb direction, or a net of 0.21-0.4 = 1.7 miles in ebb direction over 4 hours, so the net current was 1.7/4 = 0.4 kts Ebb as the average current.

9-13. (A) see Table 9-13-1. (B) and (C) see summary in Table 9-13-2, based on the current forecasts from Figure 9-13. The two optional times are near the peaks. The cycle is about 6h, so one-third cycle is 2h. So 2h before and after the peak the currents would be 0.9 times the peak values. In this exercise we are starting about 1h before and ending about 1 hr after the peak, so even without the NOAA plots we would get the right values from just the peak currents. (D), and (E) see Table 9-13-2. (F) Departing at 5 am is faster by about 2 hr.

Table 9-13-1. Mats Mats to Pt Hudson (no current) Route Plan

From WP	Lon	Lat	To WP	C (T)	D (nm)	SMG	Cur	Time
01 Mats Mats	122°40.6'W	47°57.7'N	02	010.5°	2.29	6.0	0	22m 53s
02 Approach Lip Lip	122°40.0'W	47°59.9'N	03	001.5°	1.87	6.0	0	18m 44s
03 Nodule Pt	122°39.9'W	48°01.8'N	04	348.5°	2.08	6.0	0	20m 46s
04 Midway to 05	122°40.5'W	48°03.9'N	05	351.5°	2.35	6.0	0	23m 33s
05 Marrowstone Pt	122°41.1'W	48°06.2'N	06	285.9°	2.65	6.0	0	26m 28s
06 Pt. Hudson	122°44.9'W	48°07.0'N			11.24			1h 52m 24s

Table 9-13-2

From WP	To WP	Depart 5 am, ride the ebb flowing north				Depart 11 am, buck the flood flowing south			
		SMG)	Cur	Time	ETA	SMG	Cur	Time	ETA
01 Mats Mats	02	7.0	+1.0	19m 36s	05:19	4.9	-1.1	28m 1s	11:28
02 Approach Lip Lip	03	8.5	+2.5	13m 13s	05:32	4.0	-2.0	28m 6s	11:56
03 Nodule Pt	04	8.5	+2.5	14m 40s	05:47	4.0	-2.0	31m 10s	12:27
04 Midway to 05	05	9.0	+3.0	15m 42s	06:03	1.6	-4.4	1h 28m 18s	13:55
05 Marrowstone Pt	06	6.2	+0.2	25m 37s	06:28	4.8	-1.2	33m 5s	14:28
06 Pt. Hudson				1h 28m 48s				3h 28m 40s	

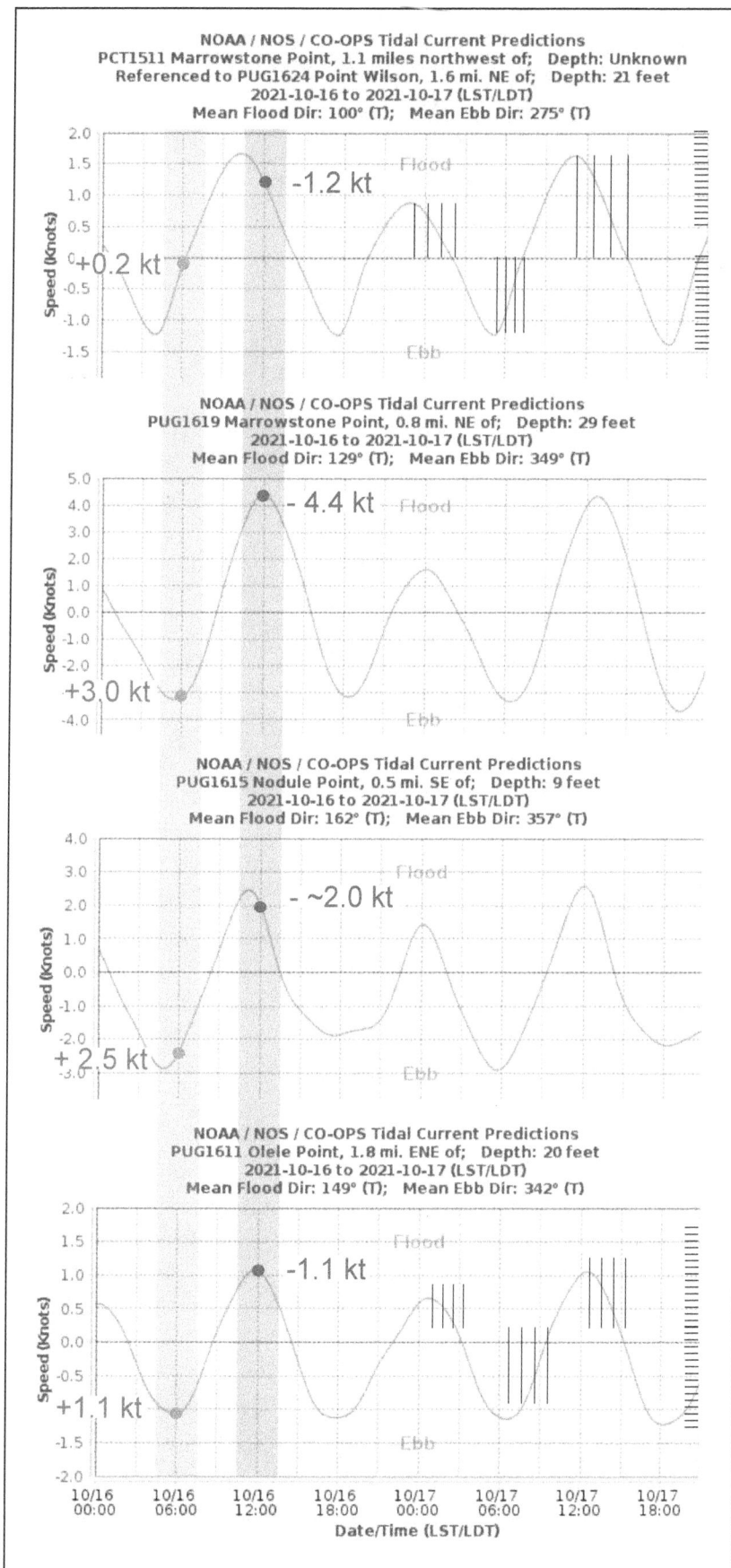

Figure 9-13. *Current forecasts along the route of Exercise 9-13, with inserted tick marks that can be used to practice with the 50-90 Rule and the Slow Water Rule*

CHAPTER 10 – NAVIGATION RULES

Answers followed by Rules that apply.

Parts A & B.
Definitions and Right of Way

10-1.	(D)	Rule 15, 17b.
10-2.	(A)	Rule 6b, 7b.
10-3.	(D)	Rule 6.
10-4.	(C)	Rule 13a.
10-5.	(D)	Rule 3a.
10-6.	(D)	Rule 12a.
10-7.	(B)	Rule 3f.
10-8.	(A)	Rule 3g.
10-9.	(B)	Rule 7d.
10-10.	(D)	Rule 13a.
10-11.	(B)	Rule 15a, 18a.
10-12.	(C)	Rule 17a.
10-13.	(B)	Rule 15.
10-14.	(A)	Rule 14.
10-15.	(C)	Rule 3d.
10-16.	(C)	Rule 17b.
10-17.	(B)	Rule 6a.
10-18.	(D)	Rule 18d.
10-19.	(B)	Rule 13b.
10-20.	(D)	Rule 15, 16, 17c.
10-21.	(A)	Rule 18a.
10-22.	(C)	Rule 18a.
10-23.	(C)	Rule 13c.
10-24.	(D)	Rule 19a.
10-25.	(D)	Rule 6, 7, 8, 19, Annex I & IV.
10-26.	(C)	Rule 17b.
10-27.	(A)	Rule 12a.
10-28.	(C)	Rule 18a.
10-29.	(B)	Rule 9a.
10-30.	(B)	Rule 19b.
10-31.	(B)	Rule 3k.
10-32.	(A)	Rule 12a.

10-33.	(B)	Rule 16, 18a.
10-34.	(A)	Rule 18b.
10-35.	(C)	Rule 15a.
10-36.	(A)	Rule 9c.
10-37.	(B)	Rule 13.
10-38.	(D)	Rule 3c.
10-39.	(D)	Rule 5.
10-40.	(A)	Rule 8a.
10-41.	(C)	Rule 3g.
10-42.	(C)	Rule 3i.
10-43.	(B)	Rule 19e.
10-44.	(C)	Rule 17a(ii).

Part C. Lights and Dayshapes

10-45.	(C)	Rule 24e.
10-46.	(B)	Annex IV.
10-47.	(C)	Rule 29.
10-48.	(A)	Rule 27.
10-49.	(D)	Rule 30.
10-50.	(A)	Rule 27b(iii), 26b,c.
10-51.	(D)	Rule 34.
10-52.	(D)	Rule 27.
10-53.	(A)	Rule Annex II.
10-54.	(A)	Rule 25.
10-55.	(B)	Rule 24.
10-56.	(A)	Rule 24.
10-57.	(B)	Rule 24.
10-58.	(D)	Rule 21b.
10-59.	(A)	Rule 13b.
10-60.	(B)	Rule 26b.
10-61.	(A)	Rule 20.
10-62.	(A)	Rule 23a.
10-63.	(A)	Rule 23a.
10-64.	(A)	Rule 30.
10-65.	(B)	Rule 24a.
10-66.	(D)	Rule 26a.

10-67.	(C)	Rule 21f.
10-68.	(B)	Rule 1, note 1 (Morse "S").
10-69.	(B)	Rule 27d.
10-70.	(B)	Rule 26.
10-71.	(C)	Rule 27a.
10-72.	(A)	Rule 36, 37.
10-73.	(A)	Rule 25b.
10-74.	(D)	Rule 26.
10-75.	(D)	Rule 27e.
10-76.	(C)	Rule 27a.
10-77.	(A)	Rule 24a.
10-78.	(D)	Rule 24e.
10-79.	(C)	Rule 24g.
10-80.	(C)	Rule 21a.
10-81.	(D)	Rule 24.
10-82.	(D)	Rule 36.
10-83.	(D)	Rule 26, Rule 24a.
10-84.	(D)	Rule 24e.

Part D. Sound Signals

10-85.	(C)	Rule 35a.
10-86.	Reserved.	
10-87.	(C)	Rule 34e.
10-88.	(C)	Rule 34d.
10-89.	(D)	Rule 35e.
10-90.	(B)	Rule 35b.
10-91.	(D)	Rule 37, Annex IV.
10-92.	(C)	Rule 35c.
10-93.	(B)	Rule 37, Annex IV.
10-94.	(B)	Rule 32c.
10-95.	(D)	Rule 35g.
10-96.	(C)	Rule 35k.
10-97.	(B)	Rule 35g.
10-98.	(D)	Rule 37, Annex IV.
10-99.	(B)	Rule 35g.
10-100.	(D)	Rule 35c.

10-101.	(C)	Rule 37, Annex IV.
10-102.	(D)	Rule 35e.
10-103.	(C)	Rule 8, 15, 16, 34a.
10-104.	(D)	Rule 19, 35b.
10-105.	(A)	Rule 35.
10-106.	(D)	Rule 33b.
10-107.	(D)	Rule 33b.
10-108.	(A)	Rule 34d.
10-109.	(B)	Rule 37, Annex IV.
10-110.	(C)	Rule 34d.
10-111.	(C)	Rule 35j.
10-112.	(C)	Rule 37, Annex IV.
10-113.	(C)	Rule 34b.
10-114.	(B)	Rule 33a (for *both* inland & international).
10-115.	(A)	Rule 35e.
10-116.	(D)	Rule 34d.
10-117.	(A)	Rule 32, 34a.
10-118.	(A)	Rule 35g.
10-119.	(B)	Rule 35c.
10-120.	(B)	Rule 37, Annex IV.
10-121.	(C)	Rule 19e.
10-122.	(A)	Rule 35a.
10-123.	(B)	Rule 35c.
10-124.	(A)	Rule 34e.
10-125.	(D)	Rule 35a.
10-126.	(A)	Rule 34d.
10-127.	(D)	Rule 37, Annex IV.

CHAPTER 11 – NAVIGATION PLANNING AND PRACTICE

Trip 1.

11-1. (A) 10 nmi. The question seeks only the luminous range; therefore eye height is irrelevant to this problem. Luminous range is calculated from the Diagram: entering from the bottom scale at the light's charted range of 15 nmi. This value intersects with the 5.5 nmi visibility curve, at which the luminous range can be read from the left scale as 10 nmi. (B) The 2014 Light List shows a range of 13 nmi, which calculates a luminous range of about 9 nmi.

11-2. This can be answered most easily from qtVlm with training mode installed (A) Chart US5WA29m (B) 1:10,000 (C) Large scale. Otherwise, use NOAA online catalog (item 1.1 at starpath.com/getcharts). The Coast Pilot no longer uses chart numbers.

11-3. Cable area. Anchoring in this area could place important power or communications cables at risk.

11-4. (A) Smith Island Light. (B) Approximately 3 nmi.

11-5. Mud.

11-6. (A) 48° 28.6' N, 123° 12.5' W. (B) 48° 25.6' N. (C) the light bears 241.5° at about .7 nmi.

11-7. The light bears 023 T at 5.9 nmi.

11-8. (A) 035.2 T (B) 015.2 M. Here is the working:

CTS = 035.2 T, Var= 020 E, CTS = 015.2 M, Dev = 2.5 E, CTS= 012.7 C.

11-9. (A) 292 R.

11-10. The northern end of Hein Bank. Is your vessel at risk?

11-11. Your present course takes you across Hein Bank, with a prominent rock shown at 2 ½ fathoms. Surrounding topography shows 3 ¼ to 4 ¼ fathoms, so let's make an educated guess that 3 fathoms will be our shallowest point. 3 fathoms = 18 ft, then subtract sounder datum of 2 ft, and add in high water of 4 ft. Our minimum expected indicated depth is about 20 ft.

11-12. Re *Coast Pilot 10*, COLREGS Demarcation Lines (CP 7), state that the International Regulations "apply on all waters of the Strait of Juan de Fuca, Haro Strait and Strait of Georgia," so you are already operating under International Rules.

11-13. (A) Present position is 48° 16.4' N, 123° 31.5' W, (B) Meeting point is 48° 21.9' N, 123° 54.2' W, (C) 290 T, (D) 16.0 nmi, (E) 4.9 kts

11-14. Correcting for current calls for 168 T, and correcting then for leeway takes this to 165 T.

11-15. Answer is D, sail is the give way in that the ship is following a traffic lane and the sailing vessel is instructed not to impede. There is close quarters. Both meet in about 44 min. Ship covering 13.3 nmi at 18 kts; sail vessel 3.7 nmi at 5 kts.

11-16. Answer is D, both must obey Rule 19d and maneuver accordingly when interacting by radar alone—even within the traffic lanes if that should arise. Needless to say, sailing vessels should especially avoid the traffic lanes in the fog as instructed in Rule 10, which applies "in any condition of visibility," not to mention that sailing with no visibility must be done carefully, with engine on so you can maneuver quickly as called for.

CHAPTER 12 – IN DEPTH...

12-1. The *Navigation Rules.* If you learn and obey the Rules you will avoid collisions with both other vessels and also with other objects, such as land. Rules for Safe Speed and Proper Watch alone will accomplish most of this.

12-2. Radar, GPS, and depth sounder.

12-3. Part A (b) natural range. Part B (c) depth contour.

12-4. The expected ocean DR uncertainty is about 5% of distance run plus the set of an unknown current of about 0.5 kts, as an optimistic estimate and 7% and 0.7 kts as a conservative estimate. (A) This gives 6.0 mile plus 12.0, which add as the sum of the squares to get 13.4 mi. (At 7% and 0.7 kts, we get 18.7 mi) (B) 14.4 from the run, and 12.0 from the current, yields 18.7 mi uncertainty with 5% and 0.5 kts. (At 7% and 0.7 kts, we get 26.3 mi.)

12-5. Parallel rulers and dividers.

12-6. Scotch Blue Painter's Tape.

12-7. (A) Use Tacking distance = 1.5 × Upwind distance. (B) 1.5 × 2 = 3, then 3/6 = 30m. That is, going direct it would be 2/6 = 20 min, but tacking takes about 1.5 times longer, so 20 + 10 = 30m.

12-8. About 2.5% of the wind speed.

12-9. Equal and opposite, or 5° W.

12-10. Geomag (see starpath.com/navpubs).

12-11. 9m23s=9.383m=0.1564h. S=1/0.1564= 6.39. Then 6.39/6 = 1.065. (A) Knotmeter is low (B) by 6.5% (ie multiply what you read by 1.065 to get the right speed). Note we knew immediately it was low because it should have taken us 10m at 6 kts and it took less.

12-12. (A) 10 min/mile. (B) 6 min/mile. (C) 100 ft/min.

12-13. ECDIS is the IMO sanctioned echart system using only official ENC or RNC, and the viewers must have identical controls. ECS is any form of echarting, using vector or raster charts, or even navigation on satellite images, using any of hundreds of echart software or firmware programs. Very roughly, the merchant marine and navy uses ECDIS; everyone else uses ECS. More specifically, passenger vessels over 500 GT and cargo vessels over 3,000 GT must use ECDIS.

12-14. (A) True. (B) True. We do not correct for leeway influence on speed as it is included in what we read on the knotmeter. (C) True. (D) False. Leeway is motion through the water so it is logged by however we are measuring this. (E) False. Offset from pure log-and-compass DR due to current depends only on the time in the current and the current itself. (F) True. Leeway offset depends on our heading relative to the wind direction. (G) False. Current changes CMG to differ from H, and SMG to differ from S; leeway change in speed is measured and accounted for in the knotmeter speed S. (H)

False. A given current will move you a given distance in a given time, regardless of your heading. (I) True. Fall off close hauled and leeway drops quickly. (J) True. With calibrated knotmeter and compass, we can solve the vector problem to get set and drift from CMG and SMG. (K) False. We can estimate it under specific conditions, but it is tricky to measure accurately, because it changes with wind speed and wind angle, sails set, trim, etc. (L) False. Although leeway increases with wind speed, leeway is also large in very light air. It goes up in both wind speed directions from the optimum wind speed the boat and sail plan is designed to. (M) True. Tidal currents go often go from minimum to maximum in 3 hours.

12-15. VMG as SMG to windward, and SMG in the direction of the active waypoint.

12-16. Waypoint Closing Velocity, also called VMG to Waypoint.

12-17. Channels 67 and 72.

12-18. (A). They cost less; they are more durable, and they are always up to date. (B) We have less stores now that stock charts that we can look at in real size before purchasing (though all are online to see in as much detail as desired.) Second, some POD papers are still not quite as good as the lithographic charts for erasing pencil lines... though this is improving with time.

12-19. (A) 20% and 20 min, or 2.7 ±0.5 and 1220 ±20m. (B) The honest, most general answer is you have no idea. The current could be running the opposite way at that time. Current predictions apply only to the stations themselves and to nearby open water, uninfluenced by land or bathymetry.

12-20. It sees around corners that radar cannot see; it tells you directly the course, speed, and name of the target vessel; it identifies the class of the vessel (tanker, tug, etc).

12-21. (A) Set = 115.4, Drift = 1.2. (B) Course to Steer = 034.1, SMG = 6.3. (C) Guess = 035, best = 034.1, error = 0.9°. Note this comparison varies with different configurations, but the assumption of equal is a good, quick working guideline.

12-22. Reference to all is Rule 19d. (A) No one. There is no right of way in the fog. (B) Large turn to the right. (C) Large turn to the right. (D) Large turn to the right. (E) Large turn to the left.

12-23. (D) Any of the above reasons can be used to justify your maneuver.

12-24. (A) is true by law; (D) is true by common sense. The other two are wrong by law.

12-25. (D) None. It is illegal and you will be fined.

12-26. 100 yards—due to Federal Protection and Security Zones.

12-27. (A) There is a specific optimum way to fold them (inside out, with the chart name and number hand lettered onto the back side at the double-fold corner.)

12-28. 1907-1525 = 3h 42m = 3.7h, and 3.7 × 7.4 = 27.4 nmi.

12-29. (A) 50 to 90 ft. (B) 150 to 500 ft. A poor fix means the unit got just enough signals to compute a fix, but it is a poor one. Both of these answers are transient, and best learned by direct measurement, ie out with a broad open view of the horizon for (A), and through one window of your house or deep fjord underway for (B).

12-30. One your instrument must be WAAS capable, and two you must have one of the specific (geostationary) WAAS satellites in view and in use in your fix. See davidburchnavigation.blogspot.com/2021/12/WAAS.html.

12-31. First the easy parts: Your masthead wind instruments might not be perfectly aligned with the centerline, or your sail trim is not the same on each tack. More complex to consider is the effect of a current, which can only be addressed after the first two items have been ruled out by tests in guaranteed still water and modest air, i.e. not too strong and not too weak.

If current is present, the effect on VMG depends on how you compute the true wind direction that you are using as a reference. In other words, when the electronics solve for the true wind direction they have to use a course and speed input. This can be S from knotmeter and C from compass, or it could be SOG and COG. This topic is beyond the scope of this book, but we can appreciate the issue by imagining tacking into a north wind, with an west flowing current. The starboard tack would have a higher apparent wind speed than the port tack. Then there is also the issue to consider that wind angle is measured relative to the centerline, but your actual COG is not aligned with the centerline in notable current. Do an Internet search on "true wind versus water wind" for an extended discussion of this complex topic.

APPENDIX

A1. Using Electronic Charts

If you intend to use electronic charting on your vessel, it will be excellent practice to solve many of these practice exercises using electronic charts in addition to the traditional solutions using paper charts. In principle you can get more accurate results with the echarts, once you have mastered the special tools available.

Electronic charts of US waters made by NOAA are free internet downloads. We maintain a portal to these that is easy to remember:

starpath.com/getcharts

The electronic navigational charts (ENC) are now the only official NOAA charts, but they also offer a way to make supplemental paper charts using the NOAA Custom Chart (NCC) procedure, linked on that page. And, indeed, mariners may choose to navigate by the NCC alone without using ENC. Made to the appropriate scale and size for the task at hand, NCC support perfectly safe navigation, essentially the same as using the discontinued traditional paper charts.

Historically, NOAA also produced raster navigational charts (RNC) that were graphic images of paper charts. Nav apps such as qtVlm can load RNC as well as ENC. You can download a copy of the 18465 Tr RNC at starpath.com/18465tr. We recommend starting with that RNC and later experiment with ENC.

Likewise after practicing with the printed 18465 Tr, you can move on to making an NCC for your own sailing region and use that. All the techniques we learn from this Workbook apply equally well to an NCC.

The main challenge to the echart navigator is what software program to use to view the charts. We are referring here to programs or apps you run in your own stand-alone computer or tablet, in contrast to console mounted navigation instruments, which have come to be known as "chartplotters," that include their own proprietary software and commercial vector charts, such as C-map or Navionics.

There are many options for nav apps, and these workbook exercises can be worked with any of them. The software is generically called a *navigation program* or *app,* although the official generic name is electronic chart system (ECS). Its primary requirement is to display and ENC or RNC, along with your live GPS position overlaid on the chart so we can watch our vessel location move across the chart as we proceed. Navigation functions include: measuring range and bearing between points; setting up waypoints for a route; along with built in functions that tell us the tide and current at any location. And there are many more features and options.

For our purposes, a dominating factor is that they must display the *official* ENC or RNC from any nation—the US no longer makes RNC, but most nations do, including Canada. We do not want to rely on third-party charts with hidden end user licence agreements (EULA) that pronounce, in one form or another, that their charts should not be relied upon for safe navigation!

To work exercises from this workbook and to learn the ropes of chart navigation with an ECS, you can use any ECS that meet the basic requirements described above. A popular one that we use at Starpath is called qtVlm. Learn about it and how to get started at starpath.com/ENC/getting_started.htm.

The plotting and measurement tools used in ECS are often unique to the product, but there are common factors and procedures that are easy to adapt to any program. There is a list of videos demonstrating each of the typical echart plotting exercises at the bottom of the getting_started link above.

ENC are notably different in content and appearance from traditional paper charts. This booklet is a quick way to learn about them.

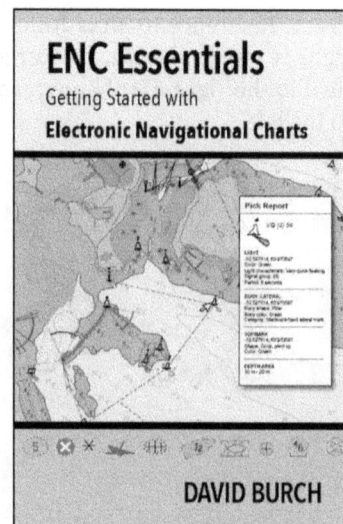

ENC Essentials

Getting Started with
Electronic Navigational Charts

ISBN 9780914025771
Paperback, 50 pages, 6" x 9"
full-color illustrations
Starpath Publications.

DAVID BURCH

A2. Interpolation

It is common in marine navigation to need an interpolated value from a table. We each need a way we are comfortable with to solve this. Here are a couple suggestions.

Suppose we know that the deviation of a compass is 20°E at compass heading 000 and it is 6.5°E at compass heading 045. What is the deviation at heading 030?

Procedure 1. Make a custom table.

(1) Write down what you know:

$$000C = 20E$$

$$045C = 6.5E$$

(2) Figure how many equal steps it takes to make a table that has your value in it. We can do this example in 3 steps, namely 000, 015, 030, 045.

(3) Figure the increment per step based on the values known: That is, $(20 - 6.5)/3 = 4.5°$ per step.

(4) Now we can make a table with our desired answer in it by just adding the increments at each step:

Compass heading		Deviation
000 =	20 =	20
015 =	20 - 4.5 =	15.5
030 =	15.5 - 4.5 =	11.0
045 =	11.0 - 4.5 =	6.5

And from this we see immediately that the deviation at 030 C is 11° E. In many, if not most, interpolation cases, it will be easy to choose the steps and make such a table. The next procedure is more systematic, which may appeal to some.

Procedure 2. Compute proportions

Consider this table of the known and unknown.

Compass heading	Deviation
A = 000 C	C = 20.0°
X = given = 30	Y = unknown
B = 045 C	D = 6.5°

We want to know Y, which we can get from proportions, namely:

$(X - A) / (B - A) = (Y - C) / (D - C)$, or

$(D - C) \times (X - A) / (B - A) = (Y - C)$.

Solving for Y and regrouping we get:

$Y = C + (X - A) \times [(D - C) / (B - A)]$.

In the last example,

$Y = 20 + (30 - 00) \times (6.5 - 20)/(45 - 00)$

$= 20 + 30 \times (-13.5/45) = 20 - 9 = 11.0$

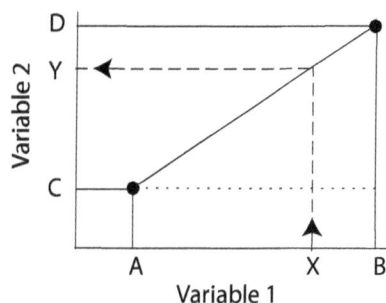

To use this method, fill in the table below and use a calculator to get the answer. For the formula to work as given, the desired unknown must be in variable 2, as shown.

Variable 1	Variable 2
A =	C =
X (given) =	Y (desired) =
B =	D =
$Y = C + (X - A) \times [(D - C) / (B - A)]$	

Example 1. Heading 310, dev = 8W, heading 290, dev 2E, what is the deviation at heading 305? It does not matter how we label E or W, but one has to be + and the other -. So call E -, then: A = 310, B = 290, X = 305, C = 8, D = -2. And we can find $Y = 8 + (305 - 310) \times ((-2 - 8)/(290 - 310) = 8 - 5 \times (-10/-20) = 8 - 2.5 = 5.5$, which is + so it must be 5.5 W.

Example 2. At 40N, sunset is at 1706 and at 45N, sunset is at 1658. What is the time of sun set at latitude 43° 15'N? First we have to get things into nice units: 1658 = 16h 58m, and 1706 = 16h 66m. Likewise, 43° 15' = 43+(15/60) = 43.25°.

So we have 40° = 66m and at 45° we have 58m, and we wish to know what is sun set minutes at lat 43.25°. We can choose A = 40, X = 43.25, B = 45, and C = 66m and D = 58m. Then $Y = 66 + (43.25 - 40) \times ((58 - 66)/45 - 40)) = 66 + 3.25x(-8/5) = 66 - 5.2 = 60.8m = 60m 48s$, and the answer is 16h + 60m 48s = 17h 00m 48s.

A3. Sources for 18465 Tr Printed Charts

Sources for Printed 18465 Tr	
Outlet	Location
Blue Water Books and Charts	Ft. Lauderdale, FL
Captains Nautical	Inglewood, CA
Landfall Navigation	Stamford, CT
Maryland Nautical Supply	Baltimore, MD
Paradise Cay	Blue Lake, CA
Starpath.com	Seattle, WA

9780914025450